The Cold War Is Over—Again

The
COLD WAR
Is Over
—Again

ALLEN LYNCH

WESTVIEW PRESS
Boulder • San Francisco • Oxford

Copyright © 1992 by Westview Press, Inc.

Published in 1992 in the United States of America by Westview Press, Inc., 5500 Central Avenue, Boulder, Colorado 80301-2847, and in the United Kingdom by Westview Press, 36 Lonsdale Road, Summertown, Oxford OX2 7EW

Library of Congress Cataloging-in-Publication Data
Lynch, Allen, 1955–
  The cold war is over—again / Allen Lynch.
    p. cm.
  Includes bibliographical references and index.
  ISBN 0-8133-1470-4 — ISBN 0-8133-1471-2 (pbk.)
    1. United States—Foreign relations—Soviet Union.   2. Soviet
Union—Foreign relations—United States.   3. World politics—1945–
4. Cold War.   I. Title.
E183.8.S65L96   1992
327.73047—dc20   91-45806
                                                                                                            CIP

Printed and bound in the United States of America

The paper used in this publication meets the requirements of the American National Standard for Permanence of Paper for Printed Library Materials Z39.48-1984.

10   9   8   7   6   5   4   3   2   1

To Tullia

Contents

PART 3
CHALLENGES OF THE FUTURE

Preface

When Nikita Khrushchev arrived home safely after his ouster from power in a Kremlin coup in October 1964, he reportedly tossed his briefcase on the sofa and told his wife, Nina Petrovna, that perhaps his greatest contribution to Soviet politics was that he had created conditions whereby the Soviet leader could now be removed from power by nonviolent means. Unlike Khrushchev, Mikhail Gorbachev was given a second chance: He survived the coup and lived to fight another day, owing in large measure to forces that his own policies, intentionally or not, had set in motion.

Why did the coup of August 19–21, 1991—actually the first even partly successful military coup in the 1,000-year history of the Russian state—fail, whereas the palace coup orchestrated by Leonid Brezhnev and his colleagues against Khrushchev succeeded? The short answer is that this time the palace coup could not be contained within the confines of the palace. Unlike Khrushchev in 1964, Gorbachev was able to benefit from the existence of a politically emboldened society and a genuinely popular leader in Boris Yeltsin, who was able to mobilize those social forces so as to deprive the junta of its legitimacy to govern.

The immediate cause of the collapse of the coup was a split within the Soviet military. Simply put, many officers were unwilling to order ordinary conscript soldiers to fire on their civilian brethren, and some feared that such an order would be ignored. The coup leaders were overly confident in their ability to cow Soviet society with an awesome display of brute force and some lip service to social issues of concern to much of the population, such as housing and the price of food. It is clear that they did not anticipate having to confront the thousands of civilians who rallied to the defense of Boris Yeltsin and of constitutional government in Russia and the USSR. Under these circumstances, and with the recent example of the disintegration of the comparably multinational Yugoslav army as a warning, the military blinked.

This overconfidence on the part of the coup plotters seems directly related to the remarkable incompetence of the coup attempt itself. The junta, aside from not fully considering the need for a massive use of force against civilians (the attempted military coup in the Baltic states in January 1991 showed that Soviet peoples could no longer be intimidated by merely symbolic uses of force), committed the stupefying error of permitting the immensely popular Boris Yeltsin to remain at large. The junta's inability (or indecision?) to cut off immediately all communications from and to the USSR enabled Yeltsin to relay his rallying cry to the rest of Moscow and the USSR by means of foreign short-wave radio broadcasts back to the country, thereby leapfrogging the internal communications blockages that the junta did apply.

Apart from the Baltic states, the coup did not take significant root outside of Moscow. Furthermore, the coup's truly active constituency— as distinct from the many fence-sitters—seems to have been limited to a relatively few leading officials in the military, police, and military-industrial complex. It is interesting that Yegor Ligachev, long thought to be Gorbachev's arch-opponent, did not publicly associate himself with the coup. The execution of the coup thus reflected primarily the efforts of the reactionary, as opposed to the simply conservative, wing of the Communist Party.

The deeper cause of the coup's collapse lies in the transformation of Soviet society that has been both the cause and consequence of the Gorbachev revolution. It must first be admitted that there is substantial ambivalence throughout Soviet society about the social consequences of economic reform. Fears of unemployment, inflation, and decreased social security are genuine and will have to be addressed by any government, reform or not. The coup leaders attempted to exploit these fears to give their doings a populist coloration. What they overlooked, to their ultimate dismay, was that in spite of this ambivalence and debate about the course of the future, there has also been a substantial consensus within the USSR and Russia about not returning to Stalinist ways. It is revealing in this respect that the junta studiously avoided all reference to Communist ideology and goals in their public declarations: Law and order, not a discredited communism, was their message. The inability of the junta to put forward any positive vision or program for the Soviet future prevented them from attracting significant popular support, or even from neutralizing opposition.

The significance of the defeat of the coup can hardly be exaggerated. Under the inspired leadership of Boris Yeltsin, the Russian people for the first time in their history were able to take responsibility for their political fate. In this respect the popular resistance of August 1991 may prove to be more important historically than the Russian Revolution itself: Whereas the Russian Revolution simply replaced an authoritarian system with a still more authoritarian order, the events of August 1991 open the prospect for genuine constitutional government in Russia and its neighbors within the former USSR.

Yeltsin's role in defeating the coup also highlighted the changed nature of relationships between the central Soviet government and its constituent republics, and thus between Gorbachev himself and Yeltsin. Yeltsin's actions affirmed the growing understanding between the republics and Gorbachev that in the future the republics would wield real sovereign power within the USSR. They had agreed even before August 19 that henceforth the republics would retain the exclusive right to levy taxes; the central Soviet government, that is, Gorbachev's government, would receive a fixed, limited percentage of revenues raised by the republics. The republics' exclusive authority to levy taxes underscored the demise of the traditional, centralized Soviet system of government. The inability of the Soviet government to meet its payroll and other financial obligations on November 29, 1991, and the subsequent assumption of union functions by the republics underscored the reality that, henceforth, sovereignty would reside in the republics and not in the union government. The establishment of the Commonwealth of Independent States by Russia, Ukraine, and Belorussia in Minsk on December 8, 1991, only gave juridical expression to this fact and formally ushered in the post-Soviet era that lies at the heart of the transformation of East-West relations that is the subject of this book.

Allen Lynch

A Note on Usage

At the time this book was sent to press the republics of the "former USSR"—this term having been introduced in the Russo-Ukrainian Treaty of August 28–29, 1991—were still in the process of hammering out a new set of political and economic relationships. The name that these governments have adopted for their common political system is the "Commonwealth of Independent States" (CIS). This nomenclature presents certain problems of usage, as the core of this book was written before the failed coup of August 1991 and the formal demise of the Soviet state. To have revised every usage of the terms "Soviet" or "USSR" would have proved tedious in the extreme both to the author and to the reader. Where the sense of the passage is affected by such terminology, I have used phrases like "the former USSR," the "central" or "union" government, and the like. Where a historical reference is made, the traditional terms ("Soviet," "USSR") have been kept, and there is no change in meaning. For most contemporary references, the term "Soviet" has been kept to refer to the central union government and relations governing more than two republics. The term "CIS" has yet to acquire common acceptance and to have insisted on it throughout the text would only have impeded the reader.

A.L.

Introduction

"When I use a word," Humpty Dumpty said . . . "it means just what I choose it to mean—neither more nor less."
—Lewis Carroll

The purpose of this book is to provoke a rethinking by the reader about the character of East-West relations, in particular, their U.S.-Soviet core. The idea developed when I heard and read all the self-congratulatory rhetoric in the West about "the end of the cold war" following the Gorbachev revolution in Soviet foreign policy and the East European revolutions of 1989. The book's underlying theme is that contrary to the general understanding, the "cold war" in East-West relations was actually put to rest between the early 1960s and the 1970s, when Eastern and Western governments codified the division of Germany and Europe. The revolutionary events of 1989 thus overturned not the cold war order but rather the *post*-cold war order in East-West relations, much to the surprise and consternation of nearly every government involved, including that of the United States. Consequently, those governments now confront forces, in the form of German unity and nationalism throughout Eastern Europe and the USSR, that the post–cold war order contained very efficiently (if at times brutally). As the epigraph above suggests, the words we use exert a powerful, often magnetic, effect on how we perceive things; hence, the importance of terminology and my insistence on reserving for "cold war" its proper place in diplomatic history.

What I seek to do throughout this book, most concertedly in Chapter 1, is to penetrate the surface of accepted rhetoric about "cold war" to expose some of the deeper complexities of the East-West relationship. The problems addressed include:

1

1. What *were* the actual issues over which the cold war was fought, and how were they resolved? What has been the relationship between cold war and the perpetuation of tension in East-West relations, long after the central disputes of the cold war had been laid to rest?

2. How did it happen that the collaboration of Ronald Reagan and Mikhail Gorbachev was finally able to contain the psychological, military, and institutional remnants of the cold war and reassert the primacy of politically defined values in East-West relations?

3. How has the unexpected and (from the point of view of most Western governments) undesired overthrow of Soviet hegemony in East-Central Europe in 1989–1990 opened entirely novel perspectives, including the question of dealing with long-suppressed nationalist sentiment throughout the region and the relationship of that nationalism to political stability in Europe, always the focal point of the East-West relationship?

4. Relatedly, how did the reforms ushered in by Mikhail Gorbachev unintentionally, and to the great dismay of the West, unleash nationalist forces within the USSR itself, so that we may now realistically speak of a political system with multiple sovereign power centers, all of which have aspirations to play significant international roles?

5. Following from this, what does it mean for the control of nuclear weapons, as well as for academic theories of nuclear deterrence, that the world's second nuclear superpower is no longer a stable state?

6. What is the impact of these "tectonic shifts" in East-West relations on the ways in which the United States defines its international interests and the threats—existing and potential—to them? How might this affect the allocation of economic and political resources within the United States in a time of fiscal stringency and crumbling domestic infrastructures?

The book is organized, prosaically, into three parts, treating past, present, and future aspects of East-West and U.S.-Soviet relations. Chapter 1, which repeats the title of the book, is essentially a "think piece" intended to clarify the way we view the essential character of East-West relations. As suggested above, I argue that we are now confronted with the collapse of the post–cold war international order and that, correspondingly, any effort to offer constructive policy advice must first clear the analytical barrier that the mental categories of the past continue to pose. In Chapter 2, entitled, "The Nuclear Family," I trace the patterns of U.S.-Soviet collaboration in the management of nuclear weapons, emphasizing the intensity of the U.S.-Soviet strategic partnership. That partnership runs parallel to the decades-long geopolitical collaboration in the division of Europe that served both superpowers so well until the East Europeans secured their freedom in 1989. I assert that the two powers' common nuclear fate will continue to shape their mutual relations, independent of political vicissitudes, and will continue to do so as the ex-USSR is transformed into a more fragmented set of political systems. Chapter 3 is an examination of postwar U.S. policy toward Eastern Europe as a test case not only of future policy toward this region but also—if Eastern Europe represented the Soviet "outer empire"—toward the erstwhile "inner empire" of a disintegrating USSR.

Chapters 4 through 7 make up the second part of the book and deal with an interrelated set of problems resulting from the Gorbachev reforms in the USSR. Chapter 4, "The Agonies of Reform in Gorbachev's USSR," provides the necessary internal backdrop to the dramatic upheavals now shaking the Soviet region. The central theme is that of the unwilled consequences of Gorbachev's reforms, as his policies—bold as they have been—have unleashed political, especially nationalist, forces beyond his initial comprehension and have led to the disintegration of the Soviet political system, and with it the end of the bipolar assumption in world politics. An important subtheme is that Gorbachev had been moving rapidly since the spring and summer of 1991 to accommodate these political forces, so much so that the West—which remained bedazzled by Gorbachev and mystified by Soviet nationalisms—found itself supporting a Gorbachev that Gorbachev himself had already abandoned. (In this respect, repeated Western efforts to bolster the integrity of the USSR at the expense of independence for the republics may well have had the effect of persuading those plotting the August 1991 coup d'etat that the West would in the end acquiesce to such a denouement.)

Turning to foreign affairs, in Chapter 5 I present the conceptual background to recent changes in Soviet foreign policy. Much of this policy-analytic work predates the Gorbachev era itself, which underscores the point that the sea change in recent Soviet foreign policy is not a mere tactical maneuver but is instead deeply rooted in a genuine rethinking of the Soviet Union's relationship to its international environment. In Chapter 6 I address the question of the irreversibility of Gorbachev's foreign policy line in more detail; I argue that even before the failed August coup we witnessed the virtual collapse of Soviet foreign policy. Profoundly rooted international and internal factors, including a revolution in political values across a broad expanse of the Soviet political spectrum, led to that collapse. I argue, furthermore, that the West will have to transcend its past fixation on Gorbachev if it is to think creatively about the future of its relations with the successor states to the USSR.

Chapter 7, on the problem of ideology in Soviet foreign policy, may seem pedantic at first glance, but in it I treat an aspect of Soviet foreign policy not usually dealt with in a systematic way, that is, the various roles that ideology has played in the Soviet Union's international relationships. (Gorbachev's remarkable defense of socialism and the Soviet Communist

Party immediately upon his restoration to power after the Communist-inspired coup attempt testifies to the tenacious hold that Marxist-Leninist categories of political philosophy have had on the champion of perestroika and glasnost himself.) My point, in sum, is that the categories of Soviet ideology retain their importance for many of those operating within a post-Soviet political system; that although the content of the ideology has changed in many important ways, the presentation of ideology is still regarded as an important tool in the struggle for power; and that Soviet ideology will for some time yet affect the manner of post-Soviet adjustment to the international environment. In the long run, however, ideology seems destined to decline as nationalist forces supplant the functions of the central Soviet government and as new generations, untutored in Soviet ways, come to power.

Part 3 looks more directly at the future, in particular at the nationalist forces that are reshaping the former USSR's international relationships and at the possible policy consequences for the United States of this transmutation of the USSR. In Chapter 8 I argue that the USSR had been disintegrating for some time before the August 1991 coup and that the United States will be affected significantly by this primordial political fact. At the same time (harking the reader back to Chapter 2) I point out that Soviet collapse will actually tend to reinforce the pattern of nuclear collaboration between the United States and those who maintain control over nuclear weapons on post-Soviet territory. However, the United States, historically unable to come to terms with nationalism in the USSR, is ill-prepared to react to a wholly new issue in international politics—the relationship of internal political order to nuclear arms control. I attempt in Chapter 9 to draw some of the threads from the book together and to suggest what they imply for the ways that Americans are, and might be, thinking about their country's future involvement in East-West relations.

Part 1

THE LEGACY
OF THE PAST

1

The Cold War
Is Over . . . Again

> *But the real reason for the war . . . [w]hat made war*
> *inevitable was the growth of Athenian power and the fear*
> *which this caused in Sparta.*
> —Thucydides, *The Peloponnesian War*

The amazing, sudden collapse of communism in Eastern Europe in the second half of 1989 caused many in the United States and much of the rest of the world to hail the "end of the cold war." The seemingly never-ending contest between the Soviet Union and the United States, between communism and democracy (or communism and capitalism), had, in this view, ended in a dramatic and conclusive victory for the United States and its allies. Even prominent "revisionists," who ascribe chief responsibility for the cold war to the United States, have conceded as much. One such critic, Christopher Lasch, has thus stated, "We ought to admit that the West won the cold war—even if it goes against the grain, our political inclinations." Mikhail Gorbachev, in this view, presided over the abandonment of the Soviet empire in Europe and pushed through political changes that "implicitly condemn the whole course of Soviet history; if these actions don't add up to a victory for the West, the term surely has no meaning."[1] None of the celebrants, or mourners, appear to grasp that the "cold war" of vivid political and popular imagery had actually ended, if not in victory, then to general governmental satisfaction, more than two decades earlier. The rapid disintegration of the Communist regimes in Eastern Europe after June 1989 surprised and even alarmed Western governments, which were much more concerned with the possibly disruptive effects of German unity and the removal of the Soviet Union as a player on the field of East-West politics in Europe than with the transplantation of democracy eastward. The reverberations of the liberation of Eastern Europe have made themselves felt across the breadth of the Soviet Union itself, with the consequent challenge to the very survival of the Soviet political union. In recent years politicians and diplomats of the West have been busy trying to prop up that union—whose downfall would have been their aim were their policies actuated by considerations of "cold war."

The Division of Europe

Whereas this attempt is a sure sign that the cold war was, by 1990, indeed over, the confusion of Western, and especially U.S., policies when policymakers have been confronted with the end of communism and of the Soviet state suggests an antecedent set of motives. Those motives have taken U.S. and allied foreign policies far beyond the simplicities of cold war in their conduct and thinking about East-West relations. In fact, the two "superpowers" and their allies have formed a limited security partnership in the most vital theater of world politics—Europe—since the late 1960s. The roots of this expanding calibration of policies may be traced as far back as the early 1950s, when the U.S. and West German governments of the time indicated their preference for the emerging postwar status quo of two German states in a divided Europe against any plausible alternative. Between the late 1950s and the late 1960s, the countries of the North Atlantic Treaty Organization (NATO) and the Warsaw Pact would formalize and then institutionalize this recognition that a Europe only half free was an acceptable foundation of East-West relations.

This preference for a divided Europe would remain a constant of the actual policies of East and West right through 1989. Western governments are still wrestling with the hell of having their (nominal) wishes granted as they seek to come to terms with an Eastern Europe that promises to upset tidy West European plans for economic and political integration and with a (former) Soviet Union whose tentative efforts to enter the modern world politically imply a flood of refugees and the creation of wholly new patterns of international relationships. It is not the governments of the West but, as Dwight Eisenhower presaged, the "peoples," in this case those of Eastern Europe and the Soviet Union, who broke the pattern of what is still commonly thought of as cold war. In this respect, it was the *post*-cold war order that was shattered by the East European revolutions of 1989.

Views of the Cold War

Why insist on terms? Does the discussion of the meaning of the "cold war" have any more than academic interest, given the fact that, whatever the analysis of the past, we are now surely in a post–cold war era and should get on with the task of building that world? In fact, our analysis of what we have been through—whether that analysis is made explicit or not—will inevitably affect our idea of what the most important problems of the present and future are. It is a cliché by now that strategists tend to plan for the last war; perhaps this should be extended to include past cold wars as well. We should be very careful, then, in weighing the only evidence that can guide us in the future, that is, our common past. This is no easy task, as the distinguished historian Michael Howard has warned us. We should beware of "false premises based on inadequate evidence," and we should know that "the past is a foreign country; there is very little we can say about it until we have learned its language and understood its assumptions."[2]

In a related vein, if it *is* the cold war, as the popular imagination would have it, that has just ended, what now are the corresponding U.S. and Soviet stakes in international politics? If the end of the cold war or simply of the most recent phase of East-West relations has resulted in the achievement of the most important U.S. foreign policy objectives, as the rhetoric of "winning" the cold war implies, then what remains to justify the commitment of U.S. lives and treasure to far-flung regions of the globe? In short, our view of what the cold war was about—the stakes involved and the policies pursued—will shape our view of the nature of the interests that have been, are, and will be involved in East-West and U.S.-Soviet relations. It will shape our understanding of the posture, active or reactive, of the policies that are called for; of the means required to secure the interests at stake; and of the implications of success (or failure) in achieving the goals of policy.

Containing Communism

If, for instance, the cold war, for the United States, was primarily about containing "communism" (or capitalism, for the Soviet Union), one would then expect that the interests of the states involved would tend to be global in character. Ideological constructs such as capitalism, communism, and democracy are universal by nature. They advance, or are said to advance, claims upon all mankind. Consequently, the sphere of competition between such ideological causes embraces the entire planet. The stakes are correspondingly unlimited, in that victory for one implies the total defeat of the other. A U.S. policy aimed at containing communism (with a view to its eventual transformation or elimination), although global in focus, would be essentially reactive in thrust, inasmuch as communism is seen as the assertive challenger to the global status quo. Indeed, this is how both sides in the East-West conflict have claimed to see the character of the East-West, or U.S.-Soviet relationship.

Given the enormity of the scope and stakes of such an ultimately irreconcilable conflict of world historical missions (going far beyond simple conflicts of interest), the means that are considered legitimate to employ would be correspondingly unlimited in scope. At the same time, the stress in U.S. (or Soviet) policy would tend to be on political-ideological means as opposed to purely military ones. In the end, it is much better testimony to the value of one's ideology to convert or render irrelevant one's opponent than to coerce him. In the event of success in this grand ideological struggle, world politics would no longer be primarily a national security issue for the states involved but rather an issue of social-economic and political development.

Containing Russian Power

If the crux of the cold war was the containment, not of communism as such, but of Russian power, one would identify corresponding differences in the interests, instruments, and reaction to success (or failure) of the parties involved. Russian power, as part of the normal warp and woof of world politics, implies a less than universal challenge to the states and social systems that make up the international system. The interests of the United States and its allies in coming to terms with the nature of Russian power would thus be more limited than if it is communism as such that is the problem. Of course, to the extent that Russian or Soviet Russian and Communist interests are equated with each other, the field and intensity of the conflict would tend to expand. Nevertheless, the possibility of using non-Soviet-Russian Communist powers (such as Yugoslavia and the People's Republic of China) to help check the extension of Soviet power in principle ensured that the Soviet challenge, however serious, would always be less total than that posed by communism.

Although U.S. interests in containing the Soviet Union are in principle more restricted than its interests would be in containing communism, the thrust of its policy would still be reactive: It would concede the initiative to a Soviet power that it sees as consciously attempting to shift the balance of global power in Soviet favor. The means employed would tend to be political-economic and political-military as opposed to purely military, although the intrusion of ideological phobias, which transcend the purely doctrinal aspects of ideology, may encourage reliance on armed force as the basis of a containment policy. In the case of success, that is, with the effective removal of the Soviet challenge to the existing world order, it is not clear what would continue to move U.S. international interests and policies. Having for so long defined its mission in world affairs in negative ways, by what it is against (whether it be communism or the expansion of Soviet power) rather than by what its intrinsic long-term international stakes are, the United States would find itself in a quandary as it sought to sort out the justification for a global foreign policy in such a post–cold war environment.

European and German Unity

If, to take another view, U.S. (and/or Soviet) policy in the cold war was driven by the nominal commitment to restore the unity of Europe, and thus of Germany, the interests involved would be much more regionally specific than in either of the two previously mentioned cases. At the same time, such a policy would be aimed at subverting the status quo in Europe, which has been recognized throughout the cold war period (and after) as the central theater (if no longer the cockpit) of world politics. The instruments of policy would vary according to circumstances, but for the Americans policy would be largely dependent on the preferences of West Germany, given the intensity of U.S. commitment to German unity. A good test of this thesis would thus be the extent to which U.S. policy consciously followed the course of West German foreign policy. In the event of success, that is, the unity of Europe and of Germany, U.S. policy would find itself in a quandary similar to that governing the demise of the Soviet challenge: With the specific goal of unity accomplished, it is no longer clear what drives the U.S. commitment to Europe.

The Balance of Power

If the cold war was about the more prosaic issue of maintaining the balance of power, albeit in a very dynamic setting following the collapse of Europe and Japan in 1945, then U.S. interests would be limited to the geopolitical "soft spots" of the balance. Metaphorically, a balance may be maintained at a single point (as in a seesaw), although considerable and increased pressure may be brought to bear from various sides over time in order to preserve the static state of equilibrium. The means used to create or preserve the balance would tend to be political-economic and political-military in character, with raw military force held in the background as a necessary, though by no means sufficient, condition for maintaining a stable and healthy balance. That is, external military force cannot over the long run be a substitute for the emergence of stable societies and polities, necessary for a plural and stable distribution of global power.[3]

Reaction to "success," if that term can be applied to the maintenance of a balance, depends on what the sources of threat to the balance of power are considered to be: the nature of certain political systems (Communist, capitalist, or democratic); an unbalanced distribution of international economic, political, and military power (bipolar, tripolar, or multipolar); the quantity and quality of weapons systems in given states or throughout the international system; or the presence of aggressive leaders of powerful states. Whatever the source of the threat, the fact remains that the responsibility of maintaining that balance can never end. As a balance is by definition a process, there is in the long run no final success, or failure, for that matter.

Preventing World War III

If, finally, the cold war was about preserving the peace, that is, preventing World War III, then the interests at stake may be related to all of the challenges mentioned above: communism or capitalism, Soviet Russian (or U.S.) power, the division of Germany and of Europe, and the maintenance of the balance of power. The means employed, however, would be considerably less varied: They entail armed force, the purpose of which in the nuclear age is to deter the outbreak of war, as opposed to winning war when it comes. The philosophy of deterrence that is thus expressed assumes the existence of a threat to be deterred: In the absence of deterrent means, an aggressive design would have taken place.

Such a view would tend to militarize the entire East-West relationship. It is then not simply the prevention of war but the broader management of political objectives that is held to be most reliably served through the threat, implicit or explicit, or even the actual use, of armed force. This deterrent perspective on the cold war, aside from taking as given a premise—the existence of an imminent threat—that sorely warrants examination, tends to reinforce the problem it purports to resolve. Not only does it reduce the spectrum of international relationships to a military dimension; it even draws the question of war and peace in largely military terms. If the causes of war transcend issues of military balance to include political ambitions—themselves rooted in particular social, economic, and political contexts—then the management of international relations is only secondarily a military issue, and thus only secondarily a subject for the application of deterrence theory.

Paradoxically, the view that the stake of the cold war was the prevention of World War III and the establishment of credible deterrence toward that end could actually have resulted in the most restrictive of all policies:

The aim of preventing an attack on the United States could have been reliably served by maintaining a minimal number of nuclear weapons capable of inflicting a devastating retaliatory attack on the Soviet Union. Had that indeed been the goal of U.S. policy, the entire apparatus of cold war—the elaborate and comprehensive military preparations, the far-flung network of military and political intervention (overt and covert), worldwide alliance systems, the various aid programs—would have been unnecessary. That this was not the case, that U.S. policy throughout the cold war embraced the totality of means that were technically and financially available, and at a very high level of material and political commitment, suggests that the cold war went far beyond the simple prevention of global war, if indeed it was about that at all.

None of the schema proposed here alone provides an adequate explanation of the cold war or of U.S. cold war policy. Each does explain an important part of both. This suggests the complexity of the subject and the importance of nuance in the analysis of something that is multidimensional in character. At a minimum, we should be clear about our premises when we review the past. Our understanding of where we have been will have a decisive influence on where we think we are and what we imagine our choices, actual and possible, to be.

Before one attempts to address a subject as ambitious in its scope as the title of this book, it is useful to recall the titles of several important books written nearly three decades ago. These include: Louis J. Halle, *The Cold War as History* (1967); Marshall D. Shulman, *Beyond the Cold War* (1965); Edmund Stillman and William Pfaff, *The New Politics: America and the End of the Postwar World* (1961); and André Fontaine, *History of the Cold War* (1970), two volumes, translated from the French, which appeared in 1965. What the authors of these works viewed as the "cold war" had clearly come to an end, or was significantly attenuating, by the mid-1960s. This should cause considerable caution, and modesty, as we raise the question a generation later—Is the cold war over?—for the very nature of the question implies, or hides, critical assumptions about the character of the East-West relationship and the sources of tension and conflict therein.

To a large part of the American public, the "cold war" has been "over" since the late 1980s, the era of Gorbachev. This notion suggests that the public projects its hopes and self-image onto the world stage and particularly onto relations with its chief international adversary, the Soviet Union. Such a projection reflects the persistent U.S. conviction that it is the nature of the Soviet *domestic* system that is largely responsible for the kind of foreign policy the Soviet Union has and that if the former changes, so must the latter and with it the entire character of U.S.-Soviet relations and of U.S. foreign policy in general. The problem here is that the phrase "cold war" has become a kind of totem of political discourse, a reflex choice of words, obscuring more than enlightening by appearing to provide a quick and simple explanation for international tensions. If the concept of cold war is to retain any analytical significance, it must first be put aside, as it were, and reduced to its constituent elements. Therefore, before one can raise the question whether the cold war is over, one first has to ask, What was (is) the cold war about?

The Nature of the Cold War

Part of the difficulty in answering this second, more substantive, question lies in the fact that the cold war was multidimensional in nature and went through several stages. The highly charged political atmosphere that was part of the cold war itself tended to cloud the meaning of the concept, as many of the participants involved attached their own tendentious interpretations to its meaning. This became most evident when either side would accuse the other of conducting a "policy" of cold war, denying that it could be an interactive process, deeply rooted in historical and geopolitical forces. In this view, the cold war represented the unilateral projection of tension and hostility by one side onto the other, which allegedly reacted in a passive, defensive, and thoroughly justified manner to the aggressive depredations of the adversary. The idea that there might have been a tragic incompatibility of interests involved (given the nature of the respective political systems and the character and magnitude of the stakes involved) does not enter into this orthodox interpretation of the cold war.

Thus Soviet officials and commentators, along with U.S. revisionist historians, have long denounced the cold war "policy" of the United States. Throughout the 1980s, Soviet commentators continued to judge U.S. foreign policy by the extent to which it deviated from its traditional cold war policy (*politika kholodnoi voyni*). The idea that U.S.-Soviet relations respond to a logic of interaction, rather than to one of U.S. challenge and Soviet response, is still largely an alien one in Soviet writings on the subject.[4] The mirror image of this view was expressed by Marshal Tito in March 1953, several weeks after the death of Joseph Stalin, when he said of the Soviet leaders, "I can say that I don't believe they will end the cold war very soon. It is likely that they will still continue it."[5] U.S. leaders of the time and later could hardly dissent from this independent Communist's assessment that it was precisely Moscow that had initiated and pursued the cold war and that it was therefore up to Moscow to end it.

Beyond this basic disagreement about the sources of the cold war (which masks agreement about its unilateral dynamics) lies a further divergence of views as to its character. In both the Soviet Union and the United States the cold war was popularly portrayed as nothing less than an irreconcilable clash of civilizational destinies: capitalism versus socialism for one, freedom versus slavery for the other. The Leninist tenet about the ultimate incompatibility of socialism with "imperialism" and the inevitability of war as long as imperialism exists was deeply rooted in the Soviet ideological arsenal. Andrei Zhdanov's "two camp" thesis of 1947 had merely put a contemporary gloss on this. More novel was the U.S. conversion to such apocalyptic visions. Secretary of State John Foster Dulles put the issue very squarely in 1953 when he observed of Soviet communism that it: "believes that human beings are nothing more than somewhat superior animals . . . and that the best kind of a world . . . is organized as a well-managed farm. . . . I do not see how, as long as Soviet communism holds those views . . . there can be any permanent reconciliation. . . . This is an irreconcilable conflict."[6] From this angle the cold war was "a contest of ultimate destinies,"[7] and President John F. Kennedy's promise in his inaugural address that the United States would "pay any price, bear any burden" in defense of freedom around the world in "a long twilight struggle" reflected that view.

For others the cold war was a much more specific and limited political contest flowing out of the way in which World War II was concluded, mainly in Europe, a contest that revolved about the reestablishment of a viable balance of power on the Old Continent. Indeed, many in this school, such as George Kennan, architect of the policy of containment, resisted applying the rubric of cold war to the carefully calibrated strategy of geopolitical containment of Soviet power in Europe, which they advanced as the main task of postwar U.S. foreign policy. Many of the attributes that would later come to be identified with the cold war—the militarization of relationships, the globalization of commitments, the ideological hysteria—were absent from U.S. containment policy as formulated and implemented in 1947–1948, though aspects of the public presentation of the Truman Doctrine were to presage each of these three defining characteristics.[8] From the Soviet side as well, excepting the ideological paranoia characteristic of Stalin's time, Soviet Western policy, as aggressive as its intentions were, displayed a fine respect for the limits of what the United States regarded as its truly vital interests.[9]

This divergence of views on the sources, nature, scope, and inner dynamics of the cold war actually serves as a reliable indicator of the multidimensionality of the problem. For there was no one cold war, fixed in space and time. What began as a rather predictable political contest to secure, or frustrate, the age-old pretension to European hegemony (the very justification for U.S. entry into both world wars) eventually turned into a worldwide ideological confrontation dependent on military, as opposed to political, instruments for its conduct. Just to grasp the issue one must distinguish the geopolitical from the ideological from the purely atmospheric sources of tension and conflict; the political objectives of the conflict from the means—political, diplomatic, psychological, economic, and military—used in their support; and the Eurocentric from the global scale and interests at stake.

The Political Collapse of Europe

If the cold war can be said to have been about something, then it was about the implications, feared and promised, of the political collapse of Europe for both the United States and the Soviet Union. The disintegration of, first, an autonomous European balance of power and, subsequently, German power thrust the United States and Russia into the heart of Europe. They were the only powers capable of reconstituting a stable equilibrium there and at the same time the only ones capable of decisively upsetting that balance to the disfavor of the other. Regardless of ideological considerations, this would have been so in 1945, given the way the war was fought and concluded. Long experience and political theory should have indicated that tension and discord were endemic in such a situation.

But does such rather traditional tension equal cold war? The term itself did not begin to acquire currency in the United States until mid-1947; it was introduced first in a speech by elder statesman Bernard Baruch and then popularized by Walter Lippmann in a series of articles attacking George Kennan's famous containment article (much to Kennan's chagrin) for its allegedly open-ended prescription for U.S. intervention against the expansion of Soviet influence around the world.[10] In retrospect, the term at first appears to reflect the general U.S. frustration that, after four years of global war and the establishment of the United Nations, power politics continued to be the leitmotiv of international relations. Lippmann specifically meant by the concept of cold war an ideologically based, globalistic foreign policy strategy based on reacting to Soviet power as such rather than an autonomous U.S. assessment of its foreign policy priorities. Hence, the strategy was, in Lippmann's preference, a geopolitically confined approach aimed at the reestablishment of stable balances of power in Europe and East Asia.

There was at first less disagreement between Lippmann and Kennan than met the eye, because the actual foreign policy then being carried out by the Truman administration reflected a carefully tailored strategy of encouraging indigenous forces in areas of vital U.S. interest—almost exclusively in Western Europe at the time—rather than an unlimited commitment to the military containment of Soviet power around the globe. A number of critical indices, including the political and economic focus of U.S. policy as represented by the Marshall Plan; the decision to support the Communist Tito and encourage national communism (rather than to "roll back" communism as such); and the cautious and ultimately noninterventionist attitude struck toward the Communist revolution in China, all suggest the limits, based on exacting geopolitical criteria, of U.S. containment policy at the time. To identify this policy of containment with the cold war, then, is to give a highly qualified meaning to the idea of cold war, especially in light of the shape that East-West relations would assume after 1948–1949.

From the Soviet angle one might argue, as André Fontaine did, that "cold war" was intrinsic to the Leninist concept of international relations and that the course of Soviet foreign policy may thus be interpreted in terms of tactical maneuver within the limits given by the postulate of systemic antagonism and irreconcilability. In Fontaine's book, the history of the cold war thus began in 1917. Some Soviet analysts have also argued recently that the origins of the cold war must be interpreted with the nature of the Soviet domestic system, specifically Stalin's despotic, "irrational" rule at home, very much in mind.[11] Such views, which root the cold war in the character of the Soviet system, say much about the essential traits of the traditional Soviet world outlook but much less about the behavioral evolution of Soviet foreign policy throughout the cold war period. As Soviet international conduct is in large measure an interactive process, an assessment of the Soviet system alone cannot exhaust the answer to the question of the sources, nature, development, and resolution of the cold war. Whatever the functions that the image and reality of cold war served for the Soviet system, and they were real enough, the cold war as an international event was much more indeterminate in its direction and in the scope ultimately assumed than its identification with a particular political system implies.

Geopolitics

Without going into historical details,[12] and being aware of oversimplification for the sake of presentation, if one asserts that the cold war was about the frustration of yet another hegemonic enterprise in Europe, then one must admit that by 1949 the elements of its resolution had been set in place, in the form of an independent West and East Germany, rooted in the Western and Eastern alliance systems, respectively, i.e., a divided

Germany (and, later, a divided Berlin) in a divided Europe. Although neither the United States nor the Soviet Union professed itself satisfied with such a scheme as the basis for a "settlement" of the war (which according to the Potsdam Agreement of July–August 1945 was to have awaited the convocation of a peace treaty with all-German representation), in fact such a solution, especially when compared to the risks ascribed to any politically realistic alternative, was eventually to prove eminently acceptable to both superpowers, both alliances, and with only partial qualification to both German states themselves.

"Facts" speak louder than words, and it is a fact that after the establishment of the two German states neither East nor West was prepared to challenge the division of Europe by offensive action. At the one point where a peaceful revision of the European schism became at least conceivable, upon the Soviet offer of March 10, 1952, to discuss terms for a neutral and unified Germany, the West reacted with remarkable uninterest. Taking into account the inevitable uncertainties about the motivations behind Stalin's actions and the conditions that might have been attached to any negotiations, the fact remains that at the one point where the Soviet leadership—faced with the prospect of West Germany's formal military integration into the Western alliance system—seemed prepared to entertain the prospect of a withdrawal from Germany, the Western allies did not deem it proper even to explore the notion with the Soviet Union.[13]

In other instances, such as the civil disturbances in East Berlin and Plzen, Czechoslovakia, in 1953 and the Hungarian revolution of 1956, Western inaction confirmed the underlying tolerance of the division of Europe, if challenging it meant a possible military confrontation with the Soviet Union. One may even go beyond "tolerance" and use the word "preference" to describe Western and Eastern attitudes to the division of Europe as the basis of East-West relations, as George Kennan discovered to his dismay in the response to his British Broadcasting Corporation (BBC) Reith lectures of 1957. Kennan had put forward a concept for the disengagement of superpower forces from Germany as part of a scheme that would reestablish a united, though neutral, Germany. The overwhelmingly negative reaction to his lectures in Paris, London, and Washington apparently surprised Kennan, who until then had been laboring under the assumption that repairing the division of Germany (and thus of Europe) was the actual policy of the West.[14] Subsequent events, especially Western refusal to block the building of the Berlin Wall, provided convincing proof to such West Germans as Berlin mayor Willy Brandt that the Western powers simply did not share West German enthusiasm for eventual reunification and that any amelioration of the conditions of the Germans in the East would have to depend primarily on a more independent West German diplomacy.[15]

The Soviet preference for codifying the territorial and political status quo goes back to the mid-1950s, when it first advanced the concept of an all-European security conference. That this reflects more than a simple desire to secure existing Soviet gains, that the Soviet government and its allies have also seen a kind of security partnership with the Americans in Europe, is shown by their eventual acceptance of the United States as a full participant in the Conference on Security and Cooperation in Europe (CSCE), which came to embody the original Soviet idea for a pan-European security conference. The nuance in Soviet appreciations of the European role of the United States is also shown by Brezhnev's remarkable acceptance of the principle of negotiated reductions of conventional forces in Europe in 1971, just four days before the scheduled U.S. Senate vote on the Mansfield Amendment proposing extensive unilateral withdrawals of U.S. troops from Europe.[16] Soviet statements in the year before the oubreak of the 1989 revolutions in Eastern Europe also confirmed this sense of partnership with the United States in presiding over a divided but stable Germany and Europe.[17] The East European states themselves, even when under Communist rule, also expressed the conviction that the presence of U.S. forces in West Germany was essential to the containment of long-term German ambitions and that precipitate U.S. withdrawals were not at all in the Eastern interest.[18]

In many ways, then, the year 1956, which saw Western inaction in face of the Hungarian revolt (as well as quiet support of the Polish Communists' defiance of Soviet leader Nikita Khrushchev), open divergence in Western aims over the Suez crisis, and Khrushchev's revision of basic Leninist tenets about the inevitability of war and a peaceful road to socialism, marks the turning point in the evolution of the cold war. Many of the elements that would later be identified as the new forces of world politics, such as growing polycentrism within alliances, the limited political utility of nuclear weapons, and the basic respect by each side for the other's vital national and alliance interests, had all been implicitly or explicitly recognized by 1956.

It would still be some time before the implications of these changes would be fully absorbed by leaders East and West. Indeed, the series of crises concerning Berlin from 1958 to 1961 may be seen as the last test of the stability of this system; during that period Khrushchev sought to undermine the West's political and military position in Western Europe as a means of ratifying Soviet hegemony over Eastern Europe (and his own power base at home). The building of the Berlin Wall in 1961 underscored the unwillingness of the West to challenge Soviet vital interests (as represented by the wall itself), the Soviet priority of defending their gains along the imperial periphery, and the virtual impossibility for offensive actions to upset the geopolitical status quo. In this light the

Cuban Missile Crisis of October 1962 merely confirms the latent stability of the East-West structure then coming into existence. Only by such a dramatic and risky "end run" could Khrushchev hope to pressure the United States into formally ratifying the division of Germany: The balance that had been established in Europe itself had proven too stable to plausibly challenge. Upon the frustration of his Cuban adventure, East and West began the long process that would, by promoting stability over system change, yield detente and the post–cold war era by the early 1970s.

Such, in simplified form, was the geopolitical essence of the cold war. The often-grandiose verbal commitment of the superpowers to "liberation" or revolution had to come to terms with the stability of each alliance system within its own sphere and with a divided Germany in a divided Europe. In this structural sense, the cold war had gelled into stable form around 1956, although it would continue to be fought for some time and on many fronts, including for a while longer in Europe itself. The series of arms control agreements and confidence-building measures instituted in U.S.-Soviet relations (see Chapter 2), as well as the group of bilateral treaties entered into by West Germany in the 1970s with its eastern neighbors, formalized the shared East-West interest in stability on the Old Continent. The extension of this detente process through the multilateral CSCE process set the framework within which East-West relations are conducted to this day, encompassing military, economic, political, and humanitarian dimensions.

The Extension of the Cold War

Outside of Europe, however, the cold war was conducted with far greater ideological intensity, less well defined objectives, and far higher casualties. The displacement of the initial U.S.-Soviet dispute over the future of Germany to the wider world reflected the progressive militarization of the cold war, the definition of specific national interests in vague, universal language and imagery, and the pervasive fear that what was at stake was no less than the existence of (one's own) civilization itself. As the above analysis has tried to show, ideological differences were not at the heart of the cold war in its initial stages. The international dispute between the United States and the Soviet Union as states in no way flowed from the differences in their social and economic systems (need for surplus markets, character of central planning, and so on). Although each superpower believed deeply in the universal validity of its own revolutionary experience, this messianic inclination could not by itself unleash the tensions that led to cold war. What the ideological

conflict could and did do was to exacerbate serious, but otherwise normal, geopolitical conflicts of interest and contribute to a complex process
whereby the policy of the adversary, now become "enemy," was endowed
with coherence, direction, and specific malevolence in a single conceptual framework, one in which far-flung events took on an ominously
strategic shape. The ideological preconceptions that each side brought to
the cold war thus had the effect of prolonging it, as in the U.S. dispute
with China and the war in Vietnam, long after the main issues of the cold
war had been effectively decided.[19]

Ironically, the truly deadly ideological disputes of this time were those
between Communist states, i.e., Soviet Union versus Yugoslavia and
Soviet Union versus China. Whereas the United States reacted with remarkable acuity to the former quarrel,[20] the ideologization of the U.S.
foreign policy vision and domestic political life that had set in after 1950
inhibited the United States from exploiting the potential inherent in a
strong independent China and then in the Sino-Soviet conflict itself. A
major opportunity, which did not return for two decades, was thus lost.
The United States could have transformed the nature of the cold war
competition by dealing with national communism in China as it had done
shortly before, in a somewhat more permissive domestic climate, with
Communist Yugoslavia. The detente that the United States ultimately
concluded with Mao's China in 1971–1972 constituted belated recognition on the U.S. part that its global containment policy had been seriously
out of phase with developments for at least a decade and that U.S.
Secretary of State Dean Acheson's intuition in 1950 that a national Chinese
communism could constitute an effective barrier to Russian imperialism,
and thus an effective foundation for a stable balance of power in Asia,
had been right all along.[21]

What *Was* the Cold War About?

So what was the cold war about? In retrospect, the question seems
much harder to answer than it probably did to contemporaries, some of
whom would probably shake their head in wonderment at the above
analysis. Yet if we address each of its putative justifications singly, any
clear answer seems to fade into the ether. First, from the U.S. side, was
the cold war about fighting communism? As long as the Soviet Union
remained the sole Communist state, this was a fairly simple proposition,
because communism and Russian/Soviet power amounted to the same
thing. After 1948, however, with the emergence of independent centers
of Communist power in Yugoslavia and then in China, the ideological
simplicity of the cold war disappeared. The United States found itself

supporting communism in its national variety precisely in order to complicate the projection of Soviet power. The Yugoslav case has been mentioned; and although the U.S. opening to China would be delayed by two decades of tragic ideological blindness, the United States did undertake, after 1956, to encourage and cultivate national communism in Eastern Europe in the form of the policy of differentiation (see Chapter 3). Therefore, communism as such was not necessarily inimical to U.S. interests and cannot prove sufficient as an explanation for the course of the cold war.

What about the argument that the cold war revolved around the necessity to create a stable balance of power in Europe as against the disproportionate Soviet power presence there? Whereas this made up the core of the East-West conflict after the war, by the mid-1950s the economic health and political self-confidence of Western Europe—always the focal point of the containment strategy in Europe—had been restored, supplemented by NATO, the powerful trans-Atlantic military arm of the North Atlantic Treaty. Khrushchev himself admitted this basic fact in his 1956 revision of Soviet doctrine, in which he admitted the possibility of peaceful roads to socialism, and in the establishment of diplomatic relations with the Federal Republic of Germany in 1955. So if the cold war continued past the mid-1950s, the need to establish a European balance of power was no longer a central issue in it. As for the position, central to West German foreign policy at the time, that the cold war was quintessentially about resolving the division of Germany in a divided Europe, the deeds of all sides would show, before the decade of the 1950s was out, their essential satisfaction with this de facto geopolitical settlement emerging out of World War II.

Although the containment of Russian/Soviet power, as distinct from communism as such, was certainly the centerpiece of U.S. cold war policy (though by the 1960s China had assumed higher priority for the United States), containment and cold war were not strictly synonymous. In Europe, at least, the task of containing Soviet power was adequately framed in terms of the Marshall Plan, a sober and pragmatic initiative that avoided the hyperbole and universalism characteristic of the cold war atmosphere of the 1950s. Even the North Atlantic Treaty, as distinct from NATO, was initially conceived as primarily a political undertaking. Only with the advent of the Korean War in June 1950 did the cold war assume the hyperbolic, militarized, and semiapocalyptic character that it has retained in the popular imagination. Significantly, powerful traces of this cold war *atmosphere,* transcending the specific issues for which the cold war was ostensibly fought, would survive their resolution and continue to haunt the present in the guise of mental images, military instruments, and institutional interests. The task of "managing" Soviet power, then, goes beyond the concept of cold war because (1) "cold war" was not originally considered requisite to that task, and (2) the task itself outlives the waning of the cold war.

Finally, was the cold war about the contest between capitalism and communism, or rather democracy and communism? Certainly, many thought so at the time. Stillman and Pfaff captured this sense well when they wrote in 1961: "A Presidential proposal for a world referendum on the issue of Communism versus the American political system would in 1947 have seemed implausible if not impertinent. In 1960, when it was in fact made, it hardly seemed remarkable: the revolution in America's thinking during the decade was imposing."[22]

The prevailing atmosphere in East and West in the late 1950s was indeed one of civilizational challenge, as Khrushchev made clear with his "we will bury you" remark and as the Americans displayed in their frantic reaction to Sputnik. The problem is that it is practically impossible to relate such Spenglerian brooding (on the U.S. side) to any specific political agenda, save perhaps whether the newly independent nations would "go" Communist or not. This is not to discount such atmospherics, for they certainly played a role in reinforcing and inflaming existing sources of tension. The analytical difficulty is in relating the issue of domestic systems to the international political agenda: There is no strict and necessary relationship between the two and much evidence to suggest that regardless of the course of the two economic/political systems, there will remain plenty of sources of tension and conflict to keep diplomats and warriors gainfully employed for decades to come.

What then *was* the cold war about? And if it is not the cold war but the post–cold war order that is now ending, how is one to interpret the undeniable changes now buffeting the international political system?

In substantive terms the cold war played itself out long ago. The issues over which it was fought—Germany, balance of power, deterrence of war, the relevance of U.S. and Soviet ideology to the Third World—have been either effectively resolved or removed to the periphery of international political life. The one element that could not quite be removed, at least until the collapse of Soviet power itself in August 1991, is that of fear, fear of ultimate intentions and existing capabilities (mainly military). The images and military instruments generated by the cold war have outlived the cold war itself; yet although they no longer bear directly on negotiable political differences, they continue to exert their influence on contemporary international relations. The image of the "evil empire" advanced by President Reagan in 1983, which is really only the mirror image of the United States that the Soviet leadership had been trumpeting for so long, expresses this well and underscores the remarkable continuity of basic imagery from Dulles's time right through the 1980s.

The military dimension, claimed to be only the reflection of political differences, continued to occupy a prominent place in East-West relations well past the time when the central issues of contention, i.e., the division of Germany and of Europe and the establishment of a stable balance of power in Europe and East Asia, had been settled. So, although the cold war proper ended sometime during the 1960s, its presence has lingered via its residue of fear and the worst-case thinking that often appears the only prudent hedge against the fearful arsenals at the disposal of East and West. We may thus safely paraphrase Thucydides, cited in the chapter epigraph, and conclude that the real cause of the cold war (and of its continuation in attenuated form) has been the growth of U.S. power and the fear this caused in Russia; and conversely, the growth in Soviet power and the fear this caused in the United States.

But if the cold war proper ended long ago and its residue is largely the atmospherics it engendered, then how should we interpret the changes that have given rise to the query, Is the cold war over? Obviously, the breakthrough in East-West relations since 1986 has been generated by the domestic and foreign policy changes introduced by Soviet leader Mikhail Gorbachev and the general responsiveness of the West to them. Gorbachev came to power clearly intent upon liquidating those tendencies in Soviet foreign policy that had led to the growing isolation of the Soviet Union during the late Brezhnev era and beyond and that served to justify U.S. treatment of the Soviet Union as a pariah state.[23] What Gorbachev and his team did was to analyze key international trends that had been brewing for the preceding decade and more and to adapt Soviet foreign policy to their implications. These trends include:

- The increased technological creativity and dynamism of the capitalist West, which has led to the information revolution and an ever-increasing economic gap with the West
- The general intractability to change in the Third World
- The progressive decrease of superpower influence, especially within their respective alliance systems
- A qualitatively greater degree of international interdependence, which refutes the purely "zero sum" (the Leninist "kto-kogo") view of international relations and highlights the impact of forms of power other than that of armed force
- The consequences of nuclear parity, i.e., the obvious limits to the political use of nuclear weapons, which raised the question of the kind of military policy the Soviet Union should have under conditions of both a continuing arms competition and nuclear parity.

The conclusions that the Soviet reform leadership drew from these trends have been encapsulated in the "new political thinking" on foreign and security policy, which may be summarized as follows (for details, see Chapter 5):

1. Nuclear war cannot under any circumstances be won; therefore, nuclear weapons cannot be an instrument of policy.
2. Security cannot be obtained through military means alone; furthermore, security in the nuclear age is mutual in character and must rely strongly on political means.
3. Nuclear deterrence as a durable guarantor of peace is rejected. Strategic parity, seen as a historical success for socialism, could cease to be a factor of stability in the face of an unconstrained arms race.
4. Peaceful coexistence as a concept is seen less as a form of class struggle and increasingly as a long-lasting condition in which states with different social and political systems will have to learn how to live with each other for the indefinite future.
5. The multipolar and interdependent character of contemporary international relations is increasingly recognized.
6. Even a conventional war, fought in Europe with contemporary military technology, would be catastrophic and must be prevented.

Most remarkably, Gorbachev undertook a sweeping reevaluation of the role of ideology in Soviet foreign policy, which Western and now even some Soviet analysts view as a fixed background condition of the cold war between East and West. Gorbachev wrote that the Soviet leadership has "taken the steps necessary to rid our policy of ideological prejudice."[24] Yevgeny Primakov, a close adviser of Gorbachev, argued in a key 1987 *Pravda* article that peaceful coexistence is no longer regarded "as a breathing space" by the Soviets. "Interstate relations," he emphasized, "cannot be the sphere in which the outcome of the confrontation between world socialism and world capitalism is settled."[25] Such active coexistence is said by Soviet analysts to imply not just the simple absence of war (the cold war itself may have ensured that). Instead it implies an international order in which rather than military strength relations of confidence and cooperation prevail and global problems—the arms race, ecological problems, Third World development—can be resolved on a collaborative basis. This has led to a more pragmatic Soviet understanding of peaceful coexistence, with "class interests" now strictly subordinate to geopolitical criteria in the daily conduct of foreign policy. Soviet toleration of the anti-Communist revolutions in Eastern Europe, including the unification of Germany on Western terms, is the decisive confirmation of this point. A central obstacle to a more genuinely collaborative East-West relationship had thus been removed. This means that the Soviet Union and the United States could actually agree on the operational significance of "normal" relations, which proved impossible during the detente of the 1970s.

The opportunity that now presents itself is not to end the "cold war," for in almost every significant respect the cold war ended over two decades ago. Rather, the possibility now exists, based upon a serious Soviet Russian reevaluation of the character of its engagement with its international environment and the collapse of even the theoretical possibility of a Soviet aggression against the West, to eliminate the residues of the cold war in East-West relations—the set of threat perceptions, military instruments, and institutional interests that were generated by the cold war in its early, substantive, geopolitical stages—and to demilitarize what will remain an uneasy and at times even tense relationship. Unfortunately, finally bypassing the cold war will not in itself resolve the normal conflicts of interest that inhere in East-West relations, as in international relations in general, and that countless times in the past have led nations to war, even if they had not been conducting a cold war beforehand. In addition, the collapse of the strict bipolar political-military order in East-West relations since 1989 has both revealed and generated an entirely new set of factors that threaten to destabilize the international system. So there is much serious and sobering work ahead for the diplomats, soldiers, and politicians. They will have to be very skilled indeed if they are not to look back upon the cold war with fond nostalgia.

Notes

1. As cited in Donald Treadgold, "Has Communism Failed?" *1991 Funk and Wagnalls New Encyclopedia Yearbook* (Funk & Wagnalls, 1991), p. 19.

2. Michael Howard, *The Lessons of History* (New Haven: Yale University Press, 1991). As cited in *New York Times Book Review,* March 24, 1991.

3. In support of this point, see Barry M. Blechman, *Force Without War: U.S. Armed Forces as a Political Instrument* (Washington, D.C.: Brookings Institution, 1978); and Stephan S. Kaplan, *Diplomacy of Power: Soviet Armed Forces as a Political Instrument* (Washington, D.C.: Brookings Institution, 1981).

4. Early signs of change may be detected in V. Dashichev, *Literaturnaya Gazeta,* May 18, 1988, p. 14; and G. A. Trofimenko and P. T. Podlesnyi, eds., *Sovetsko-Amerikanskiye Otnosheniya v Sovremennom Mire* (Moscow: Nauka, 1987), p. 5.

5. André Fontaine, *History of the Cold War* (New York: Vintage, 1970), vol. 2, p. 185.

6. Cited in Robert Dallek, *The American Style of Foreign Policy: Cultural Politics and Foreign Affairs* (New York: Knopf, 1983), p. 187.

7. Edmund Stillman and William Pfaff, *The Politics of Hysteria: The Sources of 20th Century Conflict* (New York: Harper Colophon, 1964), p. 3.

8. For the text of the Truman Doctrine, with its universal ideological defense of a rather specific policy, see Joseph Marion Jones, *The Fifteen Weeks: An Inside Account of the Genesis of the Marshall Plan* (New York: Harcourt, Brace & World, 1955), pp. 269–274.

9. See Charles Gati, "The Stalinist Legacy in Soviet Foreign Policy," in Erik P. Hoffman and Frederic J. Fleron, Jr., eds., *The Conduct of Soviet Foreign Policy* (New York: Aldine, 1980), pp. 644–672.

10. Eric F. Goldman, *The Crucial Decade—and After: America, 1945–1960* (New York: Vintage, 1960), p. 60.

11. Dasichev, op. cit.

12. See Louis J. Halle, *The Cold War as History* (New York: Harper & Row, 1967), for the most judicious treatment of the cold war as a whole. See also John Lewis Gaddis, *Strategies of Containment* (New York: Oxford University Press, 1982), for the best treatment of the subject from the angle of U.S. policy.

13. For a responsible discussion, see Adam B. Ulam, *Expansion and Coexistence: Soviet Foreign Policy, 1917–1973,* 2d ed. (New York: Praeger, 1974), pp. 504–514 and esp. 535–537.

14. George Kennan, *Memoirs, 1950–1963* (New York: Pantheon Books, 1972), pp. 229–266.

15. Willy Brandt, *Begegnungen und Einsichten: Die Jahre 1960–1975* (Hamburg: Hoffman und Campe, 1976), pp. 9–41.

16. Raymond Garthoff, *From Detente to Confrontation: American-Soviet Relations from Nixon to Reagan* (Washington, D.C.: Brookings Institution, 1985), pp. 115–116.

17. Flora Lewis, "Foreign Affairs," *New York Times,* June 12, 1988; and Sergei Karaganov, "The Year of Europe: A Soviet View," *Survival,* March/April 1990.

18. See the chapter by the Polish specialist Ryszard Woyna in F. Stephen Larrabee, ed., *The Two German States and the Future of European Security* (New York: St. Martin's Press, 1989), pp. 220–241. See also Karaganov, op. cit.

19. The most compelling analysis to this effect remains George Kennan's testimony before the Senate Foreign Relations Committee in February 1966, in *The Vietnam Hearings* (New York: Vintage, 1966), pp. 107–166.

20. *Foreign Relations of the United States, 1949,* vol. 5, *USSR and Eastern Europe* (Washington, D.C.: U.S. Government Printing Office, 1976), pp. 856–859, 886–890ff., 941–945.

21. Dean Acheson, *Present at the Creation: My Years in the State Department* (New York: Norton, 1969), p. 356.

22. Edmund Stillman and William Pfaff, *The New Politics: America and the End of the Postwar World* (New York: Harper Colophon, 1961), p. 32.

23. Dashichev, op. cit., and point ten of party conference theses, *Pravda,* May 27, 1988, p. 1.

24. Mikhail S. Gorbachev, *Perestroika: New Thinking for My Country and the World* (New York: Harper & Row, 1987), p. 250.

25. *Pravda,* July 10, 1987, p. 4.

2

The Nuclear Family: The Management of the U.S.-Soviet Relationship

The idea that the "cold war" has actually been over for some twenty years implies considerable activity in dampening rivalries and in managing conflict in East-West relations. This would be especially true of U.S.-Soviet relations, which have after all been the driving force of the cold war, as they have of East-West relations in general. Indeed, in practice, U.S.-Soviet relations in the post-1945 period, for all their undisputed tension and hostility, have taken place within a fairly specific framework of restraints that has served to moderate the superpower competition. This historical pattern of moderation in the U.S.-Soviet relationship, which flies in the face of widely accepted notions of a virtually unrestricted global contest between the Soviet Union and the United States, is the result of the logic imposed by nuclear weapons upon the conduct of the two most powerful nuclear states. Destined by their geopolitical positions and ideological values to clash, the superpowers have been prohibited by the knowledge of the catastrophic consequences of nuclear use from pushing their competition to the limit.

From the 1950s on, one can detect an emerging and progressively more sophisticated pattern of strategic collaboration between the Soviet

A portion of this chapter was adapted from F. Stephen Larrabee and Allen Lynch, *Confidence-Building Measures and U.S.-Soviet Relations* (New York: Institute for East-West Security Studies, 1986), Occasional Paper no.1.

Union and the United States: Each country has sought by means of direct and indirect signaling, diplomacy, and arms control measures of various kinds to reinforce the prohibition against conduct that might lead, if only by inadvertent escalation, to a nuclear conflict between the two. The result of this history of cooperation has been an increasingly stable nuclear relationship. Both countries have gone to great lengths to avoid a direct collision that could lead to a nuclear confrontation. Indeed, much of the rest of their foreign policies has been shaped by this common nuclear fate, often at the sacrifice of relationships with allies. However important the alliance relationships of the superpowers have been, they could not compare to the ultimate threat posed by each other's nuclear arsenals. In this respect one may even speak of a limited community of security between the United States and the Soviet Union.

The possession by the Soviet Union and the United States of the potential to destroy not merely each other but most of the civilized world as well has meant that the U.S.-Soviet relationship occupies a unique place in the international political system. "What remains constant," a seasoned British diplomat and scholar wrote, "since they are the only superpowers, is that their relations with each other are qualitatively different from their relations with their allies and with the rest of the world."[1] Henry Kissinger took up the point when he was secretary of state: "The Soviet Union and we are in a unique relationship. We are at one and the same time adversaries and partners in the preservation of peace."[2]

From this recognition of the limits that the very nature of their competition had thrust upon them, the two superpowers have behaved as if they were following the same set of rules in their interrelationship. The most important of these rules by far has been the understanding that there must be no nuclear war, however limited, between Moscow and Washington. Given the scope of the two superpowers' international commitments, and the impossibility beforehand of agreeing on limits to any conflicts that do occur, the determination to avoid nuclear war amounts to a prohibition on general war in the international system.[3]

Two significant corollaries follow from this overarching conviction that nuclear war must at all costs be avoided. First, there has been no war between the core Soviet and U.S. alliance systems or parts of them. Thus, after what may be seen in retrospect as an initial learning period about the stability of the postwar European balance of power in the late 1940s and 1950s, the two superpowers sought to institutionalize a division of Europe that, however unsatisfactory from a moral point of view, seemed to provide definite benefits of stability and peace. Second, and no less important, the Soviet Union and the United States have taken considerable pains to ensure that their broader global rivalry, especially in what became known as the Third World, did not trigger by miscalculation or overcommitment a direct confrontation between the two superpowers.

Detente

The logic of this limited partnership between the Soviet Union and the United States was captured in a most significant, but also (at least by Americans) most overlooked, agreement that was signed at the 1972 "detente" summit in Moscow by Richard Nixon and Leonid Brezhnev, the joint "Declaration on Basic Principles of Relations Between the United States of America and the Union of Soviet Socialist Republics." Aside from a passage committing both sides to recognizing "peaceful coexistence" as the basis of U.S.-Soviet relations—a concept that clouded as much as it clarified the achievements of detente—the document:

- Attached "major importance to preventing the development of situations capable of causing a dangerous exacerbation of their relations"
- Committed both governments to doing their utmost to avoid military confrontations and to prevent the outbreak of nuclear war
- Pledged them always to exercise restraint in their interrelationship and to be prepared to negotiate and settle differences by peaceful means
- Recognized that efforts to obtain "unilateral advantage" at the expense of the other, whether directly or indirectly, were inconsistent with these goals
- Established as prerequisites for the maintenance and strengthening of peaceful U.S.-Soviet relations "the recognition of the security interests of the parties based on the principle of equality and the renunciation of the use or the threat of force"[4]

These "rules" of the 1972 Basic Principles agreement are significant not for any changes that they effected, or might have, in U.S.-Soviet relations. Rather, as Michael Mandelbaum noted, "they were written down because they were already being observed."[5] The detente of 1972 thus represented a codification of understandings and practices that had become ever more deeply ingrained in the U.S.-Soviet relationship. For a variety of reasons, including the domestic political situations of both superpowers, their institutionalization did not occur until the Nixon-Brezhnev breakthrough of 1972.

A limited nuclear accommodation, a "condominium," according to alarmed foreign observers, had in fact been developing for over a decade before the Nixon-Brezhnev detente. Formal arms control agreements represented the most visible but by no means the exclusive or even the most important aspect of superpower nuclear collaboration. The three cornerstones of the U.S.-Soviet nuclear partnership were, first, as stated above, the determination to avoid a direct military conflict, however limited, because of the possible link to nuclear war; second, agreement to prevent or where that was unfeasible to restrict as much as possible the spread of nuclear weapons to other nations; and finally, recognition, however grudging, that each superpower possessed undisputed capacity to destroy and thus to deter the other, under any conceivable scenario, and that this represented a stubborn if unpleasant fact of nuclear life.[6]

Arms Control and Disarmament Agreements

Since the 1960s, the climate of U.S.-Soviet relations, and especially of its nuclear aspect, has been gauged by achievements and progress in the field of arms control and disarmament. The aims of those have been to limit the risk of war, the damage caused should war come, and the costs of maintaining an adequate defense by constraining, reducing, or eliminating the number and types of weapons fielded by both superpowers.[7] Indeed, the record of U.S.-Soviet arms control, aside from its intrinsic interest, does provide a meaningful measure of the state of superpower relations throughout the recent past. The signing of an arms control accord has generally signaled a certain relaxation of tensions in U.S.-Soviet relations. Conversely, deadlock or breakdown in arms control negotiations has reflected deeper, politically rooted conflicts of interest between Washington and Moscow. A quick and selective review of arms control in U.S.-Soviet relations bears this out:[8]

1946—Soviet rejection of the American "Baruch Plan" for the international control of nuclear weapons signals the beginning of the nuclear arms race.

1955—Soviet rejection of President Eisenhower's "Open Skies" proposal for mutual U.S.-Soviet aerial inspection of each other's territory causes the United States to go forward with U-2 aerial espionage over the USSR. Aside from its impact on Soviet perceptions of a U.S. threat, the U-2 program would provide the occasion for Soviet withdrawal from the 1960 Paris summit conference.

1959—Signature by the superpowers of the multilateral treaty on Antarctic disarmament signals a desire to limit the arms race where it is politically easy to do so.

1958–1961—Tacit observance of a ban on atmospheric nuclear testing by the Soviet Union, United States, and Great Britain reflects an attempt by all three powers to square greater public consciousness of nuclear dangers with political and propaganda advantages. Soviet resumption of such testing in September 1961, at the height of the Berlin Wall crisis, reflects a shift in Moscow's political calculations about the direction of its Western policy.

1963—Signature by the superpowers of a multilateral ban on atmospheric nuclear tests reflects the desire of both countries after the Cuban Missile Crisis to regulate their competition in a more systematic way.

1968—Signature of the multilateral Nuclear Nonproliferation Treaty formalizes the superpowers' implicit interest in restricting membership to the nuclear club.

1968—Postponement of negotiations on reducing strategic nuclear weapons by the Johnson administration following the Soviet invasion of Czechoslovakia reflects the political impossibility of engaging the Soviet Union in such talks in an atmosphere of crisis in East-West relations.

1972—Signature of agreements limiting offensive and defensive strategic nuclear systems reflects a U.S. desire to constrain future Soviet weapons deployments and a Soviet desire to guarantee military and political parity with the United States.

1979–1980—U.S. Senate debate over ratification of a second strategic nuclear arms control treaty is dominated by the question of Soviet political conduct around the world. The decision of the Carter administration to defer presentation of the treaty to the Senate for ratification reflects the recognition that the ratification is not possible in the aftermath of the Soviet invasion of Afghanistan.

1981–1982—Deferral of the arms control issue by the Reagan administration reflects the broader political desire that arms control, with the consequent implication of Soviet political equality with the United States, no longer be at the center of U.S.-Soviet relations. Nevertheless, the Reagan administration will continue de facto to observe those nuclear arms control agreements that it has publicly repudiated.

1985—Resumption of negotiations on strategic nuclear arms control reflects genuine concerns that the superpower political relationship may be getting out of control as well as the USSR's frustration at its inability to influence Western governments' military and arms control policies by refusing to negotiate.

1987—The Gorbachev about-face on the issue of intermediate-range nuclear weapons in Europe, whereby the USSR agreed to give up all of its superior number of SS-20 missiles in exchange for much smaller U.S. reductions, reflects a major political reevaluation in the Kremlin: The political effect of President Reagan's signature on any significant arms control agreement with Moscow, in effect cementing detente in the U.S. political system, far outweighs any specific military advantages that Moscow may thereby yield.

1990–1991—Soviet consent in November 1990 to surrender its quantitative military advantage in Europe, quickly followed by the Soviet military's effort to sabotage the execution of the treaty by reassigning tank units to the Soviet navy, reflects the uncertainties in the fast disintegrating Soviet political system. U.S. reluctance to conclude the practically completed Strategic Arms Reduction Treaty (a product of the Strategic Arms Reduction Talks—START), which would eventually be signed during President Bush's summit visit to Moscow in late July 1991, was based on these uncertainties.

September 1991—President Bush's announcement of unilateral U.S. measures to abolish all tactical nuclear weapons, followed quickly by reciprocal Soviet steps, indicates the intention on both sides to move as rapidly as possible to insulate the control of nuclear weapons from the domestic instabilities rocking the Soviet system. In this view, fewer nuclear weapons, stored in fewer, centrally managed sites, would strengthen unified political control over those weapons. This new stage in superpower arms control, based on reciprocal unilateral steps bypassing formal negotiating procedures, corresponds closely with the disintegration of the USSR and the reorientation of U.S. policy to take into account the reality of an unstable nuclear partner.

This uneven record in arms control, although corresponding to the fluctuations in U.S.-Soviet relations, might seem to contradict the point about the superpowers' partnership, however limited, in the management of their joint nuclear fate. One might expect to find steady progress, rather than the irregular movement on formal arms control agreements that I have identified. Yet, there is another, altogether different, level to the superpowers' nuclear relationship. That level goes beyond the issue of limiting the quantities or qualities of weapons; it is the actual behavior of the two states that could trigger the use of the weapons that may or may not be limited by arms control. And in this sphere, the evolution of constraints on the nuclear relationship has proved less dependent on the ebb and flow of U.S.-Soviet political relations. The management of the U.S.-Soviet nuclear relationship has been as much preoccupied by the question of constraining the deployment of military forces-in-being and preventing conflicts that could arise out of miscalculation and misperception as it has with the formal limitation of weapons systems as such.

Confidence-Building Measures

If the path to possible superpower confrontation can be paved by a "local" crisis that escalates out of control because of miscalculation, poor communication, or accident, then the arms control approach by itself is clearly insufficient. In this respect, policymakers in both capitals would be interested in the actual operations of military forces, especially their potential for surprise attack (which could render numerical balances largely irrelevant), and in convincing assurances about military intentions.[9] In these circumstances, politicians will be searching for predictable patterns of political and political-military activity, whether threatening or not. There would thus be an objective common interest on the part of both superpowers, assuming as we do that there is no prior intention of nuclear aggression, to establish procedures for recognizing the "normal" pattern of political-military conduct, thereby making it easier to discern significant deviations indicating a possible threat. This may be done unilaterally, as in the case of the U-2 espionage planes, or cooperatively. If the latter, such measures would fall under the category of "confidence-building measures," that is, measures designed to stabilize relations between states by providing tangible and verifiable assurances as to the purpose and character of military and political-military activity.[10] In the words of two theorists on the subject, those measures seek to communicate "evidence of the absence of feared threats."[11]

Such confidence-building measures, or CBMs, may be of several types. The first includes measures that provide short-term stability, particularly in a crisis. These are generally aimed at defusing a crisis, in some cases perhaps preventing one, by enhancing communication or reducing the danger of misperception or miscalculation. Examples of these "risk reduction" or "crisis prevention" measures are the 1963 agreement on the Hotline—concluded after the frustrating experience that both Kennedy and Khrushchev had in communicating with each other during the Cuban Missile Crisis. The Hotline provides for the transmission by wire (and later by satellite) of time-urgent information to clarify intentions (since 1985 fax transmission of photographs and documents is included). Another such measure is the 1973 Agreement on the Prevention of Nuclear War, which contains provisions for urgent consultations in the event of the risk of war between the two superpowers or between either of them and third countries. Both of these agreements were updated in 1984 and 1985, during the lowest point in U.S.-Soviet relations since the Cuban Missile Crisis. This underscores the fact that even in time of poor relations the Soviet Union and United States share a significant common interest in creating greater stability in their relationship and in reducing the prospect that any crisis in which they might be involved could inadvertently escalate out of control.

A second set of CBMs is designed to establish long-term stability. The aim here is to oblige nations to act habitually in ways that may eliminate the causes of tension and reduce the dangers of miscalculation and misperception. Such measures also strive to provide operationally meaningful obstacles to the use of military force by requiring tangible proof of peaceful intent. The 1986 agreement of the conference on disarmament in Europe, signed in Stockholm by thirty-three European states as well as the two superpowers, provides for the detailed prenotification of military maneuvers, the exchange of long-term calendars of military activities by all countries concerned, the dispatch of military observers to training exercises on a routine basis, and mandatory international challenge inspection. Such measures as the prenotification of ballistic missile test launches, agreed to at the fourth Reagan-Gorbachev summit in Moscow in May–June 1988, fall within this category of longer-term stabilizing confidence-building measures as well.

In addition to helping stabilize superpower relations in time of impending or actual crisis, a condition called "crisis stability" by the experts, CBMs have also proved useful in contributing to "arms race stability," that is, to assuring predictability in a military relationship. The more one understands about the other side's military capabilities, the less the chance of unnecessary competition triggered by uncertainty or misjudgment of strategic capabilities. The routine exchanges of data on force levels and of military concepts that have come to characterize U.S.-Soviet nuclear and conventional arms control negotiations can help to reduce the danger that actions by one side are misperceived by the other and thereby provoke an unintended, expensive, and in the nuclear age potentially catastrophic response. Had such practices existed in the 1950s, unjustified U.S. fears of a bomber gap and then a missile gap might have been avoided, and with them expensive weapons programs and heightened superpower tensions.

In a related vein, CBMs can enhance compliance with arms control agreements, and thus the level of confidence in U.S.-Soviet relations, by providing for the adequate exchange of information needed to ensure verification of specific military activities. An example of this is the provision in the 1972 strategic arms control agreement that prohibits interference with "national-technical means" (i.e., spy satellites) of monitoring compliance with the treaties. Moreover, the second strategic nuclear arms control treaty of 1979 prohibits the encryption of telemetry (i.e., the encoding of missile test-flight data, made famous by John Le Carre's *Russia House*) needed to ensure that each side is complying with treaty provisions against excessive modification of existing missile forces. This latter prohibition was significantly strengthened in the Strategic Arms Reduction Treaty signed in Moscow in late July 1991.

This discussion of "confidence-building measures" in U.S.-Soviet relatons is intended to reveal an aspect of the strategic collaboration of the two states that escapes the usual focus on nuclear arms control. Indeed, since the 1950s, the Soviet Union and the United States have been engaged in an on-again, off-again discussion of ways to instill greater confidence in their strategic relationship. On the whole, this has involved the elaboration of measures aimed at preventing surprise attack and reducing the risk of nuclear war through accident and miscalculation.

Initial U.S.-Soviet discussions on building "confidence" into their relationship centered on measures to provide greater information about each other's strategic nuclear capabilities, both as an end in itself and as a means of more effectively monitoring compliance with arms control schemes then under discussion. The "Open Skies" proposal, for example, put forward by President Eisenhower during the July 1955 Geneva summit conference, sought to lay the groundwork for both effective arms control measures and greater confidence in the stability of U.S.-Soviet relations through mutual aerial inspection of Soviet and American territory by each other's aircraft.[12] The Soviet Union, not surprisingly, rejected the idea: Why trade what would be a marginal gain in knowledge of the capabilities of the United States—an open society—as against a qualitative leap in U.S. knowledge of Soviet capabilities? Ironically, the superpowers ultimately recognized the validity of the open skies idea by legalizing aerial surveillance in the provision of the 1972 agreement coming from the Strategic Arms Limitation Talks (SALT I) that stipulated that neither side would interfere with the other's espionage satellites for purposes of verifying compliance with the agreement. Thus, though stillborn in 1955, the "Open Skies" proposal indicated a U.S. willingness to consider collaborative measures designed to create a more stable superpower relationship.

In 1958, at the Geneva surprise attack conference, the Soviet Union proposed the exchange of military observers at key points in NATO and Warsaw Pact territory in order to verify compliance with proposed agreements to limit the armed forces of the powers in Europe and thereby reduce the risk of nuclear surprise attack. Although the inconclusive adjournment of this conference left this proposal in abeyance, it eventually became, in modified form, part of the 1986 Stockholm Agreement on Confidence- and Security-Building Measures and Disarmament in Europe. More broadly, that long-overlooked 1958 conference proved an especially valuable occasion for East and West to explore many of the concepts that later played a central role in U.S.-Soviet and East-West relations, such as the role of national-technical means of verification in monitoring compliance with arms control agreements.[13]

Since the Cuban Missile Crisis, the Soviet Union and the United States have focused increasing attention on joint and individual development of measures that could reduce the risk of nuclear war through accident or miscalculation to the minimum. In December 1962, for instance, President Kennedy unilaterally offered to the Soviet leadership certain nuclear command and control systems perfected in the United States and designed to prevent the accidental or otherwise unauthorized release of nuclear weapons ("permissive action links"). His action reflected a desire not merely to reduce to the lowest possible level the chance of accidental or unauthorized nuclear launch on *both* sides—though that is important enough—but in addition to assure the Soviet leaders that the U.S. government shared their concerns about the horrors of nuclear war. In this way, Kennedy's offer was intended to serve as a kind of double confidence-building measure, one that both possessed inherent strategic value and affirmed the broader coincidence of superpower interests in strategic stability, precisely because of their political differences.

The "Hotline" agreement of 1963, mentioned earlier, established for the first time direct telecommunications links between Washington and Moscow and continues to represent a key military-technical confidence-building measure. The significance of this accord, however, went considerably beyond a crisis control procedure: It also indicated the desire of each side to bring the nuclear arms race under some sort of control and their communality of interest in limiting it. In a number of tense situations, such as the Middle East wars of 1967 and 1973, and the Indo-Pakistani War of 1971, the Hotline has been used to convey intentions and keep regional conflicts from escalating into superpower confrontations. As obvious as such a measure now seems, the absence of a Hotline was sorely felt during the Cuban crisis, when Soviet and U.S. leaders had to communicate indirectly, resorting to late-night meetings of intermediaries in Washington restaurants.[14] The value that both the United States and the Soviet Union have ascribed to the Hotline, and thereby to their joint responsibility in managing their nuclear relationship, is shown in the agreements to upgrade the Hotline in 1971 and 1984.

Related confidence-building steps in U.S.-Soviet nuclear relations include the tacit moratorium on atmospheric nuclear testing observed by the United States, Soviet Union, and Great Britain from 1958 to 1961.

Although the moratorium was broken by Nikita Khrushchev in September 1961, it would serve as the foundation for the Partial Nuclear Test-Ban Treaty of 1963 and for the series of unilateral declarations by the same three nuclear powers in 1964 on limiting their production of uranium for military purposes.

The September 1971 U.S.-Soviet Agreement to Reduce the Risk of Nuclear War is in many ways a logical successor to the Hotline accord. In this agreement, the superpowers pledged to take measures to perfect their command and control systems (a tribute to Kennedy's 1962 gesture) so as to avoid unauthorized use of nuclear weapons and to communicate with each other in the event of accidental launches or other ambiguous situations. In the political context of the time, as U.S.-Soviet relations were moving closer to detente, this agreement represented an important step in the effort to devise a regime of crisis management and crisis avoidance in the superpower relationship.[15] The 1973 U.S.-Soviet Agreement on the Prevention of Nuclear War, which provided for urgent consultations in the event of a risk of war between the United States and the Soviet Union, or between either of them and third countries, was another step in this direction.

The 1972 Incidents at Sea Agreement provides for detailed "rules of the road" when Soviet and U.S. naval vessels are sailing near each other. This agreement has proved quite effective in preventing both accidents and incidents between the Soviet and U.S. navies, which often tail each other on the high seas. The accord has been one of the most scrupulously observed undertakings between the two governments and has successfully insulated U.S.-Soviet relations from a potentially troublesome source of military confrontation.[16]

As part of the negotiations to the two Strategic Arms Limitation accords of 1972 and 1979 (SALT I and SALT II), a number of agreements were signed and measures adopted that were designed to enhance verification and compliance with the agreements themselves. These include the previously mentioned provision in the SALT I agreement banning obstruction of either nation's efforts to verify compliance with the accord through its satellites in space, as well as later Soviet consent under SALT II to furnish for the first time data on its strategic forces. Those undertakings highlight the recognition by each country of the mutual importance both of the ability of the other to verify a critical agreement and of the value of nuclear arms control itself. Perhaps most important, the SALT I agreement established a joint Standing Consultative Commission (SCC), charged with airing and resolving questions concerning the implementation of the agreement. Although the degree of effectiveness of the SCC has often been influenced by the overall state of U.S.-Soviet relations, on the whole it has worked well and has provided an important forum for resolving alleged violations and disputes arising out of ambiguities in the SALT agreements.[17] Even during the nadir of recent U.S.-Soviet relations in 1984 and 1985, the two superpowers used the SCC to hammer out clarifications of the 1971 Agreement to Reduce the Risk of Nuclear War and of the 1972 treaty limiting the deployment of strategic antiballistic missile systems (the "ABM treaty"). In effect, then, the SCC has constituted a kind of built-in confidence-building measure in the U.S.-Soviet strategic relationship.

Perhaps the most important nuclear confidence-building measure has been a formal arms control agreement, i.e., the Antiballistic Missile (ABM) Treaty of 1972, which effectively proscribes either the Soviet Union or the United States from deploying meaningful defenses against the other's strategic nuclear missiles. Ironically, the ABM treaty induces confidence about the stability of the superpower relationship by removing any confidence that either side could strike the other and emerge unscathed. By ratifying their mutual-hostage condition the ABM treaty makes inescapable the recognition that—because either country can be destroyed by the unilateral action of the other—their survival depends on mutual collaboration. In addition, by removing the prospect of effective strategic defense, however chimerical, the treaty removes the incentive for an open-ended and almost certainly destabilizing offensive arms race (which would see each side constantly trying to offset the defensive advantages of the other with further offensive innovations). All told, the ABM treaty makes explicit the insight of President Kennedy in late 1962 that nuclear security is intrinsically a mutual concern and that neither side can achieve that security without at least the tacit collaboration of the other.

The history of confidence-building measures in U.S.-Soviet strategic relations, in many cases predating the achievement of arms control and disarmament agreements themselves, underscores the way in which their mutual nuclear fate has constrained the superpowers to circumscribe their political competition in the name of "safety first."[18] Even during the height of the cold war, both countries sought to identify ways in which their inevitable contest for international influence might be insulated from the awful and unacceptable risk of nuclear confrontation. The strength of this common superpower interest is proven by the political costs that each has had to pay as a result of their mutual-hostage relationship.

For the Soviet Union, efforts to achieve a detente with the United States that would insulate the global competition of capitalism and socialism from the suicidal risk of nuclear war provoked the defection of Mao Zedong's China from the Soviet camp by the early 1960s. Mao had wanted China's global revolutionary (as well as nationalist) aspirations against U.S. "imperialism" to be based on the Soviet nuclear arsenal, in effect to implicate the Soviet Union in Chinese ambitions at the risk of nuclear retaliation by the United States. Not surprisingly, the Soviet Union under Nikita Khrushchev balked, the Soviets stopped all nuclear cooperation with China by 1959, and the Sino-Soviet relationship, and thus the Soviet international power position, has never been the same.

Correspondingly, the United States, as I will discuss in Chapter 3, was constrained to shelve its rhetorical support for East European independence whenever that objective clashed with Soviet determination to enforce its will in that region. President Eisenhower's diplomatic reassurances to the Soviet leadership in November 1956 that the United States would not intervene in the Soviet invasion of Hungary and President Lyndon Johnson's withdrawal of U.S. forces in Germany from the Czechoslovak border in 1968 on the eve of the Soviet-led invasion of that country show that the United States has been compelled to limit its foreign policy objectives when they might clash with the vital interests of the Soviet Union. Similarly, the United States did its utmost to restrain Israel in 1967 and 1973 from pressing its military advantages to total victory. U.S. actions stemmed from fear of provoking a major escalation in the Soviet armed commitment to the Arab side, which would in turn incite a heightened U.S. military guarantee to Israel and a potential direct confrontation of Soviet and U.S. forces.

The chain of nuclear escalation has been envisaged to begin not with limited nuclear use but with any direct clash of Soviet and U.S. military forces. Thus, every effort has been made by both countries to avoid or control circumstances that might find them, by accident or miscalculation, shooting at each other. When the superpowers have believed such a clash to be possible, they have subordinated all other foreign policy commitments to this overarching common interest in survival. Consequently, any effort, including diplomacy, arms control, and confidence-building measures, has been considered justified to maintain the U.S.-Soviet nuclear relationship at the safest possible level. Correspondingly, almost any interest or commitment may be sacrificed to the superpowers' imperative toward nuclear condominium. Nuclear weapons have made the security of the adversary the essential condition of one's own survival.

The two countries' experience with diplomacy, arms control, and confidence-building measures has enabled them to build a foundation of nuclear stability that has survived the gyrations in their postwar political relationship. The management of the nuclear relationship is continuous, whether political relations are good or bad and whether they are intensive in depth or extensive in scope. The lessons thereby learned seem to have assumed a progressive quality. Perhaps the foundation of nuclear stability is not as strong as it might be, but it appears to have become consistently stronger with the passage of time. Soviet and U.S. leaders and their governments seem to have built upon accumulated experience instead of having to start anew with each "crisis" in U.S.-Soviet political relations.[19]

It is interesting in this regard to reflect on the history of U.S.-Soviet relations from 1980 to 1985, a period in which those relations, and by extension East-West relations, were poor. They did not, however, prove to be particularly explosive (unlike the 1948–1951 and 1958–1962 periods). The "postdetente" period of the early 1980s was not in fact replaced by a new cold war, at least not in the sense in which that term was used in Chapter 1. Although East-West relations were not able to achieve the breadth or degree of intimacy that the founders of detente envisaged in the early 1970s, relations never deteriorated to the point of all-out confrontation and recrimination characteristic of the early 1950s. The accumulated experience of East and West, and most of all of the Soviet Union and the United States, in managing a relationship of intractable nuclear deterrence and political detente, in effect reduced the limits of outright antagonism as well as suggested the inherent obstacles to a comprehensive political-military collaboration.

From the mid-1960s until the Gorbachev period, improvements as well as deteriorations in U.S.-Soviet relations took place within a framework that was neither a comprehensive "detente" nor "cold war." The defining question for the superpower relationship was therefore not that of cooperation versus competition but rather the balance between the two and the form that each assumed. The condition of mutual deterrence and thus of mutual hostage that nuclear weapons had imposed upon the Soviet Union and the United States has been a powerful force in preserving that minimal degree of cooperation even in times of deteriorating political relations. The improvement in U.S.-Soviet political relations since 1987 and the signing of the START arms reduction treaty in mid-1991 have done little to reduce the physical aspect of the nuclear threat to each. For the indefinite future each superpower's arsenal will retain the capacity to annihilate the other's society. Furthermore, as Chapter 8 will demonstrate, the political decomposition of the Soviet Union that Gorbachev's reform policies have set in motion casts the nuclear question in U.S.-Soviet relations in an entirely new light. It is thus very likely that U.S. relations with a post-Soviet and nuclear Russia will continue to be framed by the conditions that have called into being a most unusual nuclear family.

Notes

1. Robin Edmonds, *Soviet Foreign Policy: The Brezhnev Years* (Oxford: Oxford University Press, 1983), pp. 138–139.
2. Cited in ibid., p. 139.

3. Michael Mandelbaum, *The Nuclear Revolution* (Cambridge: Cambridge University Press, 1981), pp. 72–73.

4. For the text of the "Declaration on Basic Principles of Relations Between the United States of America and the Union of Soviet Socialist Republics, May 29, 1972," see United States Arms Control and Disarmament Agency, *Documents on Disarmament, 1972* (Washington, D.C.: U.S. Government Printing Office, 1974), pp. 237–240.

5. Mandelbaum, op. cit., p. 73. See also Friedrich Kratochwil, *International Order and Foreign Policy: A Theoretical Sketch of Postwar International Politics* (Boulder: Westview Press, 1978); and Joseph Nye, Jr., "Nuclear Learning and U.S.-Soviet Security Regimes," *International Organization,* Summer 1987, pp. 371–402.

6. Mandelbaum, op. cit., pp. 109–110.

7. As established in the seminal work by Thomas C. Schelling and Morton Halperin, *Strategy and Arms Control* (New York: Twentieth Century Fund, 1961).

8. For a list and description of most nuclear arms control accords, see Andrew Wilson, *The Disarmer's Handbook of Military Technology and Organization* (New York: Penguin Books, 1983).

9. William Langer Ury and Richard Smoke, *Beyond the Hotline: Controlling a Nuclear Crisis* (Cambridge, Mass.: Harvard Law School, 1984), pp. 12–13. See also Graham Allison, Albert Carnesdale, and Joseph Nye, *Hawks, Doves, and Owls* (New York: Norton, 1985); Richard Betts, *Surprise Attack* (Washington, D.C.: Brookings Institution, 1982), p. 4; and Johan Jorgen Holst, "Confidence-Building Measures: A Conceptual Framework," *Survival,* January-February 1983, pp. 2–15.

10. For a fuller application to U.S.-Soviet nuclear relations than is given here, see F. Stephen Larrabee and Allen Lynch, "Confidence-Building Measures and U.S.-Soviet Relations," in R. B. Byers, F. Stephen Larrabee, and Allen Lynch, eds., *Confidence-Building Measures and International Security* (New York: Institute for East-West Security Studies, 1987), pp. 79–109.

11. Johan Jorgen Holst and Karen Melander, "European Security and Confidence-Building Measures," *Survival,* July-August 1977, p. 147. For a representative sample of the Soviet literature in this field, see: Radomir Bogdanov, "On Confidence-Building Measures," in Karl Kaiser, ed., *Confidence-Building Measures* (Bonn: Forschungsinstitut der Deutschen Gesellschaft fuer Auswaertige Politik, 1983), pp. 53–59; Oleg Bykov, *Mery Doveriya* (Moscow: Nauka, 1982); Evgeny Kaminsky, *Stockholm: Two Approaches to Confidence-Building* (Moscow: Novosti, 1984); I. A. Khripunov, "Mery Doveriya: Problemy i Perspecktivy," in *Diplomatichesky Vestnik* (Moscow: Mezhdunarodnye Otnosheniya, 1985), pp. 54–62; B. P. Krasulin, *Politicheskiye Garantii Ustraneniya Yadernoi Ugrozi* (Moscow: Mezhdunarodnye Otnosheniya, 1984); I. N. Shcherbakov, "Diskussiya v S. Sh. A. Vokrug 'Mer Doveriya' v Yadernoi Oblasti," *S. Sh. A.* (Moscow), no. 10 (October 1985), pp. 84–89; Vadim L. Shvetsov, *Voyennaya Razryadka i Mery Doveriya* (Moscow: Mezhdunarodnye Otnosheniya, 1984); and Vadim K. Sobakin, *Ravnaya Bezopasnost'* (Moscow: Mezhdunarodnye Otnosheniya, 1984), pp. 221–223.

12. For a detailed account of the Open Skies proposal, see Walt Rostow, *Open Skies: Eisenhower's Proposal of July 21, 1955* (Austin: University of Texas Press, 1983). For the text of the proposal itself, see "The Geneva Conference of Heads of Government, July 18–23, 1955," Department of State Publication 6046 (1955), pp. 56–59.

13. For the main Soviet and Western proposals at the 1958 conference, see conference document GEN/SA/7/Rev. 1, as reproduced in UN document A/4078 (S/4145), January 5, 1959, annexes 8 and 11 respectively.

14. Paul Bracken, *The Command and Control of Nuclear Forces* (New Haven, Conn.: Yale University Press, 1983), p. 210.

15. Raymond Garthoff, *Detente and Confrontation: American Soviet Relations from Nixon to Reagan* (Washington, D.C.: Brookings Institution, 1985), p. 1073.

16. See Sean M. Lynn-Jones, "A Quiet Success for Arms Control: Preventing Incidents at Sea," *International Security,* Spring 1985, pp. 154–184.

17. See Dean Caldwell, "The Standing Consultative Commission: Past Performance and Future Possibilities," in William C. Potter, ed., *Verification and Arms Control* (Lexington, Mass.: Lexington Books, 1985), pp. 217–229; and Sidney Braybeal and Michael Krepon, "SCC: Neglected Arms Control Tool," *Bulletin of the Atomic Scientists,* November 1985, pp. 30–33.

18. This use of the phrase is Adam Ulam's in *Expansion and Coexistence: A History of Soviet Foreign Policy, 1917–1973* (New York: Praeger, 1973), p. 726.

19. As is borne out by Gordon R. Weihmiller, *U.S.-Soviet Summits: An Account of East-West Diplomacy at the Top, 1955–1985* (Lanham, Md.: University Press of America, 1986).

3

Rhetoric and Reality: U.S. Policy Toward Eastern Europe, 1945–1989

Analysis of the U.S. relationship with Eastern Europe from 1945 to 1989 can serve two purposes as far as this book is concerned. First, the tensions between ambitious U.S. public policy objectives and the brutal realities of Soviet power in the region make U.S.-East European relations an excellent example of how U.S. policy adapted to a resistant international-political setting. In this sense, this relationship with Eastern Europe acts as a test of the proposition set out in Chapter 1 concerning the West's acquiescence in the postwar division of Europe. Second, and equally important, study of the past tendencies in U.S. policy toward Eastern Europe throw light on the likely range of choice in future U.S. policy toward a Soviet Union that has disintegrated and is being transformed to the Commonwealth of Independent States. If Eastern Europe from 1945 to 1989 can be considered the outer empire of the Soviet system, the nations constituting the Soviet Union itself were that system's inner empire. How the United States has reacted to the evolution of the outer empire should thus suggest important generalizations about the future of U.S. relations with the new Commonwealth.

During 1945–1989, the period of Soviet hegemony in Eastern Europe, a most peculiar combination of circumstances and interests affected U.S. relations in the region. Eastern Europe itself, a vital part of the USSR's foreign policy and security interests throughout the postwar period, is at best of secondary importance to U.S. foreign policy interests.

At the same time, the United States adhered to a formally declared policy toward the region, which if that policy had been realized, would have fundamentally challenged the USSR's vital security interests in the region. Yet the policy instruments available to U.S. leadership have historically been remarkably thin in comparison to both the magnitude of change and the subtlety of influence they have been supposed to promote. Any effort to reshape U.S. policy, either by scaling down long-term objectives or ignoring the region, ran into twin obstacles. The first was the character of the U.S. foreign policy decisionmaking process; the second was the stubborn reality that as long as the Soviet Union insisted on Communist governments in this predominantly anti-Communist region, Eastern Europe would remain a potential powder keg in the—by comparison—tranquil setting of East-West relations in Europe. U.S. policy thus was not able to remain unaffected by what happened between the Elbe and the Bug.

U.S. Interests in Eastern Europe

There is, in fact, a fundamental irony that runs through U.S. policy toward the countries of Eastern Europe. Taken separately, either as a region or in terms of a series of bilateral relationships, Eastern Europe would (and before 1945 did) occupy only a tangential relationship to important U.S. foreign policy interests, however broadly defined. It was in response to the rise of the Soviet Union as the chief international challenge to the United States that Eastern Europe came to assume significance in U.S. policy, first as a litmus test of Soviet intentions, later as a potential Achilles' heel of Soviet power, and from the 1960s through the 1980s as an opportunity for gradually reshaping the contours of power in a divided Europe.

Yet, as relations with the Soviet Union have improved and the Soviet threat to U.S. interests is seen to recede, whether that threat is defined in ideological, political, or military terms, then the need to accord relations with Eastern Europe any priority in U.S. efforts correspondingly declines. This is less true of U.S. West European allies, who as Europeans share a natural and deeply rooted historical concern for the economic, political, and cultural evolution of all of Europe, East and West. But U.S. interests in Eastern Europe, beyond those of a vague and idealistic sort (such as the right of all peoples to self-determination), are overwhelmingly those of a geopolitical character and thus hinge in the first instance upon the nature of U.S.-Soviet relations. Any effort, whether analytical or political, to deal with U.S. policy in the region must also deal with this basic frame, or limitation, upon U.S. relations with Eastern Europe.

Viewed historically, U.S. ties to the nations of what is called "Eastern Europe" have been episodic. Such dramatic interventions as the role played by Tadeusz Kosciuszko in the U.S. Revolution or the reception accorded the Hungarian revolutionary nationalist Louis Kossuth when he came to the United States in 1852 are well enough known. Less well known is the fact that the first partition of Poland played a minor role in the framing of the U.S. Constitution, with Federalists arguing that the lack of a strong executive authority, as exemplified by the Polish Diet's liberum veto (by which a negative vote of even one senator could block legislation), would lead to such baleful consequences as those experienced by Poland and caused by Prussia, Austria, and Russia.[1] It is also important to point out that the hero's welcome given Kossuth, rather than indicating any intrinsic U.S. interests in Hapsburg affairs, reflected the conviction that Kossuth-type efforts confirmed the universality of the U.S. revolutionary experience. That would not be the last time that Americans were to project their internal preoccupations upon the East European scene.

As a result of its participation in World War I and the promulgation of the Fourteen Points, the United States committed itself to national independence for the nations of the former Hapsburg Empire, the most dramatic example of which was the re-creation of an independent Poland. This commitment reflected a general American belief in the principle of self-determination rather than any foreign policy concept for the region itself, as the subsequent history of U.S. withdrawal from continental affairs and the progressive disintegration of regional stability show. This divorce between declaratory policy and policy commitments would reemerge in even sharper form after World War II.

The Post–World War II Period

U.S. policy toward Eastern Europe in the postwar period has been characterized by a remarkable consistency of formal long-term objectives and, at the same time, an often erratic application of workaday policy, suggesting ambiguity and even confusion about the objectives of policy in the short and medium term. Policy toward Eastern Europe has been formally based on the Yalta Declaration of February 1945, which promised "the right of all peoples to choose the form of government under which they will live" and, toward this end, "the earliest possible establishment through free elections of governments responsible to the will of the people."[2] At the same time, East European governments were understood to be "friendly" to the interests of the victorious great powers, i.e., including the USSR. In one form or another, the Yalta formulation has been confirmed repeatedly as the touchstone of U.S. policy in the area, ranging from National Security Document NSC 58/2 of December 1949—which set the basic U.S. goal to be "the elimination of Soviet control from these countries and the reduction of Soviet influence to something like normal dimensions"[3]—to Secretary of State George Shultz's December 1985 denunciation of the division of Germany, Berlin, and Europe as "unnatural and inhuman." In the same speech Shultz reaffirmed that the United States does "not accept the incorporation of Eastern Europe, including East Germany and East Berlin, into a Soviet sphere of influence."[4]

How this declaratory U.S. policy was translated into practice, indeed, the very issue of how seriously it was meant, is a very complex affair. During the war, President Franklin D. Roosevelt deliberately postponed the consideration of interallied political objectives, including those touching upon Eastern Europe, until after victory had been achieved. In Roosevelt's view (and given the late U.S. entry into the war it is difficult to argue with it), any detailed discussion of such a contentious issue as the USSR's relationship to Eastern Europe would constitute a diversion from the main—military—objective of defeating Nazi Germany. It would also risk an eventual break with the USSR, without any tangible chance of affecting unilateral Soviet decisions on Eastern Europe. At no point in U.S. policy under either Roosevelt or Harry S. Truman was the United States opposed in principle to the concept of a basic Soviet security and political interest in the affairs of Eastern Europe.

What the United States could not admit, even to itself (perhaps because it was not capable of such depth of comprehension) was that there was no middle ground between the U.S. concept of a normal sphere of Soviet influence and Stalin's minimal criteria for Soviet control. The juxtaposition at Yalta of "free elections" with governments "friendly" to the Soviet Union was thus an act of willful self-deception on the U.S. part, leading Stalin to believe that the Americans had accepted *his* concept for Eastern Europe while persuading the majority of Americans that Stalin had agreed to the U.S. concept of self-determination.[5] The casual nature of the U.S. interest in Eastern Europe was thus obscured and the groundwork laid for the escalating series of mutual recriminations that became part of the cold war.

The progression of events in Eastern Europe from 1945 through early 1948 confirmed the entirely rhetorical character of U.S. "policy" toward Eastern Europe. At no point was the United States prepared to contemplate the actual use of its immense diplomatic potential, resting as it did on U.S. military and economic supremacy, to affect the evolution of Soviet–East European relations. With the war in Europe over, the United States began the impressive withdrawal and demobilization of its armed forces, without any consideration as to the relationship between U.S. military power and Soviet policy west of Brest. In July 1945, in the face of systematic Soviet violations of the Yalta accords in Poland and throughout the lands under Soviet military occupation, the United States unilaterally withdrew its forces from the Leipzig region, in what would become the German Democratic Republic (GDR), to prearranged lines of occupation.

Indeed, U.S. military strategy throughout the war had been conducted as if in a political vacuum, with the impressive political argument for capturing Berlin and Prague being rejected by Eisenhower on purely military grounds (i.e., that as Germany was in effect defeated and the Russians would surely soon take those cities, it was unnecessary to risk U.S. lives).[6] Throughout 1945 and 1946, detailed reports by U.S. diplomats on the scene about the increasing Soviet repression in Eastern Europe went largely ignored by Washington, which had not yet written off the possibility of establishing a modus vivendi with Moscow. The alarm and general activism with which official Washington reacted to the Prague coup of February 1948 can only be contrasted to the general U.S. sluggishness, bordering on indifference, as to the pre-1948 political evolution within Czechoslovakia. That apparent lack of interest almost certainly contributed to the Soviet decision to establish Communist domination of the country.[7]

The year 1948 would prove to be a signal one in U.S. policy toward Eastern Europe. The Prague coup removed any lingering doubts within the United States about Soviet intentions and led to a U.S. strategy of treating all East European governments as simple glacis, or buffer states, for Soviet power. Few differences were recognized between the Soviet Union and the East European satellites. An economic embargo treated both with fine impartiality. The United States severed diplomatic relations with Albania and Bulgaria and downgraded relations, with justifiable reasons to be sure, with Hungary. As Stephen Garrett noted in his excellent book on the subject, the theory was "that a unified Soviet bloc was in operation and that any assistance to or normalization with a member of that 'bloc' would redound to the benefit of the total monolith." It was also felt that the "temporary" and "illegitimate" East European regimes were unrepresentative "and thus any U.S. dealings with these regimes would connive in the continued repression of those yearning for freedom."[8]

Ironically, although U.S. diplomats on the spot pointed this out, the United States removed itself from the growing tensions between the "Moscow" and the "home" Communists throughout Eastern Europe (i.e., those who had spent the war in the USSR or in the home country resistance); therefore the United States forfeited its opportunity of bringing influence to bear on the relative degree of subordination of East European policies to those of the Soviet Union.[9] By painting Eastern Europe and Stalin's USSR with the same brush, the United States in effect forfeited any chance of promoting "national communism." The latter would become the prime aim of U.S. policy in the region in response to Tito's defiance of Stalin in the spring of 1948.

The amazing turn in U.S. policy in support of Yugoslavia's rejection of Soviet domination in mid-1948 was a decisive event in East-West relations at the time and in retrospect marked a watershed in U.S. policy toward Eastern Europe. The Truman administration, which was the beneficiary of a remarkably astute analysis of the Soviet-Yugoslav rift by Laurence Steinhardt, its ambassador to Belgrade,[10] resisted all efforts to make U.S. support for Tito conditional on changes in Yugoslav domestic policy and threw its weight behind this most visible expression of national communism to date. U.S. policy merits considerable credit for both its tactical flexibility and its professionalism of execution, because Tito had long been a bane to U.S. interests in Greece and elsewhere. With the death of Stalin in 1953 and ensuing instabilities in Eastern Europe, the successful reinforcement of Tito's independent path would serve as a model for future U.S. policy toward communism in Eastern Europe (but not in Asia): The nationalizing and moderation of communism rather than its overthrow would become the twin beacons of U.S. policy, rhetoric about "liberation" and "rollback" notwithstanding.

By 1948–1949, then, the eventual contours of U.S. policy toward Eastern Europe were discernible, though perhaps only some among the Republican opposition saw them clearly at the time. The United States had decided, as the opening to Tito had shown, to work *with* existing Communist regimes, insofar as their existence and the direction of their policies might complicate the easy extension of Soviet power. Until the second half of the 1950s the U.S. government saw no candidates for such engagement except Yugoslavia and thus continued the freeze on ties with the other East European Communist states and later with China as well.

The Truman administration's agreement to work with communism in specific areas in order to contain Soviet power signified a de facto shift by the United States away from both the Yalta standard of "free elections" and the injunction in the Truman Doctrine itself in support of "free people to work out their destiny in their own way." The shift was toward a more calculated geopolitical strategy aimed at containing Soviet power rather than combating communism as such. This enraged certain Republicans who claimed to take the language of Yalta and the Truman Doctrine at face value and felt, not entirely incorrectly, that the administration had written Eastern Europe off as "lost." The Republican Party platform of 1952 denounced the "negative, futile and immoral policy of containment that abandons countless human beings to a despotism and godless terrorism" and committed the Republicans to a policy of "liberation" of the "enslaved" countries of Eastern Europe from Soviet control.[11]

Policy in the 1950s

In actual fact, any U.S. policy of "liberation" or "rollback" remained firmly in the Republican Party platform, without any demonstrable effect upon U.S. foreign policy, as U.S. passivity in the face of the East Berlin (and Czech) disturbances of 1953 and the Soviet invasion of Hungary in 1956 convincingly illustrates. Rhetorical flourishes by Eisenhower's secretary of state, John Foster Dulles, should not obscure this fact. Indeed, it may be argued that Dulles's language about "godless communism" and the "immorality" of dealing with Communists needlessly prolonged the period in which the United States was hamstrung, thereby preventing itself from reacting to the inevitable fissures in the Communist world.[12]

Certainly, the Eisenhower administration wasted no time in responding to the opportunity presented by Polish Party leader Wladyslaw Gomulka's bold defiance of a visiting Soviet Politburo delegation, headed by Khrushchev himself, in October 1956. Early the following year, the U.S. government, instead of viewing the Soviet-Polish disagreement about the direction of reform and the constitution of the Polish leadership as a "family quarrel" between common enemies, launched an impressive package of economic aid for Poland. The United States also initiated a cultural exchange program designed to reinforce perceived tendencies toward national communism there. The United States would no longer adopt an "either-or" attitude toward East European communism. (Indeed, Dulles had even condemned the neutral states as "immoral" for refusing to ally with the United States against communism.) Instead, the U.S. government would react to evolutionary tendencies within the Soviet bloc and seek to reinforce them through a variety of instruments, including economic assistance, improved trade relations, cultural exchange, and declaratory policy. Each country would be dealt with on a case-by-case basis and according to two criteria: the amelioration of domestic policies, especially in regard to economic reform and human rights; and the adoption of foreign policy positions at variance with those of the Soviet Union.

Bridge-Building or Differentiation

This policy was known under a number of names, from "peaceful engagement" and "bridge building" in the 1960s to "differentiation" in the 1970s. In principle, the policy represented a fairly sophisticated approach. No longer would the Warsaw Pact countries be treated as an immutable bloc; no longer would the U.S. government entertain any fantasies, however unrealistic, of eliminating Soviet power from the region. Yet if this new policy were to succeed, two questions needed to be squarely faced: Toward what real end were the instruments of differentiation directed, and how appropriate were the means at U.S. disposal toward advancing that end?

Any consideration of U.S. ability to conduct a purposeful, coherent, and effective policy toward an area such as Eastern Europe must first take into account the peculiarities of the U.S. foreign policy decisionmaking process. A variety of factors tended to limit the freedom of action of the professional diplomat and secretary of state in developing U.S. policy toward Eastern Europe in the postwar period, including the active role of Congress in foreign policy, the influence of ethnic lobbying groups, the tendency to appoint ambassadors according to domestic-political rather than professional criteria (or conversely, the removal of the professional diplomat from the broader policymaking process), as well as the neurosis of the U.S. body politic as far as all things Communist were concerned. Any effort to execute a strategy as sophisticated and nuanced as that of "differentiation" must operate within the constraints that such a democratic political environment imposes. Indeed, it is an open question whether—even ignoring for the moment the issue of adequacy of means— the character of the U.S. political system is capable of effectively sustaining any ambitious foreign policy strategy toward Eastern Europe.

An important test case of U.S. ability to prosecute a coherent East European policy arose in 1962 over Yugoslavia, arguably the centerpiece of U.S. policy in the region. Administration efforts to renew most-favored-nation (MFN) trading status with Yugoslavia, which was rightly viewed as an essential support of its nonaligned status, were thwarted by congressional reaction to Tito's anti-Western rhetoric in the nonaligned movement and to emigre groups arguing against "aid" to Communist governments (in the form of the actual sale of obsolete jet fighters to Yugoslavia). In essence, a long-established and vital U.S. policy was (temporarily) undermined by arguments and pressures that were effective in terms of U.S. domestic politics but that were completely unrelated to the character of U.S. foreign policy interests in sustaining the independence of Yugoslavia. In fact, the U.S. ambassador to Belgrade, George Kennan, who had provided the conceptual underpinning for encouraging "national communism" as chief of the State Department's Policy Planning Council in the late 1940s, was so distressed by the incoherence of U.S. policy and at the willful disregard of professional diplomacy that he offered his resignation.[13]

Another example of the way that the character of the U.S. political process has handicapped the execution of U.S. policy in the region is the Captive Nations Resolution, introduced in Congress in 1959 and requiring the president annually to proclaim Captive Nations Week (the third week in July) "until such time as freedom and independence shall have been achieved for all the captive nations of the world."[14] Listed, in addition to the nations of Eastern Europe (including Yugoslavia!), were various republics of the Soviet Union including (sic) Idel-Ural and Cossackia, whose existence is unknown to me. Soviet observers have identified them as having been zones of occupation and administration drawn up by the Nazis. For three decades the president of the United States, in spite of a declared policy of working with the Communist governments of Eastern Europe so as to promote their evolution *within* the Soviet bloc, had been obliged annually to go on record declaring these same governments anathema. (East European observers may thus be excused if they have at times found it difficult to understand U.S. policy toward their countries.)

This is not to argue that parochial interests can dictate overall U.S. policy toward the region. Indeed, Stephen Garrett has shown that the actual influence of Americans of East European origin on U.S. policy has been limited to the declaratory level.[15] In most cases, the executive branch has been able to resist such pressures in the formulation of policy. (In the above-cited Yugoslav case, MFN status was restored the following year.) The point is that the nature of U.S. politics has tended to reduce the coherence of policy toward Eastern Europe by mixing geopolitical with ideological and even idealistic elements. The latter two have more to do with Americans' self-image than with the actual political processes under way in Eastern Europe and their implications for specific policy interests. This has had the double effect of making it difficult to calibrate policy to the nuances of change, for better or worse, in the Eastern countries and of inducing a permanent tension between the desire to transform the distribution of power in Eastern Europe and the need to work incrementally with existing governments (and societies) to advance the prospects for mutually acceptable change.

Examples of this pattern abound. After Poland's challenge to Khrushchev in October 1956, as we have seen, the United States initiated programs of economic assistance and cultural exchange, in order to encourage divergence in Polish policy trends from the Soviet Union. By 1960, when the United States granted Poland most-favored-nation trading status, the Gomulka government had already begun a retreat toward greater orthodoxy and repression at home, without any visible sign of foreign policy dissent from the Soviet Union. Yet the "carrot" of improved trade status and warmer diplomatic contacts continued. Romania, for its part, received MFN status in 1975, well after Nicolae Ceausescu's domestic practices had made that country the most repressive of all Warsaw Pact states, including the Soviet Union. (Romania had begun resisting Soviet encroachments as early as 1962; its policy of foreign policy autonomy of the Soviet Union was, however, established independent of U.S. policy and in any case predated the MFN carrot by thirteen years.) Even Hungary, which—at least according to domestic criteria—deserved MFN status from the United States, had been engaged in an extensive reform process for over a decade before it received the conferment in 1978.[16]

Beyond this issue of assessment and timing, the very character of U.S. differentiation policy, which had sought to advance the goals of *both* domestic liberalization and foreign policy autonomy in Eastern Europe, posed dilemmas that were never systematically addressed. In seeking change in both areas, the United States avoided facing squarely the possibility that the two were in tension and of differing significance for U.S. interests. Indeed, U.S. policy often gave the impression that domestic political change within the East European countries had the same significance for U.S. policy as increasing autonomy in foreign policy, and that painful trade-offs were not necessarily involved in formulating a policy designed to encourage both trends.

Certainly, there are times when the aim of policy may be fudged without undue political stress. Such was the case in U.S.-Polish policy after 1957, when the United States extended agricultural surpluses (under Public Law 480) and then MFN status to a Poland that had shown no evidence of foreign policy dissent from Moscow and that, by 1960, had even begun to retrogress in its human rights conduct at home. In this instance, the value of supporting a more nationalistic Communist leadership was apparently adjudged superior to the specifics of either domestic or foreign policy. As already noted, in the case of Yugoslavia the U.S. government refrained from attaching any domestic conditions to its support for Tito's defection; U.S. policymakers believed that the impact of a specifically national communism, however repressive at home, outweighed the nature of the regime as far as U.S. geopolitical interests were concerned. U.S.-Romanian policy, in contrast, presents a classic example of tension and policy confusion in the execution of differentiation. From the mid-1970s through 1989, the appalling Romanian record of human rights abuses at home came to dominate the U.S. attention in U.S.-Romanian relations, as congressional and outside pressure groups sought to use the stick of MFN withdrawal as a lever to change the conduct of the Ceausescu regime. At no point in this very public discussion did the merits of Romania's relative autonomy in foreign policy enter the picture, although certainly elements within the administration and the State Department were concerned with the impact of such pressures on the Romanian position.

In truth, the very nature of a policy like differentiation, with *domestic* change as a key aim, legitimizes the kinds of U.S. domestic pressures that have at times made U.S. geopolitical interests, including its interest in encouraging the development of national communism, hostage to highly visible demands for intervention in East European domestic affairs, regardless of the practical political consequences thereof. The unwillingness of Washington to choose between advancing (and thus accepting) national communism and promoting domestic change as the *main* aim of its differentiation policy reflects the deeper U.S. reluctance to choose between a policy of incrementalism and one seeking more transformative change.

Policy Instruments

Turning from the ends of U.S. policy to its means, it becomes clear that if the nature of the U.S. political process imposes strict limits on U.S. ability to carry out an ambitious East European policy, the paucity of instruments at U.S. disposal limits it effectiveness even further. (This is as true in 1992 as it was throughout the postwar period.) The U.S. share of East European trade in the early 1980s came to less than 2 percent (compared to 4.6 percent in 1938 and 3.3 percent in 1948). In 1982, the U.S. share of trade with various East European countries broke down as follows:

Bulgaria	0.6%
Czechoslovakia	0.5
Hungary	1.1
Poland	2.4
Romania	3.1
Yugoslavia	3.6[17]

As part of total U.S. trade in 1983, trade with Eastern Europe came to about 0.6 percent. Although there has been a disparity of approximately 3:1 in the U.S. favor in terms of proportion of total trade (and thus of relative vulnerabilities), this is a disparity at exceedingly low levels, as the comparison even with the 1938 trade levels indicate.[18] Consequently, the opportunities for the United States to use its trade as a lever with the East Europeans have been severely limited. (Compare the U.S. figure of 1.9 percent to an overall East European trade turnover of approximately 40 percent with the Soviet Union in the mid-1980s and about 18 percent with other developed Western economies in 1984.)[19]

The United States has certainly made its impact felt in Eastern Europe in other ways, which range from cultural and educational exchanges to radio broadcasts and formal and informal policy statements and actions. Yet, in light of these countries' basic (and coerced) orientation toward the Soviet Union until 1989, the erratic nature of the U.S. foreign policy process, and the lack of significant policy instruments, U.S. influence has only been marginal at best, reinforcing or retarding processes that have taken shape for reasons independent of the United States. Even with a much larger U.S. economic involvement with Eastern Europe than was the case, its effective use as a diplomatic tool during the period in question would have required an exquisitely tuned diplomatic mechanism, impervious to the fluctuations of daily domestic political and ideological pressures and able to discipline U.S. policy to the geopolitics of incrementalism. Simply to state the problem in this way shows how unrealistic such a scenario is.

Ironically, it was during the Reagan administration, and especially its second half, that the elements of a more coherent East European policy began to take root. After 1985, apparently in response to the change in the Soviet leadership, the Reagan administration lent a new accent to the traditional policy of "differentiation." Deputy Secretary of State John Whitehead captured the thrust of this policy by noting that change was coming to the region so fast that by the late 1980s its countries will be "a little less dependent on the Soviet Union" and "a little more oriented to the United States." The modesty of this expectation—apparently eschewing direct efforts at transforming power relationships in the region—was underscored by the corresponding recognition within the administration that there was a need to stay within bounds so that Moscow would not see U.S. actions threatening the supremacy of communism in the region.

Furthermore, U.S. policy began openly to proceed from the understanding that, as one State Department official warned, "the idea that U.S. influence can have decisive or even major impact on Eastern Europe is not correct . . . you can [not] break down the barriers and bringing a rush of western influence into Eastern Europe."[20] This philosophy was reflected in a series of initiatives undertaken by the State Department beginning in late 1985, ranging from Secretary of State Shultz's visit to the region in December 1985 to several trips by Deputy Secretary Whitehead, who assumed responsibility for East European policy within the administration. In the cases of Poland (with which full diplomatic relations were restored in 1987) and Hungary, general sympathy was extended to the reform efforts being undertaken there. The United States even expanded its relations with the GDR, culminating in the visit of GDR Politburo member Hermann Axen to Washington for consultations with Shultz and Whitehead on May 4, 1988. (With Romania, Whitehead made clear the limits of U.S. tolerance for Romanian domestic practice, with the result that the Romanians themselves rejected their MFN status so as to avoid such pressure.)

Could such a consistently modest, incrementalist policy have been maintained? Reports that the United States had been urging its West European allies not to provide loans or other financial help to Eastern Europe unless such help was conditional on major political reform cast doubt on this, as does the fact that the United States was bankrolling the technical infrastructure necessary for the nationwide existence of a dissident press in Poland.[21] Once again, the basic tension between incrementalism and transformation had come to frame U.S. policy toward the region. The sudden, unforeseen, and in many respects undesired, collapse of Soviet authority in the region after 1989 spared U.S. officials further choice between these competing poles of policy.

Constants

For all of its vicissitudes and inconsistencies of application, U.S. policy toward Eastern Europe from 1945 to 1989 was marked by certain constant features. First, from the wartime period on, the United States has recognized that the Soviet Union had a superior and primordial interest in the affairs of the East European states, entitling it to a sphere of influence there, if the term be understood in its traditional diplomatic connotation. What the United States has not been able to accept is the imposition of a strict Soviet control over the region, which initially was seen as the precursor to Soviet efforts to establish hegemony over all of Europe and which later came to be viewed, most visibly in the form of the "Sonnenfeldt Doctrine" of 1974, as a source of latent instability that could escalate in time of crisis to an open East-West confrontation. At no point, however, has the United States been prepared to resort to the use, or even the threat, of force in order to affect the distribution of power in Eastern Europe.

Second, given the conscious abjuration of a military option, even at the height of U.S. regional and global superiority, the policy instruments available to the United States, especially economic, remained grossly inadequate in comparison to the avowed long-term aim of fostering self-determination throughout the region. The successful implementation of even the more modest short-term strategy of "differentiation" would have required a substantially higher degree of U.S. economic engagement with Eastern Europe. Yet, the unwillingness to scale down long-term aims to fit available resources continued to place U.S. policy in a state of permanent tension between the desire to transform the East European polities—which would eventually neutralize Soviet power in Europe and realize the universal idealistic aspirations of the United States—and the need to work within the constraints imposed by Soviet hegemony in order to promote a more favorable evolution of East European internal and foreign policies. Until this basic tension was resolved by forces beyond its sway in 1989, U.S. policy continued to labor in partial incoherence in the face of quixotic ends and puny means.

From 1957 to 1989, the twin standards of the policy of differentiation were the degree of domestic political relaxation in East European countries and the degree of their autonomy from Soviet foreign policy. In order to encourage both trends (where possible), the United States sought to use a combination of "carrots and sticks" to demonstrate its attitude and support (or disapproval, as in the case of the Polish sanctions). Each country was treated individually, although the ultimate purpose and unifying logic of such treatment remained the multiplication of constraints upon Soviet power projection in Europe and beyond. In practice, U.S. policy actions never proved capable of causing or stopping the movement of policy in Eastern Europe; at best (as in the case of Yugoslavia), they were able to support existing indigenous trends or to retard them, and even then only in very partial measure.

Finally, Eastern Europe has always been a sideshow in the eyes of U.S. policymakers. At most, the countries of the region were considered useful pawns in the broader strategy of containing Soviet power, never as positive values in themselves. By comparison with the main tasks of matching Soviet military power and building up an effective anti-Soviet alliance in Western Europe, the concerns of the East Europeans have always proved expendable to U.S. policy. Eastern Europe has been for the United States what Czechoslovakia was to Neville Chamberlain in 1938: a far-off land of which it knows nothing. Given the priority of these twin concerns of containment and alliance management, it is not surprising that the United States showed itself less than responsive to various East European proposals for military disengagement in Europe (such as the various Rapacki plans of the late 1950s), which should have been viewed as veiled pleas for a restructuring of Soviet–East European relations rather than merely technical arms control proposals.[22] But since every East European proposal would have required some difficult intra-alliance negotiation and restructuring within NATO, there was always a strong bias toward the status quo in U.S. reactions.

This objective preference for the status quo held for U.S. policy generally throughout the region—and for good reason. Although because of domestic politics and self-image the United States could not bring itself to admit it openly, the fact is that the division of Europe was perfectly consistent with fundamental U.S. foreign policy interests. As an insular power in relation to Europe, the United States does not require dominance over the continent or even that a majority of states there emulate its political system. Instead—and this twice proved the justification for U.S. intervention in European wars this century—the United States requires only that no single power be able to exercise its hegemony over the combined resources of the Eurasian landmass, including the western Eurasian peninsula. The reestablishment of political self-confidence and economic prosperity in Western Europe after the war and the emergence of a formidable U.S.–West European military power provided effective preconditions for denying such hegemony to the Soviet Union, whether it controlled Eastern Europe or not.

The U.S. margin for maneuver was widened still further by the emergence of a hostile Communist China as perhaps the key security challenge to the Soviet Union. A more or less autonomous balance of power has thus arisen in Eurasia, and its stability has in effect been independent of the condition and evolution of the East European nations. Global economic trends only reinforce this marginalization of the erstwhile "shatterzone" of Europe. Whereas it was always desirable for the East Europeans to shake off Soviet hegemony and evolve in more autonomous directions, this was by no means essential to the basic U.S. interest in a plural world order (meaning a plurality of power centers). The collapse of communism in Eastern Europe in 1989 and the subsequent unification of Germany, not to mention the collapse of the Soviet Union itself, only emphasizes the point.

Loss of Soviet Hegemony

At the same time, and in partial justification of the transformative direction of U.S. policy, it is now clear to all that the perpetuation of a strict Soviet hegemony in the region could in no way have resolved the explosive tensions between state and society in most of the East European countries. These tensions, even in transformed form today, have the potential to spill over to the European scene more generally. In practically every East European country, economic stagnation, the pace of social change, unsteady political successions, nationality issues, and the demand for greater meaningful participation in life of society continue to pose challenges to the ability of even the post-Communist authorities to govern effectively.

In Yugoslavia, long thought to be the most hopeful case in the region, the devolution of decisionmaking power to the republic level and below, which since the death of Tito in 1980 has threatened that country with permanent political and economic paralysis, has led to the actual disintegration of the country and brutal warfare throughout the breadth of the land. At the heart of Yugoslavia's dilemmas are nationality issues. These are particularly virulent when beleaguered governments, in the absence of effective performance, wrap themselves in the mantle of nationalism. Bulgaria's past repression of its native Turkish population, which visibly embarrassed its Soviet ally in the mid-1980s, remains a factor in Bulgarian politics today. The issue of the treatment of ethnic Hungarians in Romania (and Czechoslovakia) has risen to the interstate level, literally poisoning Romanian-Hungarian relations and leading to the recall of diplomats and the flight of increasing numbers of refugees across the Romanian border to Hungary. Historically, these have been sufficient grounds for war.

The forces of change throughout Eastern Europe, then, are continuing, the question being their precise direction and cumulative impact. At every juncture in the postwar period, instability in the East has exerted its effect upon the West and has often, as in the case of the Polish sanctions of the early 1980s, challenged the ability of the West to maintain a coherent policy in relations with the East. Clearly, the progressive evolution of the East European states toward stable post-Communist political, economic, and social structures, including greater room for the expression of autonomous national interests within specific countries, could only help stabilize the East-West relationship in Europe.

The resolution of this vital issue will also depend upon the evolution of post-Soviet–East European relations, in particular on how Russia and Ukraine will in the future define the nature of their national and state interests in Eastern Europe, now that the burden of ideologically driven security interests has been lifted from their policy in the region. The resolution will also depend on whether a stable political and economic reform can be effected within the Soviet region itself, thereby insulating Eastern Europe from the shocks of Soviet disintegration. The stakes are enormous and in themselves justify outside efforts to encourage the evolution of regional trends in a stable direction.

Unfortunately, the United States has all too often succumbed to the temptation to design ambitious overall policy schemes for Eastern Europe, whether it be the notional "liberation" concept or the more serious ideas of "peaceful engagement," "bridge building," and "differentiation," all of which posit an active grand strategy for dealing with the region as a whole (in reality they have been stratagems for reshaping the contours of Soviet power in Europe). The same excessiveness applies to future efforts aimed at encouraging "democratization" and "marketization" throughout the region. As this analysis has tried to show, such efforts vastly exceed the intellectual and political acumen of U.S. foreign policy as well as the resources at U.S. disposal. All also run into the same obstacle: In the end, Eastern Europe remains in the 1990s a vital security interest to Russia and Ukraine and a vital political interest to Western Europe but is neither to the United States, and the limits of U.S. policy in the region thus run through Moscow and, now, Berlin.[23]

The United States would do well to try to fit its East European policy to its abilities, means, and interests. Such a policy would not require grand, overarching schemes to reshape the power contours of Europe or the domestic coloration of regimes in the area but more simply an appreciation of the fragility of the processes of political, economic, and social change in the region and their resistance to easy influence from afar. Only by forgoing the hope for short-term tangible returns from its East European policy can the United States expect to cement the internal and external changes whose promotion lay at the heart of the policy of differentiation. These changes are now proceeding at their own momentum.

Eventually, the United States may have to do something that it never fully did during the pre-1989 period: to choose between international and domestic conduct as the touchstone of its East European policy. Choosing the former need not mean neglecting the latter. But it would mean raising strictly geopolitical rather than ideological criteria as the measure for U.S. policy in the region (which is no less than what the United States had been asking of the Soviet Union). In such a policy, the United States cannot directly concern itself with the internal shape and evolution of a given country's policies. Its diplomatic relations should depend upon the normal interaction of foreign policy interests and international conduct, and its economic policies should respond to normal economic criteria. Cultural ties should be viewed as the normal engagement of U.S. society with the world beyond its border and not made contingent upon, or withdrawn in response to, domestic policies deemed unacceptable in Washington.

What the United States can do, in the manner of Franklin Roosevelt's "Good Neighbor" Latin American policy, is to keep its door open to the East Europeans and respond to whatever level of relationships, especially of an economic character, the respective East European states desire. A more ambitious policy of political and economic intervention, attempting to "punish" or "reward" governments for deviation or adherence to U.S. norms, is simply beyond the political capacity of the U.S. government to manage in any consistently constructive way. Furthermore, the political fate of Eastern Europe is simply not a vital interest of the United States, as it is for Western Europe. U.S. political energies and resources are best spent elsewhere.

Although the implementation of such a noninterventionist policy may in the U.S. political context prove difficult, it should not be forgotten that almost fifty years after his death Franklin Roosevelt is still remembered with fondness and respect throughout Latin America. Were the United States able to take a longer geopolitical view of its interests in Europe along the lines suggested above, it would realize that there is no need for a single foreign policy strategy for Eastern Europe. By lowering its sights and volume, the United States may actually seize its best chance of promoting the kind of change that has been the ultimate object of its policies for more than four decades. Whether such an apparently minimalist policy can be squared with the character of the U.S. political process is another question altogether, one whose answer will say much about the maturity of future U.S. policy toward Eastern Europe.

Notes

1. See *The Federalist Papers*, numbers 19, 39, and 75, in *The Federalist* (New York: Modern Library, n.d.), pp. 118, 243, 489 respectively.

2. For the text of the Yalta Declaration, see *Documents on Foreign Relations*, vol. 8, *1945–1946* (Boston: World Peace Foundation, 1948), pp. 920–921.

3. *Foreign Relations of the United States, 1949*, vol. 5 (Washington, D.C.: U.S. Government Printing Office, 1976), p. 44. Hereafter *FRUS*.

4. *New York Times*, December 15, 1985, p. 25.

5. See Gaddis Smith, *The United States and the Origins of the Cold War, 1941–1947* (New York: Columbia University Press, 1972), pp. 133–173.

6. David Eisenhower, *Eisenhower at War, 1943–1945* (New York: Vintage Books, 1987), pp. xii–xiii, 727–732, 768–769, 771–773, 785–786.

7. Daniel Yergin, *The Shattered Peace: The Origins of the Cold War and the National Security State* (Boston: Houghton Mifflin, 1977), pp. 343–352.

8. Stephen A. Garrett, *From Potsdam to Poland: American Policy Toward Eastern Europe* (New York: Praeger, 1986), p. 68.

9. *FRUS*, op. cit., pp. 96–98; J. F. Brown, *Eastern Europe and Communist Rule* (Durham, N.C.: Duke University Press, 1988), pp. 5–6. See also the definitive work by Wolfgang Leonhard, *Child of the Revolution*, trans. C. M. Woodhouse (Chicago: Henry Regnery Co., 1958). The initial acceptance of the Marshall Plan by Poland in 1947 bears out this point.

10. *FRUS*, op. cit., pp. 856–859, 886–890 et seq., 941–945.

11. As cited in Garrett, op. cit., p. 14.

12. Bennett Kovrig, *The Myth of Liberation* (Baltimore: Johns Hopkins University Press, 1973); and Townsend Hoopes, *The Devil and John Foster Dulles* (Boston: Little, Brown Co., 1973), passim.

13. George Kennan, *Memoirs, 1950–1963* (New York: Pantheon Books, 1972), pp. 267–318.

14. As cited in Garrett, op. cit., p. 32.

15. Ibid., pp. 3–64.

16. Brown, op. cit., p. 105.

17. Figures from Garrett, op. cit., p. 76.

18. Ibid.

19. U.S. Directorate of Intelligence, *Handbook of Economic Statistics 1986,* CPAS 86–10002 (September 1986), p. 99.

20. *Washington Post,* May 11, 1988, p. A31.

21. *New York Times,* June 9, 1988, p. A11; and July 10, 1988, p. 1.

22. For the main ideas of the proposal of Polish Foreign Minister Adam Rapacki for the progressive demilitarization of East-Central Europe, see Rapacki's memorandum to the U.S. ambassador in Warsaw of February 14, 1958, in U.S. U.S. Department of State, *Documents on Disarmament, 1945–1959,* vol. 2, *1957–1958* (Washington, D.C.: U.S. Government Printing Office, 1960), pp. 944–948.

23. On April 25, 1991, Soviet Deputy Foreign Minister Yuli Kvitsinsky, speaking in Prague, affirmed a natural Soviet zone of interest in Eastern Europe. Although promising that there could be no return of Soviet dominion in the region, he stated, "The Soviet Union's legitimate interests in this region have historical and geopolitical roots and must be taken into account." *Guardian* (Manchester), April 26, 1991, as cited in Radio Free Europe/Radio Liberty (RFE/RL) Research Institute, *Report on the USSR,* May 3, 1991, p. 41. This analysis may be extended to post-Soviet Russia.

Part 2

THE DYNAMICS
OF THE PRESENT

4

The Agonies of Reform in Gorbachev's USSR

Any analysis of present-day East-West relations must begin with the astonishing fact that the Soviet Union, one of the two nuclear superpowers and a formative presence in nearly every aspect of post-1945 international relations, has imploded. In the process, the internal conditions of autocracy, whether of one person or one party, that have historically assured the rulers of Russia a dominant position in the Russian and Soviet empires as well as great power status abroad have been called into question. The expulsion of Russia in 1989 from East-Central Europe and from Germany, where it had been a dominant influence as early as the mid-eighteenth century, in one blow discredited the Soviet Union's claim to global political parity with the United States.

The collapse of the Soviet Union's (and by extension Russia's) international position is in fact a direct consequence of the internal crisis of the Soviet system, a crisis brought into being by the efforts of Mikhail Gorbachev to save the system through sweeping internal reforms. Alexis de Tocqueville observed that the most dangerous moment for a bad government is when it tries to reform itself. Such has been the experience of Mikhail Gorbachev, as it is precisely his attempted reforms that plunged the Soviet empire first into political and economic chaos and now into a confederal transmutation that has put an end to the historical unitary Soviet party-state.

In essence, in attempting to reform what he and his closest colleagues at the time (such as Eduard Shevardnadze) recognized to be a failing economic, political, and social system, Gorbachev unleashed powerful forces that were intended to support his reform efforts. Those forces, however, given the absence of sufficient consensus on basic political values, rapidly moved far beyond the point where Gorbachev or anyone else could easily control or influence them. Gorbachev repeatedly had to accommodate forces that he originally did not intend to countenance, at first in order to keep the momentum of reform moving, and later in order to preserve a union whose existence the reform process itself had come to threaten. He thus faced a most painful dilemma: He could attempt to preserve the traditional centralized union by coercion, in which case he would lose all chance of reform, to which he nevertheless remained committed; or he could compromise with the forces of republican sovereignty, as personified by Boris Yeltsin. But because those forces have been pursuing genuine independence from the union (as a basis for renegotiating a new, confederal set of relationships), such a reconciliation would really be a capitulation and the end of the Soviet Union as history has known it. The dramatic denouement of the failed coup of August 19–21, 1991, has resolved Gorbachev's dilemma in favor of the latter choice, i.e., the end of the Soviet state.

Economic Hard Times

How did this situation come about? We have learned so much so quickly since the outset of the Gorbachev era in 1985 that we tend to forget the reasons for the then-bold steps of reform pushed by Gorbachev and the plausibility, to both Soviet and Western observers at that time, of structural reform of the Soviet system.[1] Briefly stated, the system that Gorbachev inherited in March 1985 faced a fundamental crisis of development, what Gorbachev for several years euphemistically called "a pre-crisis situation." Growth rates in the economy had been declining steadily and dramatically since the early 1960s. In the early 1980s the Soviet Union had, by Gorbachev's admission, experienced an economic depression (termed "a net decrease in the absolute increment of national income").[2] The result, although not at that time a challenge to the survival of the Soviet system, imposed fundamental limitations upon the ability of the Soviet government to attain its declared domestic and foreign policy objectives. The trade-offs among military investment, foreign policy commitments, investment in heavy and light civilian industry and agriculture, and civilian consumption were becoming increasingly painful, affecting the performance of the Soviet system and even the sources of stability of the system at home and abroad. Western economists estimate that the portion of the Soviet economy devoted to consumption was actually smaller than that allocated by Nazi Germany during World War II, less than 50 percent of the total economy.[3] Even the long-term ability of the

Soviet military to maintain a military establishment competitive to that of the United States in a high-technology environment was called into question, transforming many in the Soviet armed forces into advocates of economic reform.[4]

The pattern of declining and even negative growth rates in the economy meant that the period of easy choices for Soviet politicians was over. No longer could Soviet leaders assume, as was true of the early Brezhnev period, that substantial increases in economic growth could provide for more guns and butter at the same time. Money could no longer be "thrown" at such problem areas as agriculture, which absorbed the single largest increment of state investment outside of the military during the Brezhnev period. Less money would have to be better spent, which meant difficult and painful political choices over the allocation of economic and social resources.

This rather ordinary political dilemma was compounded by the fact that the bleak situation in the economy actually demanded tremendous increases in basic investment simply to prevent a further deterioration.[5] By way of example, in per capita economic output (i.e., productivity, the true measure of an economy's modernity), the Soviet Union by the mid-1980s ranked on average between fiftieth and sixtieth in the world, placing it in the middle of Third World countries. The Soviet Union spends 2.3 times as much in energy as does U.S. industry to produce the same amount of oil and gas; 3.1 times as much for steel; 2.6 times as much for cement; and twice as much for energy in general.[6]

Indeed, the critical energy sector may serve as an index for the state of the Soviet economy as a whole. Although the Soviet Union maintains its position as the world's largest producer of oil and natural gas, with 25 percent of total world energy reserves on its territory (and 45 percent of all natural gas reserves), the trends since the late 1970s have all been downward. Aging oil fields, lack of funds for new exploitation, and profligate drilling and pumping practices (widespread use of water to pump oil, thereby accelerating the depletion of accessible reserves), have resulted in a 75 percent drop in the marginal value of pumping Soviet oil. Whereas in 1981, the Soviet Union earned seven times the cost of production for each barrel of crude oil that it exported, by 1991 it was earning less than twice the cost of production for each export barrel of oil. (The same trend may be observed with natural gas.)

As oil is the Soviet Union's single largest earner of hard currency (which permits the Soviet government to purchase Western technology—and grain), accounting for over two-thirds of all dollar-convertible receipts, it can safely be said that as oil goes, so goes the Soviet Union (and now Russia). And oil has been doing very poorly indeed, with projections that are if anything more pessimistic than performance in the recent past.[7] According to Yevgeny Khartukov, a former senior Soviet energy official, Soviet oil output has been projected to drop from 11.5 million barrels per day in 1990 to possibly 9 million by the year 2000. Net exports, which totaled 3 million barrels per day in 1990, will fall to zero by 1994 or sooner. Indeed, during the first half of 1991, Soviet oil exports declined by approximately 25 percent.[8] By 2000, the Soviet region will be running a net oil deficit of 2 million barrels per day, at current rates of Soviet domestic consumption.[9]

Returning to the present and to the economy as a whole, the Soviet economy has since 1989 been experiencing a progressive "deindustrialization." Clearly, Soviet statistics, perhaps now as never before, have to be taken with more than the usual grain of salt, but the general outlines of the economic collapse are not disputed. In the first six months of 1991, Soviet gross national product declined by approximately 8 percent, productivity by 10 percent, exports by 18 percent, and imports—due to the shortage of convertible currency—by 45 percent. In the month of May 1991 alone, the consequent lack of spare parts and of raw materials led to the closure of 300 factories.[10] The decline in the economy in 1991 and 1992 is estimated at 15–20 percent, or about twice the decline during the worst years of the American depression of the 1930s (9 percent).

The social consequences of this economic bind have been dramatic. No growth in the economy has meant little improvement in social services and in a standard of living that had long been starved by Soviet preoccupation with the military and heavy industry sector of the economy. Male life expectancy went from a high of sixty-eight years in the mid-1960s to sixty-two years by the early 1980s, an unprecedented decline in peacetime for an industrially developed country. By the late 1980s, fully 40 percent of male deaths were of working age. The Soviet Union by the early 1980s was experiencing infant mortality rates that by the admission of its minister of health, Yevgeny Chazov, put it at number fifty in the world, behind Barbados and Kuwait. (Soviet authorities stopped publishing statistics on life expectancy and infant mortality in 1975.) Alcohol consumption had risen to 43.5 liters of vodka per capita, i.e., five times that during the late czarist period. Furthermore, over 50 million Soviet citizens are now conceded by the Soviet authorities to live in 103 cities where air pollution is "dangerous," i.e., ten times the official Soviet limit. Sixteen cities have exceeded fifty times the official limits, which are themselves far more tolerant than their Western equivalents. Less than half of the industrial waste in Moscow is treated, and only 8 percent of all treatment facilities meet local standards for clean water. Two-thirds of Russian rivers, lakes, and reservoirs are too polluted for use as drinking water, according to a January 1992 report by the Russian president's adviser on ecology and health. Thirty percent of all food contains pesticides in quantities that are officially considered to be dangerous.[11]

External and Internal Problems

Such, in broad outline, was the economic and social situation facing Gorbachev in 1985 and afterward. Taken together, all of this clearly indicated that something had gone fundamentally amiss in the direction that the USSR had taken. Yet this was not all. There were international considerations of comparable concern to the Soviet leadership. The eruption of the Polish crisis in 1980–1981 sent shudders throughout the Soviet leadership, as it witnessed the disintegration of the authority of the Polish Communist Party in the face of the mass workers' movement represented by Solidarity. The message was clear, even for the most diehard reactionaries: As Konstantin Chernenko himself observed, the Polish crisis presented a negative object lesson of what happens when a Communist party loses contact with the masses. If the Soviet system were to avoid a similar fate, long festering social, economic, and even political problems could no longer be ignored.[12]

In extrabloc affairs, the Soviet Union found itself increasingly isolated in its relationships with key countries. Having failed to prevent deployment of Pershing II nuclear missiles in Western Europe, the Soviet Union in 1983–1984 unilaterally abrogated arms control negotiations with the United States on both intermediate- and intercontinental-range nuclear forces, without any detrimental effect to the U.S. position or to the political viability of key U.S. allies in Western Europe. Similarly, the Soviet government permitted itself to cast the issue of the U.S. Strategic Defense Initiative in absolute terms, refusing to make progress on strategic arms control without a prior U.S. commitment to abandoning the program in toto, thereby depriving itself of needed negotiating flexibility.

The quagmire (Gorbachev's term) of Afghanistan was demoralizing Soviet society further and complicating Moscow's relations with a number of Third World countries, especially in the Islamic world. Relations with China remained essentially frozen. In the Middle East, continued Soviet refusal to deal with Israel ensured the position of the United States as the privileged interlocutor for Arabs and Israelis alike, thus shutting the Soviet Union out of the "peace process" in the region. At the same time the Soviet leadership found itself supporting poor and increasingly threatened regimes in Angola, Ethiopia, Mozambique, and Nicaragua (not to mention Cuba, which alone cost the Soviet Union several million dollars per day). These foreign and domestic challenges came together with magnified force, with the development of the computer/information revolution, led by the world's two largest and dynamic (and capitalist) economies, those of the United States and Japan. And these challenges occurred at a time when the Soviet economy, which had never even mastered the first industrial revolution, was in full crisis.

In 1985 Gorbachev, confronted by this situation, used it to justify the reforms of glasnost and perestroika that have become his hallmark. The choice of far-reaching reforms was hardly unique in the sweep of Russian history. Imperial reformers, including Peter the Great (1689–1725), Catherine II (1762–1796), Alexander I (1801–1825), and Alexander II (1855–1881), all tried, with varying degrees of success, to modernize and rationalize Russian society through ambitious economic, administrative, and cultural campaigns. Their goal was to mobilize society to the purposes of the state and in the process to imbue dynamism and creativity into a rigid, autocratic system of rule. Yet it is interesting to note, in light of Gorbachev's fate, that all these efforts at directed reform fell short of the mark: Faced with a crisis of the autocratic system, none of the czars was ultimately prepared to renounce the autocratic principle and accede to a government of laws, in which even the sovereign's rule—and more important, his right to rule—was constrained. Every effort to elicit the creative participation of society in running the country was undermined by the inability of the imperial authority to accept an autonomous public existence for the elite classes of society.[13]

Expressing a conviction that could have been taken to heart by the Brezhnev leadership (who in retrospect seem to have been better "Sovietologists" than Gorbachev), Czar Alexander III asserted that the advent of constitutional government would mean the end of the multinational empire.[14] That is, outside of the autocratic principle, there was no evident way of binding the diverse nations that made up the Russian (and later Soviet) empire together. Russian (and later Soviet) reforms have thus contained a built-in check: Reforms designed to improve the autocratic political system were in the end always sacrificed when their disintegrative consequences for the multinational "Russian" state were pointed out. According to the census of the 1890s, ethnic Russians constituted just 44 percent of the population there. (Because of loss of territories after World War I, especially Poland and Finland, Russians in 1991 made up a somewhat higher percentage of the Soviet population, but barely more than 50 percent, according to projections from the most recent Soviet census data.)

Yet, amazingly, Gorbachev seems not to have considered the multinational composition of the Soviet state to have been an important consideration in his decisions for reform in 1985. Time and again, from 1985 through late 1987, Gorbachev approved of Communist Party declarations to the effect that the historical problem of relations among the nations (called "nationalities" in Soviet parlance) of the Soviet Union had been "resolved" once and for all. In Kiev, capital of the Ukraine, which was the largest and most important of the non-Russian republics of the Soviet Union, Gorbachev twice in the same 1985 speech identified "Russians" with the Soviet Union, indicating a phenomenal blindness to the multi-national aspect of the Soviet system.[15]

In this sense, Gorbachev ignored the single most important consideration that had repeatedly stayed the hand of past Russian reformers and caused their reforms, most of which were rooted in the same considerations as those motivating Gorbachev himself, to founder. He was thereby emboldened to proceed along a path of progressively more radical reform, which he thought was the only way to revive a failing system. As best as we can reconstruct the record of the period 1985–1988, it never occured to Gorbachev that the discrediting and dismantling of the old, neo-Stalinist structures of power and values would encourage the public emergence of nationalist claims. The logical consequence of that nationalism would be a threat to the very union that the policies of perestroika and glasnost were designed to strengthen. For the Gorbachev of 1985, the chief threat to the Soviet Union was the long-term prospect of its decline to the status of a second-rank power as a result of its inability to assimilate the global revolution in computers, information, and communications.

In this light, the "early" Gorbachev did understand, as did the imperial reformers in their time, that the system itself had reached an impasse in its development. Only a basic change in the workings of the system— akin to Peter's opening to the West, Alexander II's abolition of serfdom, or Piotr Stolypin's (Nicholas II's prime minister) 1910 wager on the entrepreneurial peasantry—could rejuvenate the system and maintain the Soviet Union's international position and prestige. For Gorbachev, this meant at first a reduction of essentially administrative methods in running the economy and a far larger latitude given to material incentive and individual initiative in the economy and the affairs of society.

Gorbachev launched this program by reaching out to society, first, the technical and creative intelligentsia, in an attempt to recruit the voluntary allegiance of "the best and the brightest" the Soviet Union had to offer. If he was to break the comfortable inertia that many in the country had come to crave after the upheavals of the early Soviet period, Gorbachev had to offer those best qualified to modernize the system good reason to collaborate with him. This implied higher salaries for the able, greater professional latitude for the Soviet "white collar class," and more freedom of expression for the creative intelligentsia. In effect, Gorbachev was trying to create the kind of dynamic civil society that all reformers since Peter the Great have tried to encourage but ultimately proved unwilling to accept, owing to the relative diminution of power for the state which the cultivation of society implied.

It cannot be said that Gorbachev underestimated the *social* dimension of political and economic reform. From the very outset and again on numerous occasions, Gorbachev made it plain that he understood that the process of reform would call into question several basic elements of the implicit "social contract" that had been established between the Communist Party and society: job security in factory and bureaucracy, relative equality of incomes, and the kind of unblinking "hurrah-patriotism" that plays so well to Russian chauvinists of all stripes. Gorbachev understood well that the crux of the matter was not his political program as such but rather the willingness of Soviet society to become a creative, risk-taking, responsible partner with the state. That response of the society has been central to Gorbachev's vision of reform. This, for the early Gorbachev, was essential in answering the question of whether the Soviet Union could be transformed into an efficient and just modern society, capable of generating the nonmilitary attributes of power that are essential to a country that retains global aspirations. In short, could a society that had become accustomed to a kind of security, to obedience and equality as primordial social values, be transformed into one that values initiative, creativity, and thus risk-taking, without undue consequences for its internal stability?

At the same time, it is now clear, and Gorbachev has admitted as much, that the Soviet reform leadership did not take the full measure of the economic crisis afflicting the country and of the depth of popular apathy. In part, this was due to inadequate information, especially on the state of the economy. Decades of willful deception in reporting on mandatory plan fulfillments had led to the point where no one in the system, including the top leadership, had an accurate picture of the state and direction of the Soviet economy. More important still, the Soviet leadership, and in the first instance Gorbachev himself, was neither able nor willing to come to terms with the profound disaffection from the Soviet system that had set in among the population in general and that had long been present among the non-Russian nations of the Soviet Union.

The consequence of this curious appraisal of the state of the union, one that was both candid and naive, was a concerted effort by Gorbachev and his allies to make a rapid transition from a neo-Stalinist political and economic system to a more traditional but still authoritarian system. These leaders were confident that there were enough unused reserves and at least passive consensus in the system to tide them over the dangerous initial period of reform. The first five years of the Gorbachev period were thus characterized by the pell-mell dismantling of the Leninist-Stalinist institutions of state and party power and, as important, of the Leninist-Stalinist version of Soviet and Russian history, before either could be replaced with substantial substitutes. The Gorbachev leadership, however, discovered that it is much more difficult to proceed from totalitarianism to authoritarianism than from authoritarianism to democracy (as occurred in Spain, Portugal, Chile, and the Philippines) because in such authoritarian systems the citizens themselves own the bulk of the country's property and are free to form private associations, thereby providing a ready-made substitute for the old order when it finally does collapse.[16] The Gorbachev leadership soon found itself in a quandary: Where it did not meet societal apathy, a result of the success of the Soviet system in destroying personal initiative, public spirit, and trust in government, it confronted nationalists who may have approved of his overall concept of reform but who were determined to expropriate it on nationalist grounds.

Glasnost and Perestroika

Perestroika has thus had both an emancipating and a disintegrative impact, although the tendencies to disintegration have generally been clearer than those of constructive reformation. The central tenets of Leninism—the ideology of the single truth and political institutions based on a monopoly of power—have been destroyed. Except for nationalism, no political force has yet emerged to replace them. (In his speech to the July 25, 1991, plenary session of the Soviet Communist Party's Central Committee, i.e., nearly a month *before* the failed coup that triggered the dismantling of the Communist Party nationwide, Gorbachev stated that in the previous eighteen months the Communist Party had lost 4.2 million members, only 2–3 percent of whom had joined another political group. This represented a precoup decline in party membership of over 20 percent.[17])

To state that Gorbachev misunderstood the obstacles to reform does not mean that he thought it would be an easy process. Nor should such a critique be taken to diminish the historical import of what his reforms have accomplished, if often in spite of themselves. From the very beginning of the Gorbachev reforms, the Soviet leadership understood that in the Soviet context change, any change, would be an intrinsically painful process. The policy of glasnost, or the opening up of information and debate, was designed to make the population aware of the painful failures of the existing structures of power and allocation of resources as the reform leadership saw them and to convince it that there was no viable alternative to the path of radical reform upon which Gorbachev had set out. All along Gorbachev realized that such far-reaching change is a long-term process, requiring a change in mind-set, what he has called the "political culture" of the nation. The process demands changes in mass attitudes and psychology as much as specific reforms in the economy and political system.[18]

Although Gorbachev recognized that such a cultural revolution would take generations to be fully successful, he explicitly took the problem of changing social consciousness as central to the process of managing change in the Soviet Union. On this point his policy has had enormous, and irreversible, impact. Gorbachev effectively discredited alternatives to the reformist path, both in terms of social acceptability and national security. He had been able repeatedly to make Soviet society aware of the unacceptable costs of past practice, thereby neutralizing politically meaningful toleration of the status quo. The effect of this strategy was dramatically underscored by Stanislav Shatalin, formerly one of Gorbachev's chief economic advisers and author of the ill-fated "Five Hundred Day Plan" to introduce a market system to the Soviet economy. "This is not a choice between London and Paris we are facing now," Shatalin told a group of Supreme Soviet members who in September 1990 were demanding guarantees of success in a free market system. "This is a choice between survival and the grave."[19]

Gorbachev had thus, within the space of five years, destroyed the capacity of traditional Soviet political culture to provide convincing explanations of social reality and credible policy alternatives. Yet the capacity of vested interests to resist change, even passively, has proven predictably strong. On the level of political tactics, Gorbachev had considerable success. He was able to deprive the vested interests of their privileged (and immune) position in the political system while at the same time providing enough guarantees for their career and personal security that they constantly hesitated before actively seeking allies against him. Crudely put, Gorbachev was the only remaining assurance of a comfortable pension for the old guard. Given the costs of upsetting the delicate balance of reformist and traditionalist forces that Gorbachev had established and maintained, an anti-Gorbachev coup would have been akin to the conservatives cutting off their noses to spite their collective faces. This helps explain both the delay—six years—in the organization of an anti-Gorbachev coup and, perhaps more important, the reluctance of most of the party leadership to take a convincingly *active* part in the coup itself.

At the same time, and here Gorbachev met serious disappointment, it became clear that no mere adaptation of the existing system could provide the active support for radical change that is now the only hope for the peoples who inhabit the Soviet region. Gorbachev had hoped that the implementation of far-reaching economic reform would save the essence of the Soviet political-economic system. In practice, however, the devastation that he has wrought on the old regime has discredited any choice associated with the framework of Soviet socialism. This is true in terms of both the social-economic content of the reforms, which became progressively more radical in order for Gorbachev to maintain the general momentum of reform, and the refusal of the non-Russian nations, and now the Russians themselves, under the leadership of Boris Yeltsin, to follow along within the framework of Gorbachev's system-saving reform. Ironically, Gorbachev himself did not grasp this primordial political fact until it was too late. The effect was to help precipitate a reactionary coup and, when it failed, to see effective power slide to the republics, especially to Yeltsin's Russia.

Cultures of Reform

What is remarkable, and only partially intended, is that there are now springing up throughout the Soviet region the seeds of entirely new cultures of reform: Most lean toward the market system and a form of political liberalism. The emergence of this new culture, or set of cultures, of reform on the surface represents the collapse of Gorbachev's dream of saving the foundation of the old order by a radical restructuring of the edifice. And yet, it is probably the prospects of these new forces for a very different kind of reform that hold out the only chance for salvaging the substance of Gorbachev's original reform vision: bringing the peoples of the Soviet Union into the late twentieth century and creating the unity that is the precondition for their peace and prosperity. By mid-1990 at the latest, Gorbachev, having taken the system so far, should have redefined his own role in the process of change. The key agent of change to date, he should have ceded genuine power to the new agents of change, spawned by his own reforms—in many instances against his original intentions and preferences. His failure to do so in time guaranteed his marginalization in the Soviet political process.

Gorbachev *did* prove himself capable of destroying the old Stalinist institutional and psychological order. For that alone, he will go down in history. Yet, by the sixth year of his reform enterprise, it became evident that Gorbachev was not the man to replace the old system with a viable alternative. The amazing political comeback of Boris Yeltsin, expelled from the Soviet Politburo with Gorbachev's approval in October 1987, and the appearance of numerous other "Yeltsins" throughout the non-Russian republics of the Soviet Union—each insisting on sovereign independence from the Soviet state—represented a dramatic defeat for Gorbachev's reformist concept, which was designed to preserve a strong, centralized

Soviet Union, not to bury it. Yet the emergence of these new forces is a natural reaction to the inability of the Communist power structure, Gorbachev included, to elicit broad support for saving the Soviet system.

The prospects for stable change now depend on the post-Soviet leaders' drawing the full implications from this fact and fully aligning themselves with the new forces for change from below. They will thereby endorse the painful modernizing change that is indispensable for the peoples and nations who inhabit what remains of the Soviet Union. Regardless of this choice, though, the Soviet system can no longer be saved: Its replacement will entail an undetermined amount of economic disruption, social dislocation, and/or political violence, whatever the political coloration of the Soviet succession. To the outside world, then, the message is clear: For as far as we can project into the future, the energies of the peoples of the former Soviet Union will be almost entirely absorbed in what are today considered to be their domestic affairs. The "Soviet threat" throughout the post-1945 period, whatever its previous validity, is dead. The implosion of power in Gorbachev's Soviet Union itself removes even the theoretical possibility of a direct, preconceived aggression against its neighbors.

This collapse of authority within the Soviet Union, as evidenced by the breakdown of the Soviet economic and political systems and the general rejection of Gorbachev's rule, has led many observers within and outside the Soviet region to predict another, indirect threat flowing from the Soviet political crisis: the onset of civil war throughout the land, with corresponding international consequences. What is the probability of such a denouement?

The Disintegration of the Union

Certainly, the drama of the present disintegration of the Soviet Union, expressed most visibly in the cession of effective sovereign power from Mikhail Gorbachev to Boris Yeltsin, can hardly be overstated. At stake has been nothing less than a historic struggle over sovereignty, that is, the ultimate source of power and legitimacy, between the central Soviet authorities and the fifteen "union republics" that together have constituted the Union of Soviet Socialist Republics. The issue has been not only about the relative distribution of economic and political power, for instance, the degree of local economic autonomy or involvement in foreign trade. On that score, there had since April 1991 actually been a surprising amount of agreement between the federal Soviet authorities and the constituent republics and even between Gorbachev and Yeltsin. Rather, the crux of the matter became, Who shall have the authority to delegate power to whom? This was dramatically underscored by the struggle between the union republics and the central Soviet government over the content of a new Treaty of Union, and in particular over the right of taxation. The republics claimed and in a historic victory in late July 1991 won the exclusive right to levy taxes in a reconstituted Soviet Union. Any future tax revenues for the central state would be dispensed only through the treasuries of the union republics, a sure sign of effective sovereignty.[20]

If, as U.S. Chief Justice John Marshall observed in the early 1800s, "the power to tax is the power to destroy," then the implications of the central Soviet government's being deprived of an independent taxation authority can hardly be overstated. The capitulation of the Soviet government on taxation demonstrates that state sovereignty, as opposed to power itself, cannot be shared in the everyday political world. It must inevitably gravitate to one or the other party, by peaceful or, if necessary, violent means. This point should not be surprising, especially to Americans. The debate over sovereignty in the United States, that is, the supremacy of federal or state law (by analogy, the issue in the former Soviet Union), was resolved by force of arms in the Civil War. Clearly, the issues that were in contention in the Soviet Union are comparable to those that have triggered civil wars elsewhere. The motivations of those who "organized" the antireform coup of August 1991 thus become clear.

It is also true that there have been present in the Soviet Union in recent years a number of factors that have historically led to mass outbreaks of revolutionary and civil violence. These include:

- A prevailing sense of disappointment, born of a hope for vastly improved conditions,[21] a hope that is now believed to have been betrayed
- The simultaneous disintegration of social and economic as well as political institutions[22]
- The reappearance of anticolonialist nationalist feelings among Russians and non-Russians alike toward the Soviet Communist system[23]
- The disappearance of a belief in the legitimacy, that is, the right to rule, of the government,[24] and now even of any supranational authority
- The complete obsolescence of the economic system in terms of its ability to promote technological progress[25]
- The resistance of the educated classes to the coercive leveling of income and opportunity[26]
- The pervasive breakdown of the machinery of government, due to a widening disparity between revenues and public expenditures[27]
- The desertion of the intellectuals from the government camp[28]

- The increasing unity among the revolutionists in the different nations making up the Soviet Union, as reflected as early as January 1991 in Yeltsin's support of the Baltic states' defiance of Soviet authority

There is, by contrast, one element usually associated with revolutionary and/or civil explosions that has not been present in the current Soviet and post-Soviet political equation, an element that historically has proved a necessary and even sufficient condition for the outbreak of sustained, mass civil violence. That element is a schism within the instruments of organized violence (in this case the Soviet armed forces, the KGB, and the police) followed by the various factions' taking up opposing sides, appealing to powerful, sympathetic forces in society, *and* being willing to use them effectively, that is, en masse and with the likely death of thousands. The curious and abortive government coup against the Baltic states in January 1991 already suggested considerable hesitancy about the massive use of force. In retrospect, it seems clear that the meekness of the anti-Baltic coup attempts in early 1991 had the effect of emboldening the general Soviet population.

The consequent ability of the Moscow population to confront the August 1991 coup in the streets, in the manner of the East European revolutions of 1989, posed a terrible dilemma for the Soviet army: On the one hand, a massive use of force was required in order to dissuade the population from further challenges to its authority; on the other hand, the military leadership could not be certain that orders to conscripted soliders to use force against civilian populations would be obeyed. The leadership feared that the consequent break in the military's ranks—as happened in Yugoslavia in June and July 1991—might actually precipitate its disintegration. This is a question that neither soldiers nor politicians nor political scientists can answer beforehand. Happily, those plotting the Soviet coup preferred to avoid the issue.

In light of the fact that there have actually been three "revolutions" occurring simultaneously in Gorbachev's Soviet Union, it is the relative absence of systematic, politically directed mass violence that is striking. The virtually nonviolent denouement of the coup reinforces the point. Politically speaking, the unitary Soviet party-state has been both disintegrating and mutating into something as yet undefined. Internationally, a major world empire is in a state of collapse. And economically, a strict, centrally planned economy has been rejected in favor of one that contains strong market elements in one form or another. Any one of these convulsions would be sufficient to trigger massive social disruption, political reaction, and civil violence. That all three are now taking place, while mass violence calculated to effect political change is not, suggests that pressures that would otherwise produce social upheaval are somehow being sublimated. (The episodic but savage ethnic violence in the southern Caucasus republics is not aimed at the reform issue as such and therefore falls outside of the scope of this analysis.)

Surely the most powerful moderating factor is the Soviet peoples' pervasive sense that civil war *is* now a real possibility. Having experienced unparalleled collective tragedy in this century—from wars and occupations to revolution, famines, purges, deportations, and mass imprisonment, not to mention three years of civil war itself just after the 1917 revolution—the peoples and institutions of the Soviet Union, most of all the Slavic peoples, simply have no stomach for the misery and suffering that revolutionary and civil violence entail. They are afraid and exhausted. In this respect, the very awareness of civil war acts as a deterrent. To realize the hold that the Soviet past has today on post-Soviet citizens, most of whom either lived this history or were raised by those who did (Gorbachev and Yeltsin count in both categories), Americans need only remind themselves of southerners' vivid memory of the American Civil War, a century and a quarter after the fact. Another instructive comparison may be made to Spain after its own civil war of 1936–1939. The recollection of the horrors of civil violence guaranteed that any post-Franco political transition, whether directed by left, right, or centrist forces, would be peaceful in character. To such a nation, anything is preferable to civil war.

What is even more remarkable in the Soviet case, which distinguishes it from the tragic fate of the Serbs and Croats in Yugoslavia, is that the various Soviet peoples share, as a matter of collective consciousness, the common experience and memory of oppression by Stalinism and its political legacy. That is, the Russians, Ukrainians, Belorussians (and even the Baltic peoples) share a community of fate that works against the expression of the kind of political-ethnic violence that has rent Yugoslavia asunder. Such a community of fate is absent in the case of the Yugoslav peoples. To the extent that Boris Yeltsin is able to continue to recast the political vocation of the Russian nation in a nonimperial direction, the prospects for civil peace throughout the USSR can only increase. Given the remarkable political maturity expressed by Russian (and Ukrainian) voters in the March 17, 1991, referendum on the future of a reformed union, i.e., that there should continue to be a political and economic association among union republics but it should be on the basis of their confederal sovereignty, these prospects should not be underrated.[29] If Russia and Ukraine can avoid forcing territorial issues—which proved the spark in the Yugoslav war of 1991–1992—their chances for stable political development should be respectable. Twice, in November 1990 and late August 1991, Russia and Ukraine have agreed to proceed from respect for existing boundaries.

Another, often overlooked, element should be added to the equation: Simple outbreaks of violence or repression, however large in scale, do not by themselves add up to civil war. For that to happen, the actual institutions that control the police and the military must divide against themselves and the resulting factions find some base of support in the population. By all accounts, the Soviet military, especially after the chastening experience of August 19–21, 1991, has little inclination as a corporate body to shoulder the unhappy responsibilities that political intervention and governance would bring. Furthermore, as the August events have shown, few citizens would support a junta that seized power, regardless of its political orientation. There is, in addition, no identifiable civilian agency or personality outside of the Gorbachev-Yeltsin axis that seems ready, willing, and able to address the crisis besetting the Soviet region as a whole and around whom elements of the military might rally. There is, probably fortunately, precious little history of political intervention by either the Russian or the Soviet armed forces: Such inexperience may help explain the amateurism of the 1991 coup attempt.

In the present situation, concern over its organizational integrity will discourage the Soviet military from intervening in politics, which would expose it as a multinational army to the political and national divisions characteristic of Soviet society as a whole. The Soviet army also has the negative object lesson of the disintegration of the multinational Yugoslav army in mid-1991 to consider. The military will now have to accommodate itself to those forces, led by Boris Yeltsin, that can under the circumstances credibly promise a strong Russia, Soviet or not. This would follow the precedent of the early 1920s, which found many members of the former czarist officer corps rallying to the Bolsheviks (ideological antipathies aside) as the last hope for a strong Russian state. The unprecedented assembly of 5,000 Soviet officers in Moscow in January 1992 appears to confirm this view. Although expressing frustration at the collapse of the Soviet Union, which they were after all established to defend, the soldiers ignored the few veiled threats that were made and rejected any hint of nostalgia for Communist politicians, ideology, or institutions. The defense minister himself acknowledged the right of the post-Soviet republics to establish their own national armed forces. In their closing resolution, the officers asked only for a limited transitional period that would preserve common security institutions and provide for a stable redistribution of Soviet military resources.[30] The Soviet military, no less than ex-Soviet civilian leaders, finds itself constrained to accept the logic of the post-Soviet era.

In the end, there may be no dramatic or clear "solution" to the crisis of authority in the Soviet area. The peoples and leaders of that region may well be condemned to live with each other. As difficult as that sounds now, the alternative is intuitively well understood and acts as a brake upon the very worst happening. The choice that had been put before Gorbachev, and the rest of the country as well, was to attempt to preserve that which can no longer be saved, the Soviet Union itself, and in the process lose all chance of reform; or alternatively, to cooperate in moving to an untested, and historically almost unprecedented, confederal system comparable perhaps to the British Commonwealth in its more ambitious visions. For Gorbachev, either choice was unacceptable, whereas the alternatives, that of chaotic disintegration or civil war itself, are unthinkable. Whatever the choice, the Soviet Union will be recast without Gorbachev, but almost certainly without civil war.

Notes

1. As developed by Seweryn Bialer and Joan Afferica, "Reagan and Russia," *Foreign Affairs,* Winter 1982/83, pp. 249–271. The authors wrote, "The Soviet Union . . . boasts enormous unused reserves of political and social stability that suffice to endure the deepest difficulties." For an analysis with more qualifications, see Seweryn Bialer, *The Soviet Paradox. External Expansion, Internal Decline* (New York: Knopf, 1986), pp. 19–40. Boris Yeltsin himself justifies such a view. He argues in his political memoir that, had Gorbachev in 1985 decided on a policy of the status quo, he could have ensured himself a quiet career for ten to fifteen years, given the enormous resources and inertia of the Soviet system. See Boris Yeltsin, *Against the Grain* (New York: Summit Books, 1990), p. 139.

2. See Gorbachev's speech to the ideological meeting of the Central Committee on February 18, 1988, *The Ideology of Renewal for Revolutionary Restructuring* (Moscow: Novosti, 1988), p. 36.

3. Confirmed by Richard Ericson, Columbia University economist specializing in the Soviet Union, and Seweryn Bialer, "The USSR Today: The State of the Union," presentation to the Harriman Institute, September 14, 1989.

4. See the detailed critique by then chief of the General Staff Nikolai Ogarkov in *Krasnaya Zvezda,* May 9, 1984.

5. For an account of the crisis in social services, see Seweryn Bialer, "Gorbachev's Program of Change: Sources, Significance, Prospects," *Political Science Quarterly,* Fall 1988, pp. 407–410, 427–430.

6. For a summary discussion on Soviet economic and social collapse, with Soviet references, see Richard Pipes, "Gorbachev's Russia: Breakdown or Crackdown?" *Commentary,* March 1990, pp. 17–18 and *passim.*

7. Leslie Dienes, "Energy—From Bonanza to Crisis," RFL/RL Research Institute, *Report on the USSR,* December 1, 1989, pp. 1–5.

8. According to Matthew Sagers, director of the energy services section of Planecon: *RFE/RL Daily Report,* August 6, 1991, p. 3.

9. As reported by Leslie Gelb, "Oil Facts and Follies," *New York Times,* May 19, 1991, sect. 4, p. 17.

10. *Le Monde,* Selection Hebdomadaire, July 11–17, 1991, p. 2, as reprinted from ibid., July 17, 1991.

11. Aaron Trehub, "Children in the Soviet Union," *Radio Liberty Research,* December 15, 1987, p. 5; and Trehub, "Social and Economic Rights in the Soviet Union: Work, Health Care, Social Security, and Housing," *Radio Liberty Research Bulletin,* RL Supplement 3/86, December 29, 1986, p. 13. See also Gail Lapidus, "State and Society: Toward the Emergence of Civil Society in the Soviet Union," in Seweryn Bialer, ed., *Politics, Society, and Nationality Inside Gorbachev's Russia* (Boulder: Westview Press, 1989), pp. 121–147. TASS, January 22, 1992, as reported in *RFE/RL Daily Report,* January 24, 1992.

12. See Elizabeth Teague, "Perestroika—The Polish Influence," *Survey,* October 1988, pp. 39–58.

13. For historical background, see Marc Raeff, *Understanding Imperial Russia: State and Society in the Old Regime,* trans. Arthur Goldhammer (New York: Columbia University Press, 1984); and Adam B. Ulam, *Russia's Failed Revolutions: From the Decembrists to the Dissidents* (New York: Basic Books, 1981).

14. For a discussion of Alexander III's attitude toward constitutionalism see W. Bruce Lincoln, *In War's Dark Shadow* (New York: Simon and Schuster, 1983), pp. 31–32.

15. Bohdan Nahaylo, "Gorbachev's Slip of the Tongue in Kiev," *Radio Liberty Research,* RL 221/85, July 3, 1985, p. 1. For a competent account of Gorbachev's persistent inability to understand nationalism in the USSR, see Hélène Carrère d'Encausse, *La Gloire des Nations ou la Fin de l'Empire Sovietique* (Paris: Fayard, 1990). See also Gerhard Simon, *Die Desintegration der Sowjetunion durch die Nationen und Republiken* (Cologne: Berichte des Bundesinstituts fuer ostwissenschaftliche und internationale Studien, no. 25, 1991), pp. 5–15 and *passim.*

16. Pipes, op. cit.

17. As reported by TASS, the official Soviet government news agency, and cited in *RFE/RL Daily Report,* July 26, 1991, p. 2.

18. For a sensitive analysis, see Alfred B. Evans, Jr., "Changing Views of Social Differentiation in Soviet Ideology," in Sylvia Woodby and Alfred B. Evans, Jr., eds., *Restructuring Soviet Ideology: Gorbachev's New Thinking* (Boulder: Westview, 1990), pp. 65–96.

19. *New York Times,* September 21, 1990, pp. A1, A6.

20. *Economist,* August 3–9, 1991, p. 45, and *Financial Times,* August 5, 1991, p. 14.

21. Alexis de Tocqueville, *On Democracy, Revolution, and Society—Selected Writings* (Chicago: University of Chicago Press, 1980), pp. 227–242.

22. Samuel P. Huntington, *Political Order in Changing Societies* (New Haven: Yale University Press, 1968).

23. Rupert Emerson, *From Empire to Nation: The Rise of Self-Assertion of Asian and African Peoples* (Cambridge, Mass.: Harvard University Press, 1960).

24. Max Weber, *The Theory of Social and Economic Organization* (New York: Oxford University Press, 1947), p. 378 and passim.

25. This is, of course, the classic Marxist framework. For an effective application to the Soviet case, see Silviu Brucan, *The Post-Brezhnev Era* (New York: Praeger, 1983).

26. Crane Brinton, *The Anatomy of Revolution* (New York: W. W. Norton, 1938). This 1938 work holds up remarkably well over the years.

27. Ibid. See also, Judy Shelton, *The Coming Soviet Crash* (New York: The Free Press, 1989).

28. Brinton, op. cit.

29. For details on the referendum, see Chapter 8, note 1.

30. As reported in *The New York Times,* January 18, 1992, pp. 1, 4.

5

The Conceptual Revolution in Soviet Foreign Policy

Our interpretation of Soviet, and now post-Soviet, foreign policy conduct depends in substantial measure on how Soviet observers themselves—politicians and, increasingly, policy-oriented analysts and advisers—have thought about the foundations and direction of Soviet foreign policy and its relationship to the international scene. It is the latter relationship that inevitably shapes Soviet policy choices. If we are to understand adequately the reasons for Soviet foreign policy conduct, we need to address the analytical and conceptual foundations of that policy. This is particularly important in considering the range of choice and change in the future foreign policy behavior of the post-Soviet Commonwealth. Our understanding of the direction of Soviet foreign policy depends critically on whether there was general support within important elite circles for the reevaluation of the USSR's international role that had taken place under Gorbachev. Understanding the cognitive world of the Soviet elite as applied to Soviet foreign policy should thus occupy a prominent place in our studies of Soviet foreign relations.

Bertil Nygren, a Swedish Sovietologist, has written:

If observable changes in Soviet foreign policy behavior are *not* reflected in cognitive changes, then we should be more careful in our judgments about Gorbachev's policies, or more skeptical about his intentions: either he is not very serious, or he is alone. If on the other hand, important cognitive changes seem to be present, then we should be more prepared to accept observable policy changes as serious and permanent; then we might very well have some "Gorbachevism" or "new thinking" even without Gorbachev.

Thus, the stronger the ideological foundation of the "New Thinking," the greater the probability that it will survive Gorbachev.[1]

One could adduce a variety of powerful political as well as analytical evidence that the foreign policy course that Gorbachev had mapped out was deeply rooted not only in his own political strategy but also in the crisis of power and influence in the USSR. Gorbachev made that crisis known throughout the Soviet system through the policy of glasnost (see Chapter 4). Indeed, the analytical and conceptual context for Gorbachev's international policies cannot be reduced to a new or altered understanding of purely international phenomena, such as the distribution of global power, the impact of nuclear weapons, or the nature of international technological change and economic growth, as important as they have been in reshaping Soviet international perspectives.

Internal and External Factors

Clearly, there is an important internal dimension as well, as the possibilities of the economy constrain the ways in which the USSR has interacted with the global environment. Alternatively, Soviet analysis of the international system may be related in significant ways to attitudes to the internal distribution of power and resources within the USSR. That is, someone favoring a major decentralization of power and demilitarization (or de-ideologization) of values at home has an interest in depicting, and influencing, a different sort of international political-military order, with a correspondingly different set of threat images, than one who is essentially satisfied with the traditional distribution of power and resources. Indeed, in the course of the Gorbachev period, this relationship between the internal and international dimensions of reform tended to become explicit, as the argument over domestic reform became couched in polemics over the nature of the external "imperialist" threat and thus of the permissible degree of internal reform.

Yet in the pre-Gorbachev period, which for our purposes extends through the Brezhnev period to the late 1950s and which embraces the intellectual origins of the "new political thinking," this external/internal relationship of the foreign policy discussion, although undoubtedly present, was difficult for the outside observer to establish and in practice probably much weaker than currently. This had much to do with the fact that, especially with the renewed repression of internal dissent following 1966 and the invasion of Czechoslovakia after 1968, the Brezhnevian political order had to be taken essentially as a given by Soviet "liberal" elites.[2] At the same time, Soviet foreign policy analysts were busily attempting to assimilate a series of remarkable international political-military phenomena that had appeared in the postwar world: the impact of nuclear weapons; the prosperity, stability, and cohesion of the West; and the emergence of a Communist China as the chief foreign policy threat to the USSR. None of these squared easily with the traditional Leninist analysis of imperialism as the wellspring of global conflict.[3]

By the mid-1970s foreign policy analysts were arguing that the influence of "external," or international, factors on socioeconomic systems, including Communist ones, was "greater than ever before." By clear implication, the increasing influence of scientific-technological innovation in the military and economic fields on domestic social structures meant that states, including the USSR, must increasingly adapt to the universal demands of what in Soviet parlance was called the "scientific-technological revolution." Soviet specialists on international relations emphasized the importance of the international system on world politics—which contradicts the Leninist view of a state's internal system as the key explanatory factor in international relations—by speaking of the "reverse influence" of the system of international relations on the policies of states.[4]

The international relations texts written in the late 1960s and 1970s reveal little of the substantive relationship to domestic preoccupations that, judging from the prominence of many of these authors in the Gorbachev reform effort, must certainly have been strong. The contemporary political visibility of such analysts of the 1970s as Yevgeny Primakov (a close personal adviser of Gorbachev and now head of the new intelligence agency), Vitalii Zhurkin (director of the Institute of European Studies), Gyorgy Shakhnazarov (a personal adviser of Gorbachev, held under house arrest with him in the Crimea during the coup of August 19–21, 1991), Vladimir Petrovskii (deputy foreign minister), and Fyodor Burlatskii (prominent political commentator, editor of *Literaturnaya Gazeta,* and head of the semiofficial Human Rights Commission), among others, bears striking witness to a direct link between international analysis and internal reform. The careers of many in the 1950s generation (the *piatidesiatniki*), who came of political age during the partial, but heady and soon-to-be interrupted, reforms of Nikita Khrushchev, have straddled the two fields. Nevertheless, it is the absence of any such overt substantive link that characterizes the Soviet international relations literature of the Brezhnev period. This literature forms an essential context to interpreting Gorbachev's foreign policy course and its legacy.[5]

The Gorbachev Soviet Foreign Policy Outlook

The Gorbachev Soviet foreign policy outlook, as introduced at the end of Chapter 1, entails (1) the nearly absolute predominance of domestic over foreign affairs; (2) a comprehensive political rapprochement with the West, led by the United States; (3) the superiority of political criteria over military ones in both nuclear and conventional arms control policy; (4) the elimination of ideological criteria in day-to-day security policy; and (5) recognition that global interdependence requires a collaborative rather than a unilateral approach to Soviet interests, including security. This revised Soviet approach to international relations is associated with such dramatic initiatives as (1) the Soviet adoption of the NATO "zero-zero" position on intermediate-range nuclear forces (INF), with disproportionate Soviet missile reductions; (2) acceptance and faithful implementation of the principle of mandatory international on-site inspection in several nuclear and conventional arms control agreements; (3) withdrawal of Soviet troops from Afghanistan; (4) a decided upgrading of Soviet support for United Nations (UN) peacekeeping activities; (5) the unilateral reduction of the Soviet armed forces by 500,000 troops and associated offensive equipment, as well as unilateral agreement to withdraw all Soviet troops from Poland, Hungary, and Czechoslovakia; and finally (6) acquiescence in the collapse of Communist authority throughout Eastern Europe, leading to the reunification of Germany on West German terms. One can, even in retrospect, view these as tactical adjustments or as evidence of a wholly new approach by the Soviet leadership to its international relations, depending on whether one can identify a corresponding conceptual change in Soviet thinking on foreign affairs.

In fact, the "new political thinking" in Soviet foreign policy may be seen as a determined effort by the Gorbachev leadership to redefine conceptually, as well as through a process of political interaction, the nature of the international environment facing the USSR and the range of appropriate Soviet choices in foreign and security policy. This revised definition of the international system reflects both a reevaluation of long-term international political and military trends, which began in the pre-Gorbachev era, and the pressing character of Soviet domestic needs. As the Soviet system proceeded on the path of structural reform, economic and political, at home, Gorbachev searched for ways of limiting the scope of demands placed on it. At the same time, the new thinking was intended to help provide Soviet foreign policy with a more appropriate set of ends and means.

The "new political thinking" in foreign policy was first of all a political rather than an intellectual or conceptual act. It reflected preestablished political priorities of the Gorbachev leadership, which in turn assiduously co-opted strains of thinking, some actually new, much developed quietly by specialists during the Brezhnev period, that suited its purposes and long-term goals. Partly, the new thinking was aimed at making more persuasive, to both foreign and domestic audiences, the course that Gorbachev set for himself in foreign affairs. Debate was also encouraged in normally reticent quarters, such as the military, in order to raise issues and elicit information that the political leadership required in making effective national decisions. Furthermore, it is now clear that Gorbachev and his closest colleagues found the worldview offered by the new thinkers in many respects a more persuasive interpretation of reality than that bequeathed them by their predecessors. But most of all, the new thinking represented a determined political effort by the Soviet leadership to recast the nature of the threat environment said to have been facing (and actually facing) the USSR and thereby to monopolize domestic Soviet discussion of the future military, economic, and political agendas of the Soviet state.[6]

There is a clear link between the revision of fundamental Soviet foreign policy concepts that took place on the specialist level throughout the Brezhnev period and much of the "new" thinking on international relations expounded by Gorbachev and his associates. Such "new" ideas as the rejection of nuclear war as a conceivable act of policy, the heightened significance attached to political factors in security policy, and increasing recognition of the multipolar and interdependent character of contemporary international relations were all put forward lucidly in the pre-Gorbachev era. The people who expressed them then became influential Soviet policy analysts. Indeed, the revised Soviet worldview represents a synthesis of tendencies present in Soviet policy circles since the 20th Communist Party of the Soviet Union (CPSU) Congress in 1956. Clearly, it has been changes in the international system as well as within the Soviet system that have triggered revisions in the formulation of Soviet foreign policy, first on the conceptual level and then in the actual making of policy itself. Because the source for many of these revisions arises from the USSR's external environment—from factors beyond Soviet control—they cannot be interpreted as simple tactical adjustments, ready to be reversed at an expedient moment. Instead, they are part of a process of international adjustment that both East and West are undergoing, and thus should be of particular concern to Western analysts and officials at an exceptionally fluid moment in Soviet and now post-Soviet relations with the outside world.

This Gorbachev synthesis may be summarized as follows: First, the Soviet leadership concluded and repeatedly made explicit to both foreign and domestic audiences that the USSR's international relationships were not to be a distraction from, and wherever possible should be a positive inducement to, the prime task of economic modernization at home. "The main thing," then foreign minister Eduard Shevardnadze said in a speech to the Soviet diplomatic community in June 1987, "is that our country not incur additional expenses in conjunction with the need to maintain its defense capacity and protect its legitimate foreign policy interests. This means that we must seek ways to limit and reduce military rivalry, eliminate confrontational features in relations with other states, and suppress conflict and crisis situations."[7] The logic of Gorbachev's policy of domestic reform led the Soviet leader to begin searching for structures of stability in critical areas, in arms control most visibly, and international organizations as well, so as to provide a durable and predictable framework for the resource choices that had to be made in the coming decade and beyond. Such stability was doubly important for Gorbachev because instability in the USSR's foreign relations would affect not only the politics of resource allocation but also the viability of Gorbachev's own political position, which assumed that far-reaching reform at home was consistent with the USSR's geopolitical influence abroad.

Second, the Gorbachev leadership had come to the conclusion that a favorable international environment could only be created on a *political* basis with the leading industrial powers, and above all with the United States. With remarkable tenacity, Gorbachev sought to strike a modus vivendi with the United States, which was the key toward establishing predictability in the USSR's foreign affairs and security requirements and would translate into a major victory for Gorbachev at home. The Soviet choice for detente thus represented more than a tactical adjustment to shifting circumstances, the "breathing spell" that some in the West detected. It also reflected a strategic and realistic reevaluation of the international environment, based on dealing with established governments in the advanced industrial world, and of the USSR's position in relation to that environment.

Third, there had been a major reexamination of security issues, led by the official confirmation by Gorbachev *and* the Soviet military that a nuclear war cannot under any circumstances be won. "The time has come," Mikhail Gorbachev said in his Political Report to the 27th CPSU Congress, "to realize thoroughly the harsh realities of our day: nuclear weapons harbor a hurricane which is capable of sweeping the human race from the face of the earth."[8] The leadership now argued, implicitly criticizing Soviet security policy under Brezhnev, a corollary: that security cannot be obtained through military means alone. Security in the nuclear age was said to be mutual in character and because of the destructive potential of modern weaponry, a common concern of all countries. Moreover, Soviet policy analysts and Gorbachev himself rejected nuclear weapons as a durable guarantor of peace. They claimed that even nuclear parity, which they continued to regard as a major historical achievement of socialism, could cease to be a determining factor for stability in the face of an unregulated arms competition between East and West. Nuclear arms control thus assumes priority as a means of reducing the external threat, limiting resource requirements for the military, and establishing a framework of stability in East-West strategic relations.

With respect to Europe, Gorbachev came to the conclusion that the USSR could not secure a significant further diminution of NATO's nuclear presence on the continent without at the same time addressing the issue of its own conventional posture and operational doctrine. Toward this end, Gorbachev admitted the need to reduce "asymmetries" in the conventional arms balance in Europe, thereby admitting the problem posed by Soviet superiority in forward-based tank forces for further arms control in Europe. Most dramatically, in December 1988 he announced a unilateral reduction of Soviet forces by 500,000 troops (200,000 in the European USSR and Eastern Europe) and the intention of making the remaining forces unmistakably defensive in orientation.

Interestingly, in a series of journal articles published in the latter half of 1987, a number of political-military analysts developed the concept of "reasonable sufficiency" and applied it to the East-West arms relationship.[9] Parity, they wrote, is not a simple quantitative concept. What counts is the ability of the USSR to deliver a devastating counterblow, not the precise numerical balance or the parallel development of weapons systems on both sides. The realities of the nuclear balance are such that deterrence is very stable within a broad range of weapons balances. The criterion in Soviet nuclear weapons procurement should be the capacity to maintain a reliable retaliatory force, *not* what the Americans have per se. In the process, the authors were evidently seeking to lay down new criteria for Soviet military and arms control policy that, by establishing *minimum* standards for credible deterrence, would help to demilitarize Soviet thinking about security and in the long run release considerable resources tied up in defense for domestic economic and social development.

That these views are not merely voices in the wilderness is shown by the vigorous reaction by the Soviet military beginning in the second half of 1987 to much of the civilian discussion of nuclear weapons and policy, which by then had gone beyond the bounds of specialist discussion and had come to absorb the special attention of the highly visible Writers Union.[10] When the rhetoric is separated from the analysis, what appeared to concern the military is not the specific interpretation of deterrence offered by the civilian specialists but rather its public articulation, which they fear will have the effect of discrediting their mission within the armed forces and ultimately undermine their socializing role in Soviet society. It would now appear that this is exactly what Gorbachev, surveying the military stranglehold over much of Soviet culture, had in mind.

A related point, brought to the fore by the U.S. Strategic Defense Initiative (SDI) program, concerns the future stability of the superpower arms balance. If even the maintenance of parity may not ensure stable deterrence, because of the pace of military-technological development and the possible qualitative leaps in the balance, and if superiority is not an attainable objective, then more efforts must be devoted to restraining the military competition. A revised view of military sufficiency, as indicated above, would provide the USSR with greater flexibility in pursuing arms control options to institutionalize constraints on (primarily U.S.) military-technological development and its translation into fielded weapons systems. The volte-face in the Soviet position on the INF issue thus proved to be only the first shot in a series of such efforts to provide a more predictable, less threatening, and ultimately less costly strategic environment. An important debate with serious consequences for key institutional actors had been launched. In that process, concepts were evidently seen as deeds too.

Fourth, the Soviet concept of peaceful coexistence was revised. Key Soviet policy analysts and officials now interpreted peaceful coexistence less as a form of class struggle, the traditional Soviet viewpoint, and more as a long-lasting condition in which states will have to learn how to live with each other for the indefinite future.

As Primakov noted in a key article in *Pravda* in the summer of 1987, peaceful coexistence was no longer regarded "as a breathing space" by the Soviets. "Interstate relations," he emphasized, "cannot be the sphere in which the outcome of the confrontation between world socialism and world capitalism is settled."[11] Such "active" coexistence is said to imply not simply the absence of war but instead an international order in which not military strength but relations of confidence and cooperation prevail and "global problems"—the arms race, ecological problems, Third World development—can be resolved on a collaborative basis.

Gorbachev wrote that the Soviet leadership had "taken the steps necessary to rid our policy of ideological prejudice."[12] If this would lead to a more pragmatic understanding of peaceful coexistence, with "class interests" strictly subordinate to geopolitical criteria in the daily conduct of foreign policy, a central obstacle to more genuinely collaborative East-West relations would have been removed. Certainly, it would mean that the United States and the Soviet Union might actually agree on the operational significance of "normal" relations, which proved impossible during the detente of the early 1970s. "New rules of coexistence," as Gorbachev put it in a key article on September 17, 1987 (reported to have been drafted by Deputy Foreign Minister Petrovskii), might then be drawn up.[13] Soviet officials, both pro- and anti-Gorbachev, have themselves recognized the centrality of this point for the integrity of Gorbachev's foreign and domestic policy vision and program. Speaking to the Soviet diplomatic community after the June 1988 party conference, Foreign Minister Shevardnadze explicitly declared the secondary significance of ideological/class values in contemporary Soviet foreign policy. According to the TASS account, Shevardnadze said, "the new political thinking views peaceful coexistence in the realities of the nuclear century. We are fully justified in refusing to see in it a special form of class struggle. One must not identify coexistence . . . with class struggle. The struggle between two opposing systems is no longer a determining tendency of the present-day era."[14]

The implications of Shevardnadze's remarks were underscored with dramatic effect when Yegor Ligachev, at the time the "second secretary" of the CPSU, joined the issue in early August 1988 in the first open challenge to Gorbachev's foreign policy vision. At the end of a speech on domestic affairs, in which he again cast scorn on market-oriented reforms, Ligachev suddenly turned to foreign policy and declared: "We proceed from the class nature of international relations. Any other formulation of the issue only introduces confusion into the thinking of the Soviet people and our friends abroad. Active involvement in the solution of general human problems by no means signifies any artificial 'braking' of the social and national liberation struggle."[15] Having earlier failed to curb the scope of Gorbachev's reforms on domestic grounds, Ligachev seems to have turned to foreign policy, where he may have hoped to find a more receptive audience. He evidently saw foreign policy as the "weak link" in Gorbachev's strategy: By attacking foreign policy reform, he hoped that domestic reform might be scaled down and vested party interests respected.

That the leadership was sensitive to the interdependence of foreign and domestic policy is shown by Gorbachev's Politburo ally Aleksandr Yakovlev's quick and brisk defense of the new foreign policy line several days later, when he reiterated the subordination of class interests to "all-human" interests such as survival in the nuclear age. At issue is the right to define the nature of the threat environment facing the USSR and thus the nature and level of the Soviet political and military response to it. If "class" values remain paramount, then the threat from the class enemy remains high and the USSR cannot afford the relative diminution of Soviet military expenditures, the (again relative) demilitarization of Soviet foreign policy, especially in the Third World, and therefore the reorientation of political values implied by Gorbachev's domestic economic reform. In this way, a debate over arcana of ideology is really a struggle for the acceptable framework of choice in reform, in both foreign and domestic policy, and bears directly on the prospects for reform at home. It is thus not coincidental that on October 4, 1988, shortly after one of Gorbachev's periodic "purges" of the top leadership, including the reassignment of Ligachev, Vadim Medvedev, the new party secretary for ideology, issued a ringing defense of the Gorbachev line on this point.[16]

Gorbachev's November 2, 1987, speech commemorating the seventieth anniversary of the Bolshevik Revolution included a synthesis of many of the analytical and political tendencies discussed in this chapter.[17] Perhaps most remarkably, however, Gorbachev raised therein a series of questions that go to the heart of the traditional Leninist theory of international politics. In response to those questions, Gorbachev implied that it is no longer necessary for the Soviet Union alone to contain the "aggressive" nature of imperialism; domestic forces within those societies might now be strong enough to "block [imperialism's] more dangerous manifestations." Second, Gorbachev suggested that capitalism may no longer require militarism for its economic survival and political stability (in that case, it would no longer be "imperialist"). Third, he suggested that the capitalist system is not in the long run dependent on the exploitation of underdeveloped countries (a policy of "neocolonialism"). Finally, Gorbachev implied that Western awareness of the nuclear threat can find expression in state policies, thereby leading to a more stable international system.

Simply to discuss such ideologically charged points implicitly challenged central Leninist tenets on the nature of imperialism and the wellsprings of conflict in world politics. The debate over the nature of imperialism, i.e., whether it can be restrained only by external (Soviet) power or by forces intrinsic to it ("bourgeois democracy"), has fundamental implications for the kind of external threat said to be facing the USSR. If imperialism can be contained by internal forces, then the requirements of Soviet security policy (and defense spending) are reduced accordingly. That Gorbachev raised these issues and provided even partial responses shows that the new flexibility in Soviet rhetoric and policy stemmed from a fundamental reevaluation of the relationship between the Soviet Union and its external environment. Taken together, and in light of the analytical background with its roots in the Brezhnev and Khrushchev periods, one may even speak, at the eleventh hour, of the emergence of a new Soviet theory of international relations.

The Soviet Ideological Change

The remarkable innovations in Soviet international policy reflect a shift in both the role and content of Soviet international ideology. This shift has been caused by the interlinking of Soviet internal and foreign policies. A change in the perceived capacity of the international system to threaten vital national interests has become an important precondition for the character, scope, and pace of domestic reform. The latter requires a redistribution of political authority, reallocation of material values, and (relative) decentralization of federal power, which has served in the past as the vehicle for the expression of the raw power interests of those who have ruled the Russian nation.

In this ideological change in foreign policy, in its thrust, both international and internal factors have played a role, although it has been the internal political and economic reform that has acted as the catalyst. The reevaluation of internal sources of power and legitimacy that constitute the essence of the Gorbachev reform has demanded, and also made possible, the assimilation of the understanding of the international system that had been put forward well before the Gorbachev period. Although the exponents of the new understanding were not heeded earlier, they are now influential, perhaps especially so in the post-Soviet era. Taken together with the intrusion of a series of highly pragmatic political considerations—in particular those relating to events in East-Central Europe and the absence of means by which the Soviet leadership could have exercised any restraining influence without jeopardizing the course of reform within the Soviet Union itself—these factors led to a vigorous and progressive exclusion of *traditional* ideological considerations from the conduct of Soviet foreign policy. (For details on this point, see Chapter 7.)

What, then, is the political foundation of this new ideology of Soviet external policy known as the "new political thinking"? In fact, until late 1991, it was far from clear, as much of both ideology and policy remained in a stage of flux. This has led some observers both in and out of the Soviet Union to argue for the essential vulnerability of the new political thinking. They note the fragility of a political and philosophical reorientation that is based mainly on a nuclear threat, which is after all only one component of a whole matrix of interrelated problems. If, ironically, the new security policy is maximally successful, that threat could be significantly diminished, thereby undermining the very foundation of the new approach.[18] Thus, precisely because this new ideology has yet to strike root throughout established political structures, its future is closely tied to new structures of political-institutional authority and legitimacy, which have been central to the Gorbachev reform enterprise but which still coexist uneasily alongside the old. The fate of the new thinking is thus intimately connected with the institutionalization of economic and political reform and the establishment of more effective decisionmaking mechanisms for addressing problems and issues of a national and Commonwealth—as opposed to sectoral, institutional, or local—character.

Yet if the fate of the new foreign policy philosophy is closely bound to one set of policies and practices, it is much less certain that future foreign policy conduct can revert to past patterns of hegemonial influence, regardless of the ideological foundation of the political leadership. In this respect, the relative narrowness of the support enjoyed by the new political thinking as an ideology loses much of its significance. The collapse of communism throughout East-Central Europe and the unification of Germany within NATO have revolutionized the entire context of Soviet and post-Soviet foreign and security interests in the heart of Europe—for Soviet observers the central theater of world politics. The political, military, and economic means by which the Soviet Union asserted its superpower status throughout the postwar period have in effect shriveled up. Any future leader, Russian or Commonwealth, will have to adapt to these profound constraints on their international influence. Thus, whereas the character of the adaptation to reduced circumstances will depend in important measure on the regnant philosophy of international relations, the necessity to do so seems now a foregone conclusion. (For details, see Chapter 6.)

Indeed, what is remarkable about the collapse of the Soviet Union's international position is how little resistance has been voiced from a very broad range of the political spectrum. The very concept of superpower is broadly rejected by many from "left" to "right" in the Soviet political system. They see such status, and the set of ambitions and commitments that it engenders, as running counter to the primary need to resurrect the Soviet state and/or the Russian people. On the official level the late Marshal Sergei Akhromeyev, Gorbachev's military adviser, forcefully rejected the concept of "limited sovereignty" in future Soviet–East European diplomatic relations, arguing that the Soviet Union must adapt to the East European revolution of 1989. Correspondingly, Yegor Ligachev has time and again reaffirmed the essential interest of the Soviet state in disarmament and reduced military budgets as the precondition for the comprehensive reforms required to save the Soviet (and by implication the post-Soviet Russian) system.[19] This general consensus on the near absolute priority of internal social, economic, and political development, combined with the impressive set of political and material limitations on Russian and Commonwealth external policies, should serve to reenforce the foreign policy tendencies of the Gorbachev period. Indeed, the worldview presented by the new political thinking would appear to provide a convenient, if not convincing, rationale for making a virtue out of the painful necessity of accommodation. It is interesting that foreign policy concerns played little role in the attempted coup of August 1991; in fact, the junta took pains to reassure the world about the continuity of Soviet international policy.

In many respects events in East-Central Europe and the Soviet response to them have constituted the acid test of change in Soviet foreign policy thinking and conduct. Originally, Gorbachev's laissez-faire policy toward East-Central Europe, aside from reflecting both Soviet preoccupation with its own domestic affairs and increasingly mature political leaderships (both popular and governmental) throughout East-Central Europe, was apparently based on two key assumptions: (1) that Communist parties would preserve a powerful say in government, and (2) that there would be no tampering with the Warsaw Pact. In the meantime, the pace of events forced Gorbachev's hand on the first point, as shown by Solidarity's triumph in leading the Polish government—with the effective neutralization of the Communists—and the self-destruction of the Communists in Hungary and throughout most of the rest of Eastern Europe. On the second point, the Warsaw Pact, the issue has been more complicated, but again Soviet policy has been compelled to concede the game by acquiescing in the reunification of Germany on West German terms and in the dissolution of the military and political structures of the Warsaw Pact by mid-1991.

It can no longer be disputed, as is also clear in the case of the non-Russian nations within the USSR itself, that Gorbachev vastly exaggerated the consensus on Soviet-type values within Eastern Europe, including within the respective Communist establishments themselves. Yet, there was clearly no way to intervene forcefully in East-Central Europe without at the same time calling a halt to the reform process at home. The political dynamics of his own reform thus prohibited Gorbachev from making the effort to intervene—even politically, economically, or ideologically—in East-Central European reforms (and later in revolution). Therefore the future of socialism in the USSR had been divorced from the fate of socialism abroad, and the Marxist-Leninist "world historical process" dropped as a desideratum, at any level, of Soviet foreign policy.

Ironically, the opposition to Gorbachev's foreign policy that has been voiced from reactionary quarters, especially in the military, has actually tended to underscore his foreign policy analysis and the irreversibility of the foreign policy changes over which he has presided. This criticism, which began to be heard around the time of the June 1990 party congress, has reflected an effort to exploit understandable confusion over Soviet international policy—especially the rapid unification of Germany—as a tool of domestic politics rather than to offer an alternative foreign policy program. Indeed, the most telling criticism of the Gorbachev foreign policy has played upon the Soviet peoples' weariness (and wariness) of "foreign entanglements," in the process actually reinforcing the progressive Soviet withdrawal from global affairs that has characterized Gorbachev's foreign policy. Such was the substance of the charge leveled against

Shevardnadze throughout the fall of 1990, i.e., that he might countenance the involvement of Soviet troops in a Persian Gulf war.

Nevertheless, the critics in this highly charged symbolic debate (Soviet arguments about the fate of Eastern Europe are reminiscent of the old U.S. dispute over "who lost China?") failed to advance a persuasive programmatic critique of the USSR's international position. Thus, in spite of having made Soviet Gulf policy a burning domestic issue in early 1991, the critics were unable to affect the pro-UN (i.e., pro-U.S.) direction of Gorbachev's policies. Indeed, the nominal issue in these debates is the manner and timing of Soviet adjustment to its reduced international circumstances, not the adjustment itself. In this regard, the CPSU International Department's January 1991 report on policy toward Eastern Europe pointedly excluded ideological criteria from its discussion of Soviet security interests in the region. In short, Gorbachev has succeeded in transforming the very framework of foreign policy discussion, so much so that even dissent tends to strengthen its underlying strategic postulates.[20] As Chapter 6 will show, the issue is not whether there will be a return to some alleged adventurism in Russian or Commonwealth foreign policy—"the hammer and sickle"—but whether any leader, present or future, can regain the power to act upon, rather than just react to, the country's international environment, i.e., to be the hammer or the anvil.

Notes

1. Bertil Nygren, "New and Old in Gorbachev's 'New Thinking,'" *Nordic Journal of Soviet and East European Studies* 6:1 (1989), p. 5.

2. Cynthia Roberts and Elizabeth Wishnick correctly noted the tendency in the works of many—including mine—to overlook the domestic aspect of the new Soviet international analysis. See their review article, "Ideology Is Dead. Long Live Ideology?" in *Problems of Communism,* November/December 1989, p. 58.

3. Interestingly, criticism of China's Cultural Revolution was at times advanced as a veiled critique of the Stalinist heritage in Soviet politics. See Fyodor Burlatskii (now a key exponent of reform), *Mao Tszedun i ego nasledniki* (Moscow: Mezhdunarodnye Otnosheniya, 1979).

4. Fyodor Burlatskii and A. Galkin, *Sotsiologiya. Politika. Mezhdunarodnye Otnosheniya* (Moscow: Mezhdunarodnye Otnosheniya, 1974), pp. 235, 237–238; Gyorgy Shakhnazarov, "Politika skvoz' prizmu nauki," *Kommunist,* no. 17 (1976), pp. 111–112; Pavel T. Podlesny, "Vvedeniye," in Genrikh A. Trofimenko and Podlesny, *Sovetsko-amerikanskiye otnosheniya v sovremennom mire* (Moscow: Nauka, 1987), p. 5.

5. For a representative list of their writings at the time, see the bibliography in Allen Lynch, *The Soviet Study of International Relations* (Cambridge: Cambridge University Press, 1987), pp. 174–195. Dusko Doder and Louise Branson brought

to light a revealing story, that points to the political relevance of the dissenting-establishment views of foreign policy in the pre-Gorbachev period. Upon meeting West German Chancellor Helmut Kohl after the funeral of Konstantin Chernenko, Gorbachev asked, "Kuda driftuyet Federalnaya Respulika?" Use of the American-ism "drift" suggested to the West German deputy foreign minister present, a Soviet expert, that Gorbachev either was studying English or had accepted the jargon of Moscow think-tank experts. Dusko Doder and Louise Branson, *Gorbachev: Heretic in the Kremlin* (New York: Viking, 1990), p. 67.

6. For a similar viewpoint see Stephen M. Meyer, "The Sources and Prospects of Gorbachev's New Political Thinking on Security,"*International Security* 13:2 (Fall 1988), pp. 125, 128, 134, 137, 156.

7. See Shevardnadze's candid speech to the Soviet foreign policy community in *Vestnik Ministerstva Inostrannykh Del SSSR,* no. 2 (1987), pp. 30–34, in which he clearly set forth the priority of internal economic development in all of the USSR's foreign relationships.

8. Mikhail S. Gorbachev, *Political Report of the CPSU Central Committee to the 27th Party Congress* (Moscow: Novosti, 1986), p. 78.

9. In addition to Vitaly V. Zhurkin, Sergei A. Karaganov, Andrei Kortunov, "Vyzovy Bezopasnosti—Starye i Novye," *Kommunist,* no. 1 (January 1988), pp. 42–50, see Zhurkin, "O razumnoy dostatochnosti," *S. Sh. A.,* no. 12 (December 1987), pp. 11–21; Igor Malashenko, "Parity Reassessed," *New Times,* no. 47 (1987), pp. 9–10; and Malashenko, "Reasonable Sufficiency and Illusory Superi-ority," *New Times,* no. 24 (1987), pp. 18–20.

10. See Thomas Nichols, "Intellectual Pacifists Criticized by Military Officer," *Radio Liberty Research,* RL 308-87, July 28, 1987; Nichols, "The Military and 'The New Political Thinking': Lizichev on Leninism and Defense," *Radio Liberty Research,* RL 80/87, February 26, 1987; Eugene Rumer, "Soviet Writers Clash Over Morality of Nuclear Deterrence, *Radio Liberty Research,* RL 299/87, July 13, 1987; Dominique Dhombres, "Le general et les pacifistes vegetariens," *Le Monde,* May 10–11, 1987, p. 5; and D. Volkogonov, "The Most Just War," *Kommunist,* no. 9 (June 1986), pp. 114–123 (JPRS translation UKO-86-016, October 21, 1986, pp. 130–140). For background, see F. Stephen Larrabee, "Gorbachev and the Soviet Military," *Foreign Affairs* (Summer 1988), pp. 1002–1026.

11. "Novaya filosofiya vneshnei politiki," *Pravda,* July 10, 1987, p. 4.

12. Mikhail S. Gorbachev, *Perestroika: New Thinking for Our Country and the World* (New York: Harper & Row, 1987), p. 250.

13. For Gorbachev's article, entitled "The Reality and Guarantees of a Secure World," see *Pravda,* September 17, 1987, pp. 1–2, translated in FBIS, *Daily Report. Soviet Union,* FBIS-SU, September 17, 1987, pp. 23–28.

14. *Pravda,* July 26, 1988, p. 4, as translated in FBIS-SU, July 26, 1988, p. 30.

15. *Pravda,* August 6, 1988, p. 2, as translated in FBIS-SU, August 8, 1988, p. 39.

16. Central Television, August 12, 1988, as cited in Elizabeth Teague, "Kremlin Leaders at Loggerheads," *Radio Liberty Research,* August 16, 1988, p. 5. For Medvedev's remarks see *Pravda,* October 5, 1988, p. 5.

17. The following quotes from Gorbachev's speech come from the TASS English translation provided by the Soviet embassy to the United States, "October and Perestroika: The Revolution Continues," pp. 39–55.

18. As discussed in Sylvia Woodby, *Gorbachev and the Decline of Ideology in Soviet Foreign Policy* (Boulder: Westview Press, 1989), pp. 58–59.

19. Akhromeyev has stated in this respect, "Limited sovereignty must not exist and ideology must no longer find a place in interstate relations." *La Repubblica,* November 22, 1989, as translated in FBIS-SU, November 30, 1989, p. 106. For Ligachev's most recent statement, see the Associated Press, June 8, 1990. For a particularly strident cri de coeur against the loss of Eastern Europe, see the statement of Soviet Army General Albert Makashev at the founding conference of the Russian Communist Party on June 19, 1990, as summarized in *Le Monde,* June 21, 1990, p. 4. It is interesting to note, however, that the criticisms of Gorbachev at the 28th CPSU Congress in July 1990 did not dwell on the collapse of communism in Eastern Europe (based on the Harriman Institute's review of Soviet television throughout the party congress and *New York Times,* July 5, 1990, p. A10).

20. "O razvitii obstanovki v Vostochnoi Evrope i nashei politike v etom regione," *Izvestiya TsK KPSS,* no. 3 (1991). For an evaluation, see Suzanne Crow, "International Department and Foreign Ministry Disagree on Eastern Europe," RFL/RL Research Institute, *Report on the USSR,* June 21, 1991, pp. 4–8. AP quoted Colonel Viktor Alksnis as calling for a "parliamentary inquiry with a criminal investigation" of Shevardnadze on December 24, 1990. On the debate over Soviet Gulf policy, see Suzanne Crow, "The Gulf Conflict and Debate over Soviet 'National' Interests," RFL/RE Research Institute, *Report on the USSR,* February 8, 1990, pp. 15–17.

6

The Transformation of
Soviet Foreign Policy

The collapse of Communist power throughout Eastern Europe in the fall of 1989 and the subsequent resolution of German unity on West German terms signify the political collapse of Russia in Europe.[1] The decline in the capacity of the Soviet Russian state to influence the settlement of geopolitical issues of vital interest to it has proven so rapid and so thorough that its political influence in what Soviet observers continue to call the central theater of world politics is lower than at any time since the mid-eighteenth century, when the Russian state first emerged as a truly European power. The defeat of Russia by Japan in 1905 did not fundamentally affect its standing as a European power, if only by dint of its sheer mass and its desirability as an ally. Even during the nadir of Russian power in purely physical terms during the 1920s and 1930s, the Soviet state inspired fear and hope far beyond its borders in ways that seem nearly incomprehensible in the last decade of the twentieth century. Only the remarkable political personality of Mikhail Gorbachev has obscured a disintegration of international influence that in its scale and scope finds no precedent in the leisurely and controlled declines of the British, Ottoman, Spanish, and Austrian empires.

A shorter version of this chapter entitled "Does Gorbachev Matter Anymore?" appeared in *Foreign Affairs,* Summer 1990. Copyright © 1990 by the Council on Foreign Relations, Inc.

Consequences of Reform

The reunification of Germany and reestablishment of the historical divide between Russia and Europe almost perfectly reflect the logic of the reform process that Gorbachev set in motion at home as well as abroad. In his effort to reform a failed Soviet system root and branch, Gorbachev unleashed powerful forces of an economic, social, political, and nationalist character. In principle those forces should have supported his reformist program, but in practice, because of the absence of any kind of internal or external consensus on Soviet-informed values, they rapidly moved beyond the point where Gorbachev and the Soviet leadership could control or even easily influence them. In response, and in order to preserve the essential momentum of increasingly radical reform at home, Gorbachev found it necessary to accommodate political tendencies that he certainly did not intend to countenance at the outset of his rule in 1985. Through a series of bold initiatives, which often seem to accept the adversary's terms, he attempted to redefine the nature of the challenges that the Soviet state was facing. He hoped thereby to recast the very terms of political discourse and retain the advantage of monopolizing the definition of political alternatives.

In foreign policy, this strategy worked to dramatic effect in the case of the intermediate-range nuclear forces in Europe: There disproportionate Soviet nuclear force reductions served to aid the cause of detente in the U.S. political arena and actually removed a significant military threat to Soviet ability to prosecute nonnuclear operations in the event of a future conflict in Europe. More recent and dramatic applications of this political strategy may be found in Gorbachev's failed effort in February 1990 to preserve what he still referred to as the "vanguard" role for the Communist Party by acceding to a competitive political environment and the remarkable attempt to redefine relations among the Russian and non-Russian nations of the USSR through a new treaty principle, which envisaged several kinds of federal or confederal arrangements amongst the constituent union republics. The Soviet concession to the U.S. insistence on retaining 30,000 more troops in Europe than the USSR, as well as the rapid Soviet agreement to the U.S.–West German formula for resolving the issue of German unity, may be seen as additional dramatic moves. Such actions are evidently aimed at revolutionizing the political-psychological context of apparently irreconcilable conflicts of interest, much in the way that Anwar Sadat's visit to Jerusalem transformed the stakes and interests in the Egyptian-Israeli relationship. Thus, the USSR under Gorbachev had been expecting that the momentum toward the demilitarization of the East-West relationship would make irrelevant the details of relative force balances and tactical concessions. The willingness to tolerate the complete integration of East Germany with West Germany also suggests that the USSR, faced with inexorable historical forces, was hoping to benefit from a transformed German-Soviet relationship in the future, in which its influence would be felt as part of some all-European process—of which the USSR would be considered an integral and equal part.

Yet hopes, however compelling, remain hopes. Quite apart from the question of whether the putative partners of the Soviet Union (or Russia) at home and abroad share such visions of its future political mission, the instruments with which such nontraditional policies of persuasion might be advanced are almost entirely lacking, with little chance of their appearing in any near-term future. There is simply no way back to Eastern Europe for Russia, which confronts the unsettling prospect of practically all of its erstwhile allies, certainly all of the important ones, reclaiming their European heritage, which they define in explicit contradistinction to Russia. By mid-1991, all Soviet troops had left Hungary and Czechoslovakia, with those in East Germany and Poland not far behind. The future ability of Russia to make its preferences felt in the councils of Europe, where it really matters, will depend on economic performance, on the productivity and competitiveness of the Russian economy. Simply to state that proposition underscores the difficulty of the Soviet successor state's international position.[2]

Up to now, the West has been a grateful beneficiary of the weakness of the foundations of Soviet power and the rethinking of traditional Soviet categories of interest and priorities that have characterized Gorbachev's foreign policy. Much concerned opinion has been expressed in the recent past about the fragility of Gorbachev's domestic political position and the implications that his removal from power would have upon Western international interests. Certainly, it cannot be denied that the neutralization of Gorbachev—which effectively began after Boris Yeltsin's leadership in defeating the coup of August 1991—will have a significant impact upon the calculation of interest and the decisionmaking process in the post-Soviet political system. Gorbachev had, at least until the fall of 1990, proved central to the scope and pace of reform, both domestically and internationally. Beginning in April 1991, he attempted to reassert his centrality in an entirely novel way: in guiding the cession of sovereign authority from the central Soviet state to its constituent republics.

Nevertheless, it is very unlikely that, *at this stage* of East-West relations and of the comprehensive crisis with which the Commonwealth system is confronted, a change in the leadership or in the pace, scope, and even character of domestic reform would have a corresponding impact on the tenor of East-West relations and of the most vital Western, especially U.S.

geopolitical, interests. The reasons for this relative optimism stem from the nature of the U.S. stake in East-West relations and from the impact that Gorbachev has had to date on Soviet foreign policy and by consequence on East-West relations themselves.

The Importance of Gorbachev

It would of course be absurd to maintain that the political leadership of Mikhail Gorbachev did not prove central to the basic reorientation of Soviet foreign policy that has taken place since 1985 and thus to the transformation of East-West relations that has ensued. However, in order to gauge the likely future relationship between the composition and course of the post-Soviet political leadership and the range of meaningful choice in Russian and Commonwealth foreign policy, it is important to delineate as carefully as possible the ways in which Gorbachev has exercised an impact on Soviet foreign policy. One should assess especially the ways in which many of the forces encouraged and unleashed by Gorbachev may serve to constrain future Russian international behavior. One's goal should be to apply to the analysis of Soviet external policies the kind of rigorous sociological analysis that Moshe Lewin has done in the field of Soviet domestic politics and society.[3] That is, one should search out the deeper, "international sociological" factors that in their cumulative and interdependent impact will inevitably serve to shape the range of foreign policy choice open to any government. This concerns not only those forces impinging upon the country from the international system itself but also those internal forces, involving both the material and the moral resources of the state and people, which affect the capacity of the state to define and achieve its objectives beyond its own frontiers.

Viewed from this angle, events have come to the point in the Soviet region where there can no longer be a question of a return to some mythical "status quo ante" in either domestic or foreign policy. Whatever the future direction of Russian politics, the depth and strength of sociopolitical factors reflecting the nature of the country as a complex modern society exclude a return to a neo-Stalinist political and institutional order. Quite apart from the question of whether contemporary Russian society, with a large, well-educated urban population all too familiar with international standards of living and performance, could sustain such a regression, any leader proposing such a path would have to address another question: How could a return to hypercentralized methods of administered economics and politics address any of the problems that are now universally recognized to be afflicting post-Soviet society and thus prevent the inevitable and permanent removal of the country to the margins of international economic and political life?

The failure of the large number of Soviet politicians and officials who were unsympathetic with Gorbachev's vision of radical reform to deal with the issue of the future power status of the USSR had long prevented them from translating their opposition into an alternative political program. This tended to preserve Gorbachev's authority over the party-state apparatus until very late in the game, i.e., the fall of 1990, and at the same time prevented the antireform forces from attracting significant social-political backing among the population at large. This fact underlay the failure of the coup in co-opting support, or even neutralizing opposition, in August 1991. The logic of the Soviet reform is thus rooted not simply in a massive failure of performance, which has resisted every previous effort at merely administrative reform, but in sociological forces that have in a classic Marxist way outgrown their institutional integument and thereby rendered it obsolete.

The impact of such "sociological" factors in the domain of Soviet foreign policy is much more profound. Aside from the ways in which economic failure and the overriding priority of domestic affairs have affected the foreign policy agenda, there is—and has always been—a vast international society that is beyond Soviet control or even easy influence and to which the Soviet state has had to adapt. This was recognized as early as 1929 by Foreign Minister Maxim Litvinov in a statement to the Executive Committee of the Soviet Communist Party:

> Unlike other Commissariats, the Commissariat for Foreign Affairs cannot, unfortunately, put forward a five-year plan of work, a plan for the development of foreign policy. . . . In . . . drawing up the plan of economic development we start from our own aspirations and wishes, from a calculation of our own potentialities, and from the firm principles of our entire policy, but in examining the development of foreign policy we have to deal with a number of factors that are scarcely subject to calculation, with a number of elements outside our control and the scope of our action. International affairs are composed not only of our own actions and aspirations, but of those of a large number of countries . . . pursuing other aims than ours, and using other means to achieve those aims than we allow.[4]

The impact of these international factors has perhaps never been as marked as today, as Russia's manifest domestic weaknesses, given the nature of the contemporary international political economy, strike at the heart of its capacity to project its influence beyond its borders.

Paul Nitze captured the consequence of such an analysis in a speech given at the John F. Kennedy School of Government at Harvard University in December 1989. Nitze adjudged the possible failure and replacement of Gorbachev, on which he did not pronounce, as "tactically" but no longer "strategically" significant. "Any successor to Gorbachev," he argued,

> would have to deal with today's situation—with the whole panoply of Soviet problems and constraints on policy those problems create—as much as Gorbachev will have to do if he continues in power. . . .
>
> The force of many of the changes we have seen follow each other so dramatically over the last few months has created such an alteration in the world scene that Gorbachev or any other Soviet leader will have to adjust to it.

Thus, before entertaining ideas of a collapse of East-West relations now that Gorbachev has been removed from the scene, one should keep in mind the complex of internal and international factors that will continue to influence the decisionmaking process of any post-Soviet leadership in foreign affairs. Among the domestic factors are included economic and political forces that tend both to limit and to reorient the commitment and allocation of domestic resources to foreign ends; among the international factors are counted an internal-conceptual reevaluation of Soviet interests, deeply rooted international-systemic tendencies, and specific policy choices made by the West, in particular by the United States during the Reagan administration.

The overriding factors that have served to change and constrain Soviet international conduct, as Chapter 4 has suggested, are those rooted in the breakdown of the Soviet system and its progressive inability to achieve its stated goals at home and abroad. The traditional, ideologically infused, vision of Soviet interests and objectives is now recognized to have been incapable of even diagnosing the miasma into which the USSR had fallen. The resultant decline, and in some areas even collapse, of the key indices of economic and social performance have raised issues of domestic reconstruction to such a commanding priority that no more compelling advocate of the primacy of domestic policy can be found than the former foreign minister, Eduard Shevardnadze.[5] The urgency of repairing the economic, social, as well as what Soviet leaders have called the "moral," damage to Soviet society inflicted by decades of Stalinist and neo-Stalinist political practice has caused international concerns, including relations with former allies in Eastern Europe and "socialist" outposts along the U.S. periphery, to be strictly subordinated to domestic considerations.

Factors Beyond Political Control

Beyond the general constraining impact that the necessity for domestic reform has had upon the formulation and execution of Soviet international interests and policy, there are quite specific economic and political forces that have reinforced the clear superiority of domestic over international affairs for the Soviet, and now post-Soviet, leadership. They include, first, the effect of the failure of the Soviet economy on the sheer ability of the Soviet state to engage in and sustain external commitments demanding substantial material resources. An economy that has yet to master the first industrial revolution and that, according to Gorbachev, suffered from progressively declining growth rates over twenty years and then an effective depression in the early 1980s is in no position to sustain the role of a major international power—economically, politically, or even in the increasingly discounted coin of military power.

Second, and running deeper than the relatively simple question of resource constraints, there are indications across the political spectrum of a strong desire to redefine basic values, to make what might be called a "kinder, gentler" country. Political movements ranging from the social-democratic "left" through Gorbachev to many even in the Russian nationalist "right," have called for a de-ideologization and demilitarization of values, with a corresponding shift in power from the party-state through intermediate institutions to individuals, and from the center to the periphery in economic, political, and nationality affairs. These changes entail a very different kind of foreign policy orientation and international environment than existed for most of the pre-Gorbachev period. In other words, the more benign the international political-military environment is and is perceived to be, the wider the scope for far-reaching domestic reform. Correspondingly, the prime task of foreign policy in this reformist vision is to facilitate the creation of such an international environment. Although certainly valued for its own sake, that environment is also necessary for the reformists' ability to shape the domestic political agenda. Invoking the foreign threat is no longer functional for the promotion of internal objectives. Cohesion, it is now recognized, has to come from within. In fact, the effort to instill such cohesion by creating an external bogeyman would be seen as a mark of the failure of the current reform effort.

A third element, one that not only underpins the revisionist course in Soviet foreign policy but also argues strongly for its continuation under any likely future political dispensation, is the fact that, in spite of all of the actual differences within the Russian political class and the society over the scope and pace of reform, the diagnosis of the Soviet crisis that Gorbachev made manifest through the policy of glasnost is very broadly accepted. Even Yegor Ligachev, who was for long seen as an alternative to Gorbachev, could argue his case only within the framework of perestroika, which Gorbachev had established as the dominant language of contemporary Soviet political discourse. Ligachev's speech at the special meeting of the Soviet Communist Party in February 1990 was widely interpreted as an assault on Gorbachev, but it actually bore witness to Gorbachev's strength (within the existing Soviet political class, that is). Ligachev accepted the analysis of the crisis of the system that Gorbachev had advanced, he accepted Gorbachev's reform strategy as the only realistic choice, and he supported Gorbachev personally as the man for the job.[6] Whatever his reservations about the reform program that Gorbachev set in motion, and in particular about the social and political consequences thereby entailed—and those reservations were certainly considerable—Ligachev and those like him operate within a political framework that had been determined by Gorbachev himself. This meant both that for them there was no apparent alternative to Gorbachev, either in terms of programs or individuals, and, perhaps more important, that there is a very strong consensus on the need for serious reform of some kind and thus on the near-absolute priority of domestic economic, political, and social development. (It is significant that Ligachev, although nominally retired from politics, did not publicly associate himself with the August 1991 coup.)

As suggested at the outset, the factors that have shaped and constrained contemporary Soviet foreign policy have been not only internal but international ones as well. It is important to remember, as Chapter 5 has detailed, that there had long been present in Soviet academic and political elite circles what some have called an "intellectual underground" of foreign policy experts. Throughout the Brezhnev period they forged an analysis of the international system and correspondingly of Soviet foreign policy that transcended the strict class/ideological terms of reference so characteristic of orthodox Leninist theory of international politics. These analysts, many of whom occupied influential positions as advisers and officials in the Gorbachev administration, attempted systematically to assimilate the meaning of such novel developments as the impact of nuclear weapons on world politics; the prosperity, stability, and cohesiveness of the West; the emergence of a Communist China as the chief external threat to the USSR; and the cost and difficulty of projecting and sustaining influence in far-flung, unstable regions of the Third World that were peripheral to any definition of Soviet geopolitical interests. The increasingly pragmatic, skeptical, and in the end even pessimistic thrust of such analysis was reinforced in the course of the 1970s by the impact of such forces as the information revolution, which was clearly passing the USSR by; the collapse of any strict bipolar order of international political influence; and the costs to the USSR of staying at a remove from an ever more interdependent, and obviously mutually profitable, international economic order.[7]

Of course, the simple existence of intellectual and analytical currents emphasizing the importance of geopolitical versus class/ideological interests, the complete political disutility—even in nonuse—of nuclear weapons, and the value of engagement in interdependence versus (always relative) autarky did not by itself translate into meaningful political influence within the Soviet system. One therefore has to venture into an analysis of those properly international forces and policies that, by increasing the opportunity costs of existing Soviet policy, served to accelerate the dynamics of internal change—which had been retarded by the prolonged institutional debility of the late Brezhnev period. Here one has to acknowledge the impact of the policies of the early Reagan administration, whatever the precise intentions of those who formulated its Soviet and arms control strategies. Because policies adopted by the Reagan administration coincided with the depth of Soviet political and economic stasis, their effect was to clarify certain choices before the Soviet leadership and actually to facilitate Gorbachev's clear break with the recent Soviet past in foreign policy.

The Effect of Reagan Administration Policies

The first such impact is one that is usually overlooked in Western discussions of the U.S.-Soviet relationship in the Reagan period. The strong ideological tone that the administration adopted early on upon its assumption of power in 1981, combined with its determined effort to move all arms control issues to the periphery of U.S.-Soviet relations, eventually—after Soviet observers came to believe what they were seeing—shattered a strong preexisting consensus among Soviet politicians and academic advisers alike that there were strict limits to hostility intrinsic to the U.S.-Soviet relationship. The Soviets, frustrated by the policy of the Carter administration, had initially welcomed the election of a Republican president and considered his party a more reliable partner than the Democrats for detente. That Reagan should take such a tack was deeply unnerving and served to discredit the prevailing political and intellectual paradigm of U.S.-Soviet relations in the Kremlin and in the political class at large.[8] This proved to be a necessary though by no means a sufficient condition for the sea change in the Soviet approach to the United States and to the outside world in general that was to take place under Gorbachev.

More specifically, and in reinforcement of this bracing ideological shower, the promulgation of the Strategic Defense Initiative in March 1983 triggered a Soviet overreaction. That overreaction, rooted in a growing sense of alarm at all major internal and international power trends, proved essential to forcing a formal reevaluation of the relationship of Soviet military power to Soviet security interests. The record of the deliberations leading to the SDI decision indicated that such a reevaluation was not the intention of the Reagan administration itself. Nevertheless, that was its ultimate (and rather immediate) effect. SDI alarmed the Soviet political-military leadership by threatening to call into question its entire decades-long accumulated investment in strategic nuclear offensive weapons, thereby rendering nugatory the military and political consequences of parity with the United States. At the same time SDI opened up an apparently limitless high-tech arms competition for which the leadership realized the USSR was most ill-prepared and in which it would constantly be reacting to the terms as set down by the United States.

Soviet political-military analysts and the Soviet leadership were aware after the SDI announcement that the traditional, quantitatively oriented approach to the arms race and to arms control had reached a dead end. Not only was an armaments policy predicated upon quantitative parity becoming prohibitively expensive, but it also seemed about to become quite dangerous indeed. An unlimited or substantially unregulated arms competition in high-tech offensive and defensive strategic systems, with a poor and deteriorating U.S.-Soviet political relationship in the background, might through some qualitative breakthrough signal the end to whatever stability nuclear deterrence had brought to East-West relations. In this regard, it is interesting to note that only after the promulgation of the SDI program did Soviet observers, including Gorbachev himself, begin to question the relationship between parity and strategic stability.

It is also at this time that one finds the first Soviet statements that recognize the desirability (as distinct from the fact, which had been admitted long before) of the relationship of "mutual assured destruction," at least as a transitional security order, that had come to characterize nuclear deterrence between the Soviet Union and the United States. It is hard to imagine that the promulgators of SDI could have envisaged the traumatic impact that its announcement would have on a Soviet leadership that was without compass at home or abroad. The Soviet leaders transformed the SDI into a lever that served to advance a rethinking of interests and concepts—already begun but not yet brought to fruition.

A similar effect, one that reinforced these tendencies, could be discerned in the administration's successful deployment of intermediate-range nuclear missiles in Europe after November 1983 in the face of sustained Soviet opposition; U.S. policy toward Afghanistan; as well as its general determination to maintain a high level of military spending, particularly in high-technology items. (Indeed, on the last point one of the major Soviet concerns about SDI related to the numerous spin-offs in the field of high-technology conventional defense that Soviet analysts predicted.) The success of NATO's INF deployments decisively discredited Moscow's diplomatic strategy: The Soviets had tried to undermine NATO by appealing to Western popular opinion and movements and by seeking to pit the interests of the key NATO capitals against each other. Besides the diplomatic defeat that the Soviets thereby suffered, the NATO success also meant a dramatically increased threat to the Soviet military's ability to prosecute its preferred conventional option in Europe. (That threat was exaggerated by an often hysterical propaganda campaign. By 1984 it had significantly demoralized much of the Soviet population, affecting even labor productivity.) In Soviet eyes the value of seeking security through military means and at the expense of the security of others was put in question.

Similarly, U.S. support for the Afghan resistance materially raised the cost of the Soviet military presence in that unfortunate country, thereby making the maintenance of the status quo in Afghanistan increasingly untenable for a Soviet leadership with so many more pressing domestic issues at hand. Again, it is not true that the United States was able to force a reversal in Soviet policies. Gorbachev himself had referred to Afghanistan as a "bleeding wound" upon the Soviet body politic in February 1986, several months before the Stinger anti-aircraft missiles that had such a devastating effect upon Soviet air power were to arrive in Afghanistan. The crucial point is that all these U.S. policies and actions, including the rhetorical and budgetary commitment to continued high levels of military spending, coincided with a kind of latter-day "scissors crisis" in Soviet foreign and security policy. That crisis was characterized by the obviously declining political utility of the existing set of Soviet policies with their steadily rising and equally obvious costs, both material and political. The interaction of these international and internal factors and policies served to sharpen the choices and costs of existing policies for the Soviet leadership. By the mid-1980s, the choices had become so stark, relative to the past, and the opportunity costs of not making them (or making the wrong ones) had become so high, that it actually became easier for Gorbachev to make the clean break with the past than would otherwise have been the case.[9]

The Logic of Reform in Foreign Policy

Thus, a variety of elements within the Soviet system, in the driving forces of the international political and economic system, and in the policies that the Soviet government was confronted with coming from the outside world (in particular the United States) worked to shape the series of policy choices that the Gorbachev (or some other) administration would have to face upon assumption of power in 1985. As in domestic policy, Gorbachev and the remarkable team of advisers with which he had initially surrounded himself put their stamp on the post-Brezhnev-era foreign policy of the Soviet Union. Yet it is also true that almost any Soviet leadership facing the combination of internal and external dilemmas that beset the USSR by the mid-1980s would have to have moved toward a reorientation of energies to domestic affairs and a dramatic amelioration of tensions with the West, primarily with the United States. It is important to recall, as indicated above, that Gorbachev's foreign policy philosophy of "new political thinking" reached far back into the Brezhnev period for its intellectual roots. Discussion of the very concept of new political thinking also predates the Gorbachev period, beginning in work published in late 1983–early 1984, a year and a half before Gorbachev's assumption of authority.[10] Furthermore, Soviet intentions to commit to a turnaround in U.S.-Soviet relations were strongly expressed by the Chernenko leadership in the fall of 1984, reflecting the realization that the previous, essentially unilateralist, policy toward the United States had failed in all important respects.[11]

In addition, before drawing too stark a contrast between all of Gorbachev's foreign policy and that of his predecessors, the fact remains that in a most important respect Gorbachev was the first Soviet leader since the mid-1970s to have been able to realize the Brezhnev agenda in U.S.-Soviet relations, i.e., to reestablish arms control as the central, defining element of the superpower relationship. (Of course, this was done by Gorbachev for very different ends from Brezhnev's: not to limit existing force levels as a foundation for a more secure global ideological and geopolitical competition, but rather to transform the U.S.-Soviet political relationship as a complement to reform at home. Since detente for the Brezhnev leadership was in important ways a substitute for reform at home, the contrast in objectives between past and recent Soviet policy clearly overrides the similarity in political tactics.)

Finally, few students of Soviet affairs would when pressed deny that the Soviet political and military "threat" that Gorbachev is understood to have substantially dismantled had long been exaggerated in the West for purposes of building defense budgets and maintaining intra-alliance cohesion. Nor would they deny that as a matter of practice (and as I argued in detail in Chapter 1) most Western governments, with only the possible and partial exception of the West German, were fundamentally satisfied with what had become the postwar status quo of a divided Germany in a divided Europe (yet they publicly remonstrated the USSR for that division). The fact is that a comprehensive, geopolitically oriented detente could have been initiated and maintained with Brezhnev's USSR if only important domestic forces in the United States had accepted the original, highly competitive concept of detente that the United States itself had put forward (but did not advertise) in 1972 and claimed as a decisive contribution to a "generation of peace."

All the recent talk about the "end of the cold war" obscures the fact that, as Part 1 demonstrates, in substantive political terms the cold war had been put to rest by both East and West in the course of the decade running from the late 1950s to the late 1960s. That period ended with both parties agreeing that (1) a stable balance of power—economic, political, and military—had been created in Europe, and (2) the de facto resolution of the German question in the form of two German states in two alliance systems was satisfactory. In substantial measure, what had come to drive the East-West relationship were not the substantive political issues over which the cold war was originally fought and eventually resolved. It was instead what outlived the issues—the images, and powerful ones at that, in the form of threat perceptions; instruments, in the form of military forces; and institutional interests, in the form of military-industrial complexes—that largely shaped the East-West relationship.

What Gorbachev has done, and this is his decisive contribution to Soviet foreign policy and to East-West relations, is to address directly these secondary, epiphenomenal aspects of the cold war and to see to it that parochial instrumental or institutional interests could no longer drive the political agenda in East-West relations. Given the character and the scale of his domestic tasks, Gorbachev had to assert and maintain the primacy of politically determined interests and criteria in Soviet foreign and security policy and attempt to extend the scope of politically induced change across the East-West international agenda. The classic early instance of this strategy involves the issue of INF in Europe, alluded to earlier. Disproportionate Soviet reductions served to transform the U.S. domestic debate on relations with the USSR and established detente as the only viable policy for the foreseeable future. Henceforth, the one politically realistic debate could be over the terms of that detente, not over its desirability. That is the explanation for Gorbachev's impatient determination to conclude a quick arms control agreement precisely with Ronald Reagan's administration and puts into relief what would otherwise be seen as a dramatic Soviet capitulation.

In the same vein, Gorbachev's remarkable acquiescence in the disintegration of Communist power throughout Eastern Europe, which was certainly not his original intention (he believed almost until the end that reform and Soviet-informed values were compatible), reflected his understanding that only by clearly dissociating the fate of internal political orders in East-Central Europe from the nature of Soviet security interests in the region could he hope to prevent either a backlash against his own position at home or the inevitable pressures for intervention, which would have had the same effect. The de-ideologization of Soviet policy in Eastern Europe certainly reflects a historic decline in Soviet political influence in the region and, by extension, on the international stage at large. At the same time, it was the only way to maintain course on the now transcendent Soviet political objective: i.e., the comprehensive reconstruction of the Soviet economic, social, and internal-political order. That reconstruction itself was seen as the precondition for the future power status of the Soviet state, both within and without the present frontiers of the USSR.

Much the same may have been intended in the obviously reluctant Soviet acquiescence to German reunification on West German terms. What appears by traditional categories of evaluation to have been a capitulation on a world-historical scale, i.e., the remove of the USSR as a political-military presence from the heart of Europe, seems instead to have represented a dual effort: to accommodate inevitable forces of change and in the process to redefine the very significance of the USSR's problems—whether they relate to Germany, military security, or ideological security—and thereby to transform the stakes and commitments entailed. That is, if Germany can no longer be coerced, perhaps it can be won over. The extension by Germany of more than $45 billion in various forms of financial assistance to the USSR (between unification and January 1992) represents an important payoff for a more enlightened Soviet policy.

It is precisely in this sense that Gorbachev has proven decisive in effecting a veritable breakthrough in East-West relations. He has been the right man at the right time. Yet his successors are no longer in a position, domestically or internationally, to prove so decisive to the future of East-West relations, at least as far as their intersection with fundamental U.S. foreign policy interests is concerned.

First, since 1986, there has developed an expanding network of binding international treaties and agreements, especially in the field of arms control, which dramatically raises the political price that the successor states would have to pay should they be tempted to reverse the course of policy that Gorbachev had chosen. The resolution of the Stockholm conference on disarmament in Europe in September 1986, which dealt with the elaboration of a series of military confidence-building measures in Europe, is an early—and thus powerful—illustration of the point: Apparently irreconcilable political-military differences between the USSR and the United States were amicably and quickly reconciled in the face of the political alienation that both would have had to face throughout Eastern and Western Europe in the event of a collapse of the conference. The dramatic progress in both bilateral U.S.-Soviet and multilateral all-European political, economic, and military agreements since then, and the incorporation of detailed verification mechanisms into the latter, raise that price for any future post-Soviet leadership. And because that price includes not only spoiled diplomatic relationships but also valuable economic ties as well as the prospect of renewed political-military competition without allies, it should prove a most effective deterrent.

Second, and to a large extent due to the impetus provided by Gorbachev himself, the course of political events in Europe, including Eastern Europe, is no longer within the control or even easy influence of the Russian state. There is simply no way for Russia to retrieve its position in Eastern Europe, at least not in any way resembling the hegemonic pattern of Soviet influence in the postwar period. Third, in spite of Gorbachev's admirable intentions to recast the foundations for the exercise of Soviet international influence, the fact remains that the means, above all economic ones, for the Commonwealth states to reassert an illusory status quo ante will be quite difficult to obtain and utilize. It had already become difficult for the Soviet Union to preserve a modicum of political influence in what Soviet leaders continued to regard as the central theater of world politics: Europe.

Finally, under any likely future political dispensation, domestic affairs will retain a near absolute priority on post-Soviet resources and energies. The political energies of the post-Soviet leadership are almost completely absorbed simply with the preservation of some minimum of cooperation that might be consistent with the nationalist aspirations of the peoples of the former USSR, Russian and non-Russian alike. Preoccupation with what Soviet propagandists have called the "international relations" of the USSR itself practically assures the remove of Soviet Russia from the main lines of international relations for the foreseeable future.

Yet what about a break with existing policies? Such a break, however unlikely it appears at the moment, is implicit in the current post-Soviet political situation, as the August 1991 coup attempt demonstrates. What if there were a successful Russian "nationalist" coalition of disaffected elements in the military, Communist Party apparatus, and blue-collar workers whose job security and already precarious standard of living are threatened (however temporarily) by genuine market reform? Certainly such a reactionary political denouement would represent the antithesis of everything that Gorbachev, Yeltsin, and the more radical Soviet reformers have to date stood for. The attempt to establish "order" and protect the interests of the allegedly exploited Russian nation, which can be discerned in some of the Russian "nationalist" literature and political activities, especially in the Baltic states, would jeopardize the personal and political fortunes of those who have committed Russian society to the path of radical reform, and many innocent bystanders as well.

Such a turn could spell the end of the already uncertain prospects for Russia to pull itself into the late twentieth century, but it probably would not, could not, materially reverse the fundamental direction of Russian foreign policy or East-West relations. Quite apart from resource constraints at home and systemic constraints abroad, an explicitly nationalist leadership that sought to reassert control over the entirety of the former USSR would provoke such a hostile reaction from the non-Russian half of the multinational Commonwealth that the consequent civil turmoil along nationalist lines would paralyze the state and absorb any remaining energies that it might wish to devote to international affairs. This "worst case" alternative to Gorbachev (or now Yeltsin), which some have advanced as a spur to efforts to assist the Soviet leader and avoid an international setback, would actually seem to complete the marginalization of Russia from international life. That marginalization—as alarming as it is for Soviet Russia—has proved essential to the transformation of East-West relations and the establishment of one Europe.

It is not the overthrow of Gorbachev, or now Yeltsin—followed by aggression against the international community—that is the chief threat to international stability. It is, rather, the possible spillover of explosive social, political, economic, and nationalist currents from within the post-Soviet system onto the international arena. Any given leader has little to say about the shape and ultimate direction that such forces will take. Although it may be preferable, given what we know, or do not know, about the nature of the post-Soviet political system, that a Gorbachev-like leader remain at the helm of the Russian state and in particular of its international policy, the irreducible U.S. interest in a plural distribution of geopolitical power in Europe is now assured for any foreseeable future, independent of the course chosen by Moscow. (The West European stake is somewhat different, since countries in that region are naturally sensitive to questions of the relative balance of political-economic power within Europe; for the United States it only matters that such a balance exists. Thus, the management of the German issue is at heart a matter for the Europeans to deal with.)

Nevertheless, the analysis given here should not yield a prescription of fatalism, as the argument that the most important internal and external forces buffeting the post-Soviet system are systemic in character and will tend to shape the range of choice faced by any leader actually provides the foundation for a stable long-term relationship between Russia and its neighbors. That relationship is rooted in powerful geopolitical and economic reality rather than in any one man's political skills, however extraordinary. The sooner the West can broaden its vision of Soviet, or rather post-Soviet politics, the sooner it can assume the responsibilities of a sober, long-term analysis of the foundations and consequences of the peace.

Notes

1. The author has been inspired here by Hajo Holborn, *The Political Collapse of Europe* (New York: Knopf, 1951).

2. For some general indicators of Soviet economic performance, see Chapter 4.

3. Moshe Lewin, *The Gorbachev Phenomenon: A Historical Interpretation* (Berkeley: University of California Press, 1988).

4. As cited by Vernon Asparturian in Roy Macridis, ed., *Foreign Policy in World Politics* (Englewood Cliffs, N.J.: Prentice-Hall, 1962), p. 134.

5. See Shevardnadze's candid speech to the Soviet foreign policy community in *Vestnik Ministerstva Inostrannykh del,* no. 2 (1987), pp. 30–34.

6. For the text of Ligachev's speech, see Foreign Broadcast Information Service, *Daily Report. Soviet Union,* February 7, 1990, pp. 77–79.

7. For an exegesis of this view, see Chapter 5. For an exhaustive treatment, see Allen Lynch, *The Soviet Study of International Relations* (Cambridge: Cambridge University Press, 1987 and 1989).

8. See P. T. Podlesnyi, "Vvedeniye," in G. A. Trofimenko and P. T. Podlesnyi, *Sovetsko-amerikanskiye otnosheniya v sovremennom mire* (Moscow: Nauka, 1987), p. 5.

9. For a Soviet analysis that implicitly supports this interpretation, see Vitaly Zhurkin, Sergei Karaganov, and Andrei Kortunov, "Vyzovy Bezopasnosti—Starye i Novye," in the authoritative CPSU journal *Kommunist,* no. 1 (January 1988), pp. 42–50. The argument runs parallel to a key ideological speech by Gorbachev aide Aleksandr Yakovlev arguing that the military competition is a trap laid by the West to exhaust the USSR economically and that consequently the USSR should refuse to play tit for tat in this sphere, concentrating instead on its economic, social, political, and ideological development. *Vestnik Akademii Nauk,* no. 6 (1987).

10. Anatoly Gromyko and Vladimir Lomeiko, *Novoye Myshlenie v Yadernyi Vek* (Moscow: Mezhdunarodnye Otnosheniya, 1984).

11. For one account, see Dusko Doder, *Shadows and Whispers: Power Politics Inside the Kremlin from Brezhnev to Gorbachev* (New York: Random House, 1986), pp. 218–244.

7

The Continuing Importance of Ideology

"We have got to do everything possible . . . to insure that the party is reformed . . . that it becomes a vital force for perestroika.
. . . I am convinced that socialism is correct. . . . The October Revolution . . . was a real revolution . . . a genuine national revolution.
. . . Some sentence of Lenin's in which he said that socialism is the vital creativity of the masses, that is the model that we have to implement, this is something that Lenin said. . . . This is my way of saying things in normal human language."
—Mikhail Gorbachev, August 22, 1991, the day after being delivered from the coup directed by the Communist Party against him (*New York Times*)

In Chapter 5, I argued that the new Soviet international outlook was notable for bypassing traditional Soviet ideological criteria, especially with respect to security, in the daily conduct of foreign policy. This is a fundamental point, and the ideological revolution in Soviet foreign policy has made itself felt in practically every area of the USSR's international conduct. During his first term as foreign minister, Eduard Shevardnadze time and again made clear to *internal* Soviet audiences composed of the Foreign Ministry staff and members of the Soviet diplomatic corps the priority of what he termed "common sense" over ideological considerations.[1] Soviet political observers, who have always encouraged the borrowing of Western technical accomplishments, by 1988 spoke openly of "the need to assimilate the entire positive baggage of [Western] political thought . . . all of the humane and effective forms of its social structure, its entire rich experience in solving social and national problems." Gorbachev himself forcefully stated that the Soviet leadership was striving "to expunge ideological prejudice from our policy."

In addition, long *before* the dramatic collapse of Communist power following the failed coup of August 1991, the state examination in Marxism-Leninism was abolished in all Soviet universities (January 1990), and in July 1991 the Soviet Communist Party approved a draft version of the party's charter that jettisons its Leninist political heritage.[2] Furthermore, the dramatic progress in East-West relations since 1985, which includes an across-the-board improvement in Soviet external relationships, startling reversals in Soviet military and arms control policies, and, most striking, the laissez-faire policy toward Eastern Europe, culminating in the collapse of Communist authority throughout the region, has clearly reflected a decline in the level and character of ideologically driven hostility in Soviet foreign policy and East-West relations as a whole.

Political and Analytical Significance of Ideology

Before we address the nature of this change, it is fair to consider its political and analytical significance. After all, regardless of the motivations involved, the observable shift in the center of gravity of Soviet policy has enabled East-West relations to move on issues and in fields long thought to be intractable or not susceptible to political and diplomatic intervention. Many in the West and the East are happy to exploit all existing opportunities for improved relationships, whether of ideological provenance or simply a coincidence of short- to medium-term political interests. And who can blame them? As U.S. Secretary of State James Baker has observed, the possible fragility of the reforms set in motion by Mikhail Gorbachev is no reason to refrain from actual engagement; on the contrary, "locking in" politically binding and self-enforcing agreements now would tend to constrain any future leadership, should the political and ideological foundations of current reform policy change.[3]

Whatever truth such an evaluation may have on the political level, it fails to speak to the deeper issue of the sources of change in Soviet conduct, including ideological change, and thus pleads agnostic as to the stability of change and the future scope of choice. While the politician may thrive with such a levelheaded approach, the student of Soviet foreign relations must seek to penetrate the entire complex of considerations affecting the course of Soviet policy, including its critical ideological component. The abandonment of ideological criteria in the application of security policy did not per se mean the "end of ideology" in all aspects of the USSR's international relationships; nor will it in the post-Soviet era.

One first has to come to terms with the several roles that ideology has played in past Soviet policy. Only against that standard can an accurate assessment of the nature and relative importance of ideology and ideological considerations in Soviet policy, and thus of the nature of contemporary Soviet and post-Soviet political processes, be made.

If we understand ideology as both a set of conscious assumptions and purposes, derived from a given philosophical and political tradition, with corresponding authoritative "texts" (formal and informal), and a part of the set of the total historical, social, and personal background of the given political leaders and citizens, we can then identify a number of functions that political ideology has served in the case of Soviet political behavior. There is little doubt that in the long run it is this latter aspect, what Vladimir Shlapentokh has called "public ideology," which exercises a decisive impact on the framework of acceptable choice in a given political system. At the same time, in a Soviet-type ideological system the formal "party ideology" itself exercises an important influence on the public ideology.

Most important, the accepted ideology provides the *categories* with which reality is both perceived and interpreted. In the Soviet Union, where the party-state exercised a privileged monopoly over the educational system and means of mass communication for seven decades, these basic epistemological and philosophical categories were formed since early school years and were systematically reinforced throughout the individual's experience of socialization. The categories are deeply rooted and resistant to change, even in the face of striking changes in the existential experience and in the content of the ideology itself. Such ideologically determined categories of thinking thus tend to be very effective in shaping cognitive and analytical processes, especially over the long term, although they are also very abstract.

The basic categories of importance for the Soviet political experience fall under the general theory of materialism, as codified by Marx and Engels and later modified by Lenin, and are divided into two main subheadings: The first is dialectical materialism, which contains both a philosophy of dialectics, which Marx derived from the German idealist tradition, and a system of political economy, which Marx derived from the great British economists in the Smith-Ricardo tradition. The second is historical materialism, which attempts to apply the categories of dialectical materialism to the particular field of human relations within society. The categories that follow from these philosophical schools are indeed very general, yet because of that, quite difficult to alter. The postulates of dialectical materialism also yield three basic "laws" of social reality: the transformation of "quantitative" changes in degree to "qualitative" changes in kind, hence the eventual development of history by revolutionary "leaps"; the "unity of opposites," which inclines one to see all social phenomena as interrelated; and the "negation of the negation," based on the triad of thesis-antithesis-synthesis. That triad alerts one to the importance of conflicts of interests as the motor of historical change and progress.

The persistence of these mental categories, furthermore, does not simply stem from their high degree of generality (becoming in effect nonfalsifiable propositions) but also from their apparent fit with much of the existential world. They seem especially apt when compared to competing philosophical categories, such as the tradition of Anglo-Saxon empiricism and the corresponding liberal assumption of linear historical progress. From these three basic "laws" of the dialectic follow certain basic insights into the nature of social phenomena; those insights are likely to persist well into the post-Soviet future, independent of the policies being pursued at any given moment. In the Marxist-Leninist cognitive universe, the most important of these insights are the following: that social phenomena, as with phenomena in nature, do not exist in isolation but are rather dependent on other such phenomena; that social phenomena must be studied in their movement and development; that whenever one confronts apparent opposites, one must search for, identify, and analyze their positive interrelationship; and, finally, that one must look for contradiction in the processes of society and of nature, because contradiction is the motive force behind all development. Contradictory forces, furthermore, are not generally equal; one force is dying at a faster or slower rate and is at the same time resisting the force(s) that is (are) rising.

Wolfgang Leonhard provided some striking illustrations of the effect that such categories have had on the thinking of committed Communists. Writing of his time as a young functionary in the wartime and early postwar leadership of the German Communist Party, Leonhard observed that he and his comrades were not at all impressed by the obviously higher Western standard of living. He wrote that at that time he thought that "historically, declining societies have always had a higher standard of living than those which are just coming into being." Again, commenting on why the Western concept of freedom had no effect on those like himself who were secretly dissenting from the official Stalinist line, Leonhard wrote:

This opposition was conducted within our world of ideas, in our own terminology, and was concerned with our own problems. It had nothing to do with Western sympathies or Western conceptions of freedom. For us, freedom meant insight into historical necessity. We were free because we were the only ones who possessed this insight on the basis of scientific theory; whereas people in the West who lacked this scientific theory and simply confronted historical evolution with an unreasoning, desperate opposition, to the point of simply being the playthings of that evolution— these were the ones who were unfree.

Recent interviews conducted among veteran Communists in the Soviet Union and in other ruling and nonruling Communist parties bear witness to the lasting grip of the basic ideological categories upon the thinking of those educated in the Marxist-Leninist tradition. This grip is independent of their actual stance toward given policy issues and affects even those veteran Communists who, like Boris Yelstin, have abandoned the Communist Party in pursuit of new political frontiers.[4]

The second, "historical," aspect of materialist theory involves the specific focus on the relationship and tension between the productive forces of society and production relations within society as the engine of history, with the class struggle as motif and catalyst. It is precisely economic forces that are seen as fundamental, or determining, in the nature, scope, and pace of social development. Furthermore, to close the circle, these forces operate according to the dialectical principle of contradiction (thesis-antithesis-synthesis).

From the vantage point of the sociology of knowledge, which is our proper concern here, the point is not to measure Marxism-Leninism in its basic epistemological aspects by the Soviet claim of its scientific validity. We should instead view it as a mundane theory of reality that should be adjudged in terms of its ability to shape core epistemological assumptions and political sensibilities. By that standard, the basic Marxist ideological concepts have proved at least as effective in informing fundamental political beliefs, preferences, and range of choice as have many basic Western perspectives and should certainly not be dismissed as analytically inferior to the cognitive maps of non-Soviet (or non-Marxist) politicians and students of politics. Given the cognitive importance of this most general function of the political ideology, one should be careful before embracing too broadly the thesis of the end of ideology in Russian political life, either foreign or domestic.

These conceptual/analytical aspects of ideology are often confused with its utopian aspect, its concern with ultimate purposes. Correspondingly extreme conclusions are drawn about the role that ideology has played in Soviet internal and international politics. The scope of the epistemological components of the Marxist-Leninist ideological framework is such that they operate in effective dissociation from its teleological function. The strength of the ideology does not lie in any given prescription or expectation for the day-to-day world of political events. Rather, as far as international relations are concerned, the ideology directs one to a preoccupation with the domestic, especially economic, dynamics of societies as the touchstone of international change and to the assumption of conflicts, not harmonies, of interest as normal in political life in general and in international relations in particular. These are sensible postulates, as the course of world politics daily demonstrates.

Other Aspects of Ideology

There are other aspects of ideology to be taken into account. These operate on different levels, and some may more easily lead to dysfunctional behavior than others. For example, the natural and "filtering" aspect of ideology has in the specific Soviet context often been systematically exploited (or abused) by the ruling party-state through its traditional monopoly of the means of mass communication. Although in the short term at least, that kind of filtering may be susceptible to direct propaganda, in conditions of relatively open social communication, such as that prevailing under glasnost, overt efforts to manipulate specific political beliefs (as distinct from basic intellectual categories) would appear to produce a substantial degree of disorientation and eventually a certain loss of credibility in the specific political aspects of the ideology, and hence in the political authorities. It is an open question, then, whether this filtering function of the ideology can survive the (relatively) free flow of information intact. The experience of other societies and of institutions (e.g., the Catholic church) suggests, however, that substantial adjustments can be made in the phenomenology of the ideology without challenging its underlying ontological or epistemological foundations.

In addition to these conceptual aspects of Soviet ideology, which in their structure apply to all individuals and all institutions and societies, Soviet ideology has served more explicitly political purposes. The theory of Marxism-Leninism, which unites the cause of communism in Soviet Russia with the fate of all mankind (and thereby of "universal human values") through the vehicle of the "world historical process," has been consistently exploited by the Soviet leadership as one means by which to justify, or legitimate, the privileged position that it has historically arrogated to the Communist Party of the Soviet Union within the USSR and until most recently within the "socialist world system" as well. Until the collapse of communism in Eastern Europe in the fall of 1989, such ideological considerations lay at the heart of the Soviet definition of its security interests in the region. At the same time, the existence of "fraternal" Communist regimes in East-Central Europe, by underscoring the international vocation of communism, served to buttress the Soviet Communist Party's claim on power within the Soviet Union itself.

The best known examples of this highly utilitarian exploitation of ideology include Stalin's doctrine of "socialism in one country" (contra Trotsky); the Stalinist thesis of the "ever aggravating contradictions under socialism," justifying total repression; Khrushchev's declaration of the noninevitability of war, justifying peaceful coexistence and its concomitant internal policies; the Brezhnev Doctrine, asserting ideological conformity in East-Central Europe and in the Soviet Union; and, more recently, Gorbachev's "new political thinking," with its intimate tie to reform at home. The corollary to this legitimating function of the ideology is the disciplinary political purpose to which it has been put by Soviet leaders seeking to define the acceptable language of political discourse and thereby to dominate the political agenda of the country. Changes in the specific political content of the ideology need not as such challenge this disciplinary aspect of ideological politics, which one finds in various forms across political systems. Finally, it is clear that Soviet ideology has been used repeatedly and self-consciously by the Soviet leadership to justify policies made for reasons independent of ideological considerations and to affect foreign perceptions of Soviet policies. Again, changes in the content of the ideology need not alter the roles that ideology performs or the purposes to which it may be put.

Soviet ideology has thus exercised an important conceptual and analytical influence on the way that Soviet political man understands politics and society. On this level the ideology is rather resistant to change. Furthermore, ideology in general and Soviet ideology in particular are not incompatible with generally recognizable rational and pragmatic behavior, given the basic postulates of the ideology. Certainly, there are distortions in the Soviet ideological belief system, but this is true of all belief systems. The only relevant issue here is the degree of specificity desired and the acceptability of what is sacrificed. More serious are the effects of ideological distortion, conscious or otherwise, on the daily world of observable phenomena.

As far as international affairs are concerned, the most egregious distortion, and the most easily falsifiable by events at home and abroad (the latter becoming generally apparent only of late), has been what has justifiably been called the two-camp view of world politics, which is based on rejecting the idea that socioeconomic changes might be unconsciously taking place in all societies (including the USSR) faced with certain similar difficulties of development. The traditional orthodox Soviet thesis has been that genuine peace can come only with the final victory of a particular social system (i.e., communism) led by a particular political party (i.e., the Communists), which will lead to a fundamental, ideologically driven struggle for survival in international relations, a struggle that has not proved conducive to long-term conflict resolution.

It is exactly at this level, i.e., of the prevailing dogma on the nature of international conflict, where the most striking changes in both the role and the content of Soviet international ideology have been occurring during the Gorbachev years. That such a change took so long in coming, in the face of sustained accumulated evidence to the contrary, may be explained not by the flawed nature of Marxist-Leninist philosophy (flawed though it may be), but rather by the institutional aspects of the Soviet political ideology: the institutional commitment of the Communist Party of the Soviet Union and the personal commitment of its leadership to a particular political application of the ideology; the general difficulty of accepting new or modified values as they become ingrained within the system; and the impact of Soviet international performance on the politically credible balance sheet of "costs and benefits."

Old and New Thinking Contrasted

It may prove helpful to recall the gist of what might be termed the "old" political thinking. In June 1985, a usually authoritative Soviet voice ("O. Rakhmaninov") took issue with the East European states (Hungary, Romania, and the GDR) that had begun to maintain that in a time of deteriorating East-West relations, such states had a special role to play in maintaining stability, perhaps even serving as a kind of honest broker between the Soviet Union and the United States. Rejecting such notions, Rakhmaninov thundered: "What question can there be of any mediation between the USSR and the United States if on the key international questions the foreign policy of the USSR and of the Marxist-Leninist nucleus of world socialism is identical?"[5] This passage reflects the tight correspondence in the orthodox Soviet view between the future of communism in the USSR and the fate of communism around the world, as revealed through the "world historical process." With exceptional clarity, the statement of Rakhmaninov serves as the perfect foil against which to measure the divorce that is now being completed between the fate of socialism in Russia and "the world historical process." This divorce is the essential ideological contribution of the "new political thinking."

Indeed, the way in which Soviet foreign policy and security interests have been recently defined and executed were changing to a most dramatic extent, before the final demise of the Soviet state in December 1991. These changes, captured under the rubric of the "new political thinking," have been interpreted as signifying the practical end of ideological influence in Soviet foreign policy.[6] In fact, the remarkable innovations in both the concept and application of Soviet international policy happened *not* because ideology was less important but rather because it was more important than ever. However, the content of the ideology, as it affects foreign affairs, changed, as have the ways in which ideological considerations intrude upon foreign policy. Furthermore, this shift in the two aspects of ideology—role and content—occurred because of the intensity of the relationship between Soviet internal and foreign policies, as a change in the attributed capacity of the international system to threaten vital Soviet interests had become an important precondition for the character, scope, and pace of reform at home. A less threatening international environment has become essential to all those throughout the Soviet and post-Soviet political spectrum who are seeking to decentralize political authority, demilitarize the allocation of material resources, and in general concentrate upon the internal regeneration of Russia. (See Chapters 5 and 6.) The consequence was a vigorous and progressive exclusion of *traditional* ideological considerations, but not of ideology as such, from the conduct of Soviet foreign policy.

In the past the sound argument was often made by students of Soviet affairs that ideology played the role that it did in Soviet foreign relations because of the nature of the Soviet political order, i.e., of the institutional order of the Soviet party-state and of the distribution of political power (and position) that followed from it. Many of the actions of the Soviet party-state leadership, Leonard Shapiro observed in 1963, "are to be explained not in terms of ideology [as such], but in terms of the one party rule which Lenin created, in other words, as a result of a necessity engendered by the organizational forms of rule which have been set up."[7] Of course, the insistence on one-party rule is itself strongly influenced by ideological' considerations; party-ideological and party-institutional considerations are thus practically indistinguishable from each other.

The effective demolition of the Soviet Communist Party that Gorbachev has accomplished; its replacement by a multitude of nationalist programs throughout the USSR and its successor states; and finally, Soviet acquiescence in the dismantlement of communism in East-Central Europe—all signaled the end of this proprietary role of the Soviet Communist Party and thus of its coercive ideological function in society. Boris Yeltsin's decree as the popularly elected president of Russia in July 1991—*before* the coup whose failure precipitated the expulsion of the party from political power—to ban all Communist organizations from the workplace represented but the death knell of a process begun by Gorbachev himself. In the sphere of international relations, the collapse of the party-state system meant that for the USSR as early as 1989, in the execution of its foreign policy, it no longer made a significant difference that the Soviet Union was also (if nominally and not for long) a Communist state.

Our conclusions about the role of ideology, past and present, in Soviet foreign policy depend of course on the level of analysis we employ. There are, as I have shown, multiple conceptual and political functions that ideology has performed in Soviet political life, domestic as well as foreign. Here, one can posit substantial continuity in the content and role of Soviet ideology in foreign affairs. Furthermore, one can identify important continuities with the past in the recent ideological revision. Those continuities have often been interpreted as decisive signs of a break with the past. For example, the distinction that is now so often made between interstate and international relations was central to Khrushchev's and Brezhnev's concept of peaceful coexistence, now criticized by numerous commentators. The meaning of this distinction, which on the philosophical level remained wholly unchanged under Gorbachev, is that class-based (i.e., ideological) criteria and interests have a status decidedly inferior to that of traditional "state" interests in the sphere of interstate relations. The sphere of international relations, by contrast, is where the historical contest between capitalism and socialism as socioeconomic systems (as distinct from their separate representation in sovereign states) takes place. And in the area of interparty relations, the principle of proletarian and/or socialist internationalism is still said by avowed communists in the former USSR to prevail.[8] (Their ability to act on such principles, however, may be regarded as practically nil in the post-Soviet era.)

Although the whole thrust of Gorbachev's foreign policy thinking and action has served to diminish even further the importance of these latter spheres in terms of actual policy, the essential Marxist-Leninist ideological framework for interpreting world politics persists.[9] This is true both within the remnant of the party itself and, more important now, in the minds of most post-Communist Soviet politicians, whose political and intellectual training is almost exclusively Marxist-Leninist in character.

Likewise, the identification of pragmatic impulses in the formulation and execution of policy cannot as such be taken to mean an absence of ideological influence on policy. Ideology and rational conduct may be perfectly compatible with each other. Furthermore, the close relationship that is now asserted between internal and foreign policy may be taken as a truism that applies to all countries; it is only the character and dynamics of that interrelationship, not the tie itself, which existed throughout Soviet history, that demand to be examined. (In addition, any discussion of Soviet "national security" interests as something apart from ideological influence begs the point that the very concept of "Soviet" is itself infused with ideological content, and that ideological criteria themselves have often played an important role in the definition of Soviet security interests, as in the case of Eastern Europe throughout the postwar period.)

Finally, even the notion of "universal human values" as the touchstone of policy is philosophically fully consistent with traditional Marxist-

Leninist thinking. Orthodox Marxists have always maintained that it was precisely and exclusively through the class-based historical process that genuinely human values could be realized. Only through full proletarian consciousness could man resolve the alienation from his "species-being" that is characteristic of his existence in class-based society. It should be noted that even Eduard Shevarnadze, in his first term as Soviet foreign minister, defended the primacy of universal human values—by which he explicitly relegated class or ideological values to second rank—as a new "general line," valid under "contemporary circumstances." As circumstances change, so do general lines, as they have before in the Soviet past. Gorbachev ally and now radical democrat Aleksander Yakovlev, at the time party secretary for ideology and himself a prime mover behind the "new thinking," has stressed the continuity in the basic Soviet conceptual approach toward international relations. The emphasis of Soviet policy on cooperation and interdependence, he told an Academy of Sciences audience in April 1987 in a key speech on ideology and the social sciences, "does not reduce by one iota the problems of ideological antagonisms between socialism and capitalism." As Andrei Kozyrev, now Boris Yeltsin's foreign minister, put it in dismissing the "illusory reality" of ideological lull outside the [inter]state sphere," the "deideologization of inter-state relations cannot, of course, cancel the struggle and exchange of ideas on the international level."[10]

The Primacy of Politics

Until most recently, international security for the Soviet leadership also meant ideological security. If ideology was especially important in the past because of its role in defining the relationship between external and internal security, it follows that as the character of that interrelationship is being reexamined, the role of ideology cannot fail to be affected. As one official put it:

> The Soviet Union has always linked its security with the victory of socialism on an international scale. We believed that the Soviet Union's position in the world would be more reliable if more states were to embark on the road to socialism. . . . This has brought about a situation when the country was drawn into a competition for world spheres of influence which requires tremendous material resources. . . . The future of socialism should be decided primarily within Societ society and resources must be released for the needs of perestroika, which are now swallowed by competition with the USA in the "Third World." . . . This is hardly acceptable in conditions of the country's grave financial and economic situation.[11]

This passage underscores the point that the new international ideology of the "new political thinking" was above all the product of a determined *political* effort on the part of the Gorbachev reform leadership to redefine the nature and role of the international environment for the Soviet Union in a time of profound structural change (and upheaval) at home. Certainly, new thinking provides the political leadership with a more convincing analytical framework for intrepreting important international and global political processes than that offered by the reductionist ideology of "scientific communism" (i.e., attributing the sources of international conflict to the nature of particular—"imperialist"—kinds of states). At the same time, the new thinking, by challenging existing assumptions throughout the political system, is designed to elicit better information for a leadership determined to reshape Soviet policies from top to bottom. It is also intended to provoke normally reticent quarters, such as the military, to release information and to make plain the data and assumptions upon which their claims upon Soviet resources and political attention have so long been based. This is the function that the small but growing body of civilian experts on military affairs (such as Alexei Arbatov of the Institute of World Economy and International Relations and Andrei Kokoshin of the Institute of the USA and Canada) have to date successfully performed.[12]

Finally, and perhaps most important, the ideology of new political thinking is an integral part of the process by which the reform leadership seeks to dominate the discussion of the acceptable boundaries of reform and thereby advance its ambitious domestic program. This program, which in intention amounts to a constitutional and social revolution, obviously requires a redistribution of political power and a reallocation of resources that would be considered impermissible by the orthodox Leninist ideology of imperialism. Leninist ideology, after all, posits a persistently high level of threat to Soviet interests resulting from the *nature* of imperialist socioeconomic systems; since the nature (as distinct from the conduct) of imperialism can never be affected by internal or external forces—its noxious consequences can only be mitigated by its containment or abolition (by violent means if necessary)—the Soviet region is, according to this vision, permanently condemned to the status of a garrison state as long as "imperialism" exists.

Effecting the reallocation of political power and material resources that has been the goal of the Gorbachev reform requires—which is also true for a post-Communist confederal union—breaking the stranglehold of (traditional) ideological and military interests on Soviet society, something that Khrushchev, who also sought relief from certain Leninist constraints, failed to do. This in turn requires the effective repudiation of the Leninist ideology of imperialism as the intellectual and political foundation of the Soviet (and now post-Soviet) approach to international affairs. The result has been not the end of ideology in foreign policy but a substantially new one.

It is important to stress that the new political thinking, although in essence an ideological instrument of domestic reform, has also been shaped by profound international as well as internal processes and problems, as Chapters 5 and 6 have shown. The role and interaction of these international and internal factors in pushing Soviet policy and thinking to new lines reflect processes that are well beyond governmental control or even easy influence. The new policies and thinking that have been produced as a result thus do not represent simple "tactical" adjustments in approach, ready to be reversed at an expedient moment. Their import, and their consequences for post-Soviet politics and politicians, run far deeper than that. This has been well understood by all sides in the Soviet political class, which sees in the ideological presentation of policies a crucial vehicle in the struggle for power. The political prospects of this contest are tangential to the purposes of this analysis; it is beyond doubt, however, that the end of ideology in post-Soviet politics can come only with the end of politics and in particular of the Soviet legacy in the successor republics. Indeed, in the final analysis, the chances for the new ideology of foreign policy to strike root in the post-Soviet system depend in the long run on the prospects of the internal reform that it is designed to advance. Above all, the answer hinges on whether the social forces, including those of a nationalist character, that have provided the occasion and pressed the need for reform can find adequate expression in the institutions, new and old, of post-Soviet power. That would constitute an adequate guarantee against a reversion to any kind of neo-Stalinist political-institutional order and thus of a corresponding ideology.

Notes

1. *Vestnik Ministerstva Inostrannykh Del,* no. 15 (1989), pp. 27–46.

2. I. Yanin, "Vozvrashcheniye k Prostym Istinam," *Mezhdunarodnaya Zhizn',* no. 2 (1989), p. 125; Mikhail Gorbachev, *Perestroika* (New York: Harper & Row, 1987), p. 250; *Izvestiya,* February 5, 1990.

3. *New York Times,* October 24, 1989, p. A13.

4. Wolfgang Leonhard, *Child of the Revolution* (Chicago: Henry Regnery, 1958), pp. 483–484 and 487–488; *New York Times,* January 22, 1989, p. A1ff.

5. *Pravda,* June 21, 1985.

6. Sylvia Woodby, *Gorbachev and the Decline of Ideology in Soviet Foreign Policy* (Boulder: Westview Press, 1990).

7. In R. N. Carew Hunt, *The Theory and Practice of Communism* (London: Penguin Books, 1963), p. 17.

8. Marshal Sergei Akhromeyev, the late military adviser to Gorbachev, had stated: "Limited sovereignty must not exist and ideology must no longer find a place in interstate relations. It will, however, survive in interparty relations." *La Repubblica,* November 22, 1989, as translated in FBIS-SOV-89-229, November 30, 1989, p. 106. It is noteworthy that during the fourth Reagan-Gorbachev summit, in Moscow in May–June 1988, Gorbachev made a determined effort to incorporate language on "peaceful coexistence" into the joint statement and was visibly disappointed at the U.S. demurral. See Joseph Whelan, *The Moscow Summit, 1988* (Boulder: Westview Press, 1990).

9. For an earnest effort to square the "new political thinking" with dialectical philosophy, see V. Altukhov, "Dialektika tselostnogo mira i novoye myshleniye," *Mirovaya Ekonomika i Mezhdunarodnye Otnosheniya,* no. 9 (1989), pp. 53–65. Altukhov is an editor of *Voprosy Filosofii.* See also Altukhov, "Gosudarstvennye, Natsional'nye i Klassovye Interesy vo Vneshney Politike i Mezhdunarodnykh Otnosheniyakh," *Mirovaya Ekonomika i Mezhdunarodnye Otnosheniya,* no. 2 (1989), pp. 66–72.

10. *Vestnik,* op. cit.; Aleksandr Yakovlev, "Dostizheniye kachestvenno novogo sostoyaniya sovestskogo obshchestva i obshchestvennye nauki," *Vestnik Akademii Nauk SSSR,* no. 6 (1987), pp. 75–77; and Andrei Kozyrev, "East and West: From Confrontation to Co-Development," *International Affairs* (Moscow), no. 10 (1989), pp. 7–8.

11. Igor Malashenko, "Interesy strany: mnimye i real'nye," *Kommunist,* no. 13 (1989), pp. 119–120.

12. For a representative sample of their work and that of their colleagues, see the successive volumes of the IMEMO yearbook entitled *Disarmament and Security* (Moscow: Institute of World Economy and International Relations, 1986–1990).

Part 3

CHALLENGES OF THE FUTURE

8

Soviet Collapse and U.S. Foreign Policy

The USSR, the *Union* of Soviet Socialist Republics, has disintegrated. This became clear early in 1991, when Mikhail Gorbachev, the president of the USSR, saw it necessary to hold a referendum on the need to preserve the union (which took place on March 17, 1991). The results of the referendum (more precisely the set of referenda, due to the parallel Russian and Ukrainian items challenging the Gorbachev motion), which approved of the continuation of a "union" of republics only on the basis of genuine sovereignty for these constituent republics, underscored the fragility of the federation.[1] The consequent rapid sequence of agreements on the nature of a future union between the central government and nine consenting republics, beginning on April 23, 1991, had seen the Soviet government effectively acquiesce to the republics' demands for real sovereign power. By late July 1991, the Soviet government had even consented to divest itself of its ability to levy taxes, thereby ratifying the evisceration of the central government's independent capacity to govern and the reversal of the historical relationship between the Kremlin and its constituent parts. (In a sense, this simply confirmed a fait accompli: Through the first five months of 1991, the republics had turned over only 30 percent of required revenues to the central government.[2])

Portents of Disintegration

Other portents of Soviet disintegration abound and, taken together, underscore the argument of those plotting the August 1991 coup that reform could no longer be squared with the preservation of the historical Soviet Union. On June 7, 1991, the Ukrainian republican government declared that it had "seized" all union (i.e., Soviet government) assets on its territory. The Ukranian Council of Ministers, fearing that, contrary to previous agreement with the central government, vital economic properties on Ukrainian soil were not being transferred to the Ukrainian government, declared: "All legislative acts and decisions of the Union bodies concerning property on the territory of the republic are not valid if these decisions are taken without clearance of the state bodies of the Ukraine."[3] In a case with international ramifications beyond the borders of the USSR, on July 29, 1991, Russian President Boris Yeltsin signed a to-then unprecedented treaty with Lithuania, according Lithuania full diplomatic recognition as a sovereign subject of international law in exchange for Lithuania's guaranteeing the civil rights of Russians living in Lithuania and the economic survival of the isolated Russian enclave of Kaliningrad (formerly Prussian Koenigsberg), which is cut off from the body of the Russian Federation by Lithuania and Poland.

The treaty represented a diplomatic coup for Yeltsin as well as a considerable embarrassment for the Gorbachev government, in that it established a model—on a republican basis—for a negotiated settlement with the Baltic states that the Soviet government itself had proved so reluctant to entertain. The signing of the treaty therefore underscored the increasing remove of the central Soviet authorities from the political forces that have been inexorably recasting the mold of the USSR.[4] On a more prosaic level, the central Soviet authorities had by mid-1991 lost track of the vital sector of oil exports, insofar as these were by then largely initiated and controlled by republics, refiners, oil production associations, joint ventures, and import-export companies. This led the Soviet government to exaggerate by perhaps as much as 100 percent the decline in oil exports in the first half of 1991.[5]

"Disintegration" of the USSR means that the central Soviet state had lost the ability to formulate, decide, and execute policies affecting the allocation of resources—economic, political, social—throughout the breadth of the country it claimed to rule. The series of emergency presidential decrees that Gorbachev had increasingly relied upon in attempting to govern the country were consistently ignored and, what is more, ignored with relative impunity. The inability of a government to punish those opposed to it as well as to reward those who support it is a sure sign of debility and of the effective disintegration of its authority, even if it continues to govern in name. The idea of "disintegration" takes on added significance in the Soviet case in that it is precisely the mission of integrating not merely the state and society but also the numerous nations that make up the USSR that has distinguished the Soviet Russian state historically both from its contemporary Western counterparts and from its Western imperial antecedents. The term "disintegration" should thus be taken to mean a specific breakdown in the integrative capacities of government, and not necessarily a catastrophic societal upheaval of the sort now so widely predicted. The latter may be a consequence of the former, but it is a distinct phenomenon for purposes of analysis.

Indeed, what is striking about the Gorbachev period is the absence of mass, politically directed violence of the kind ordinarily associated with the transformations under way in the Soviet Union. At least four revolutionary transitions are now occurring in the region: from political totalitarianism to pluralism; from a centrally planned to a market economy; from hegemony of the Russians, or more precisely, of those who claimed to rule in their name, to a more confederal relationship among the nations of the USSR; and finally, from a superpower to an ordinary power on the world stage. Any one of these taken singly could be considered as having revolutionary consequences for the state and society in which it is taking place. The fact that all four are occurring simultaneously and in the absence of sustained mass violence must be without precedent in the modern state. It may even be that political science and economic theory do not have the categories to understand what in the economic and political spheres are entirely novel experiments: No market economy has ever been created from the ground up; no Communist government has gone so far in countenancing reforms that in principle and by consequence undermine the vital essence of the Communist system. Be that as it may, the rapid decline in the governability of the Soviet system had, by mid-1991, *before* the coup become evident. The international as well as the internal ramifications of this remarkable political implosion will affect the United States and its allies, whether they wish it or not.

The problem for the outside world is that the disappearance of the second (still nuclear) superpower will impinge on the stability of the post-1945 order in East-West relations. As we saw in the first chapters of this book, it was the Soviet and U.S. blocs that underwrote that stability. The magnitude of the change implied by the collapse of the USSR may be grasped by spelling out its four main political aspects. (1) In constitutional terms, the unitary (though in form federal) state that has been the USSR has ceased to function and been replaced by an incipient and practically unprecedented experiment in confederal government. There is a vast emptiness now in what was the heart of Soviet power. (2) In historical terms, the collapse of the Soviet state has also meant the end of one of the world's great empires, i.e., the comprehensive hegemony of "Russia" over its neighbors. (3) In political-economic terms, the abandonment of strict central economic planning without an alternative in mind or in place (what some have called *katastroika,* i.e., central planning without a center) has reinforced the movement toward political decomposition. (4) And in foreign policy terms, these internal forces, together with real changes in Soviet thinking and international circumstances, have led to the collapse of those conditions that have for centuries guaranteed the rulers of Russia not only a hegemonic position over the nations inhabiting the empire (including the Russians themselves) but also their great power status internationally.

Impact on the United States

What are the consequent challenges to the outside world, including to the United States, of this seismic shift in the weight and role of the Soviet Russian state in domestic and world politics? In thinking through this problem, it may prove helpful to consider two sets of relationships that cut across both basic aspects of the current transformations in the Soviet Union and their implications for U.S. foreign policy interests and conduct. These are, first, the ways in which the United States has been affected by, and reacted to, comparable instances of imperial disintegration in the nineteenth and twentieth centuries; and second, the ways in which U.S.-Soviet relations have been affected by the fact that the USSR has been a specific kind of multinational (but also unitary) state. The insights yielded by this twin set of perspectives should help to frame the likely range of future conduct in relations between the United States and the USSR and/ or its successor state(s).

On the first point, every breakdown of a major world empire—from the Spanish to the British—has had an important impact on U.S. foreign policy. In many cases, the consequences of decolonization have caused considerable embarrassment for the United States, in its relations with both the metropole power and the emerging independent states. For better or worse, such major events in U.S. foreign policy as the Louisiana Purchase, 1803 (acquired from the French empire), the Monroe Doctrine, 1823 (in reaction to the anticolonial revolutions in Latin America), confrontation with the USSR over the Belgian Congo, 1960, the Vietnam War (after the failure of the French to subdue their former colony), and the identification of U.S. interests with apartheid in the early to mid-1970s in the face of the collapse of the Portuguese empire in southern Africa have their origins in the transformation of a major imperial relationship.

Even the purchase of Alaska in 1867 was possible because of the desire of the Russian empire to liquidate its overextended North American holdings. Although the latter instance may not serve as precedent in the current crisis of Soviet Russian imperialism (however, Boris Yeltsin has hinted that Russia proper might sell four small islands that Japan claims, as a way of removing an irritant in Soviet-Japanese relations), all of these examples show that even during the period of alleged isolationism in U.S. foreign relations, the United States has not been able to remain unaffected by the breakup of major empires. How much more true must this be in the case today of the USSR, chief postwar rival of the United States.

The Historical Legacy of U.S. Policy

On the second point, i.e., the impact of the multinational character of the Soviet state on U.S. foreign policy, the truth is that at no time in the U.S. relationship with Soviet Russia, including the periods of nonrecognition and cold war, has the imperial character of the Soviet state had a significant effect on U.S. policy toward the Soviet Union. Throughout the seventy-odd years of Soviet history, the U.S. public and U.S. officials have held an image of the Soviet Union that is largely a reflection of that held about the United States. (Would they be flattered to know that the same is true of the Russian people and much of Soviet officialdom?) The Soviet state, however detested, and Soviet society were seen in essentially unitary terms, akin to the United States, with the differences between Ukraine and Russia held akin to those between, say, New York and Texas, i.e., largely regional and folkloric in nature and certainly not having any fundamental bearing upon the stability and conduct of the state.

During the period of nonrecognition, 1917–1933, it was not the denial of *national* self-determination that prevented official U.S. dealings with the Soviet government. (In fact, the United States withheld recognition of the Baltic states' independence from Russia until 1922, in the hopes that the restoration of constitutional government in Russia would thereby reestablish the continuity of the—imperial—Russian state.) Such obstacles to U.S. diplomatic recognition of Soviet Russia as Soviet repudiation of czarist debts, the Bolshevik seizure of U.S. property, Soviet-inspired propaganda in the United States, and official Soviet atheism did seriously retard the normalization of U.S.-Soviet relations in the 1920s. Yet once these problems had been resolved or put aside (as they would be in 1933), the repression of national self-determination within the USSR would not serve to complicate the course of relations between Moscow and Washington.

U.S. objections to the undemocratic nature of the Soviet system would remain a hindrance to any genuinely intimate set of relations with Moscow, but these objections were rooted in a general revulsion at the dictatorial character of the Soviet regime and never at the specific subjugation of the nations, Russian and non-Russian, that composed the USSR.

The Soviet dictatorship was seen as one over individuals or even classes, but never in any politically important sense as a dictatorship over a multitude of nations, as was, by contrast, the czarist system ("the prison house of nations," in words that Lenin helped make popular).

It would be strange, actually, if Washington had insisted on a revision of the terms of national incorporation into the USSR as a condition of normal relations. Traditionally, states have relied upon the standard of effective control of territory as the basis for according diplomatic recognition. The existence of a British "empire," after all, had never occasioned any serious difficulties in relations with Washington. Furthermore, by the 1930s, the United States had evolved the "Good Neighbor" policy in its relations with Latin America, whereby Washington removed the question of the internal political coloration of governments in the region from its bilateral diplomatic agenda with them. If this was so in an area that Washington had always considered to be one of vital interest, it should not be surprising that the United States would be much less concerned about raising such internal considerations of the USSR, a distant power in those days, to a precondition for transacting international business. The focus on the purely interstate level of the relationship would be further reinforced by the rise of Fascist Japan and Germany in the early 1930s, and the coincidence of interest between Washington and Moscow in trying to arrange for the international containment of Fascist ambitions.

What is important for our analysis is not that Washington should choose to develop its relations with the central Soviet authorities but that there should be no recognition by the United States that the USSR, by virtue of its being a multinational union, was a special kind of state and that consequently the problem of self-determination for the people of the USSR had to be understood in terms of self-determination of the nations of the USSR as well. This blind spot toward nationalism in U.S. consciousness toward the USSR is well illustrated in the following observation by Vera Micheles Dean, a generally perceptive student of Soviet affairs of the early postwar period. On the prospects for U.S.-Soviet relations, Dean wrote in 1948, "A community of views still persists between the United States and Russia on long-term problems like the necessity for termination of colonial rule."[6] This identification of Russia with the Soviet Union and the inability to associate colonialism with the Soviet system have been consistent traits of U.S. official, public, and many academic analyses of the USSR and have served to frame the range of choice in U.S.-Soviet relations as well as constrict our field of vision concerning national developments in a multinational USSR.

Throughout the early period of U.S. recognition of the USSR, from 1933 on, the United States fully accepted, as the foundation for U.S.-Soviet relations, the official Soviet view of the USSR as a single, legitimate state entity based on the voluntary union of its constituent national parts. (The three Baltic states, which were coerced into the USSR in 1940, that is, six years after U.S. recognition, were not part of the USSR upon recognition and thus fall into a different legal and political category for the United States from the other twelve Soviet republics, all of which were equally coerced into the Union. Thus, the United States refused to recognize the incorporation of the Baltic states into the USSR, a position that would have no legal foundation were it applied to the rest of the USSR, given the terms of recognition in 1933, i.e., recognizing the USSR as it then existed.)

This tendency on the part of the United States to deal exclusively with the central Soviet authorities in Moscow, at the exclusion of the nations that make up the USSR, has been a consistent one in U.S. foreign policy even when, as in the year and a half leading up to the August coup, the power of the center had been progressively usurped by the republics. Indeed, in certain respects, U.S. policy has been more respectful of Soviet interests than has the Soviet leadership itself: The Soviet constitution provided each of the fifteen union republics with its own ministry of foreign affairs. Never, even during the depths of the cold war, has Washington entertained the possibility of establishing diplomatic relations with the union republics, something that would have been entirely legal under the old Soviet constitutions. At a minimum, Washington could have obtained a propaganda advantage by demonstrating, in the event of a Soviet veto, the purely fictional character of the voluntary union that the USSR has claimed itself to be. At a maximum, the United States could have put itself into a much more favorable position to assess national developments within the USSR and to react with intelligence and calculation to the fissiparous forces that are now reconstituting the USSR. That the United States never seriously contemplated a policy toward the USSR analogous to that of "differentiation," which was applied to Communist Eastern Europe after 1956, underlines once again how invisible the multinational structure of the USSR has been for the United States in its dealings with that country. (Only in the aftermath of the abortive coup did Washington make the first moves toward recognizing the new realities of the post-Soviet political landscape: official [and tardy] recognition of the Baltic states in September 1991 and, in late November 1991, the decision to establish diplomatic relations with independent Ukraine. The establishment of the eleven-member Commonwealth of Independent States in December 1991 forced Washington's hand as far as the rest of the republics were concerned.)

Thus, the entire course of U.S.-Soviet relations, including the period before recognition in 1933, the early recognition period itself, certainly the years of wartime alliance from 1941 to 1945, and the cold war years, never found the United States making the multinational character of the Soviet state a significant desideratum in its official Soviet policy. Although the U.S. intelligence agencies did assist certain of the western populations of the USSR in the late 1940s, primarily the western Ukrainians and the Baltic peoples as they resisted the reimposition of Stalinist rule, this never affected the formal assumptions of official U.S. policy toward the USSR. The problems that the United States had with the USSR could be negotiated or otherwise resolved with the central Soviet leadership; U.S. policies were directed toward affecting *that* leadership's calculus of costs and benefits in its own U.S. policy, not toward undermining its dictatorship at home and certainly not toward affecting the framework of relations governing the incorporation into the USSR of its constituent nations. Even the ceremonial rhetoric of "liberation" of the "captive nations" of the USSR (as the congressional resolution of 1959 had it) was dropped from presidential rhetoric upon the initiation of detente with the USSR in 1972.

More recent conduct by U.S. administrations confirms this judgment. During the early Jimmy Carter administration, National Security Adviser Zbigniew Brzezinski asked for the nuclear targeting plans for "Russia." When presented with the targeting plans for the entire Soviet Union, Brzezinski objected, noting that he wished to be able to target specifically *Russian* sources of power and thereby help to disintegrate the multinational USSR, whose population is only half Russian. The absence of such plans, and the general perplexity that Brzezinski's request induced, again shows the general unreadiness of official Washington to think through the realities and implications of a multinational USSR. Brzezinski's request in turn demonstrates another characteristic of U.S. analysis of the USSR, that is, the identification of the Soviet system with the interests of the Russian people. The rise of Boris Yeltsin, in part on the argument that the Soviet system exploits the Russian nation at least as much as any of the others making up the USSR, effectively refutes this.[7]

Reagan-Bush–Era Policy Toward Gorbachev's USSR

Even the language of the "evil empire," as employed by Ronald Reagan in the early 1980s, does not reflect any appreciation for the special, imperial character of the Soviet state. By evil empire Reagan and his sympathizers meant just that the Soviet Union was a bad, though large, state, not that it was specifically imperialistic in the manner in which it organized relations among the nations of the USSR. It was as if the USSR were a unitary empire, after the fashion of the founders' own vision of the great "American empire." The rapid improvement in U.S.-Soviet relations, from the Geneva summit meeting of November 1985 through seven other summit meetings involving presidents Reagan and George Bush with Mikhail Gorbachev, resulted in the personalizing of the U.S.-Soviet relationship, as the United States came to identify its state interests with respect to the USSR with the political interests of Mikhail Gorbachev. This had the effect of accepting Gorbachev's own political agenda for the transformation of the USSR as the basis of U.S.-Soviet relations. Because Gorbachev's reform vision has been so closely linked with his determination to preserve the structure of the union as it has existed for nearly seventy years, this meant that the United States, for all intents and purposes, endorsed Gorbachev's efforts to preserve a union that was rejected by nearly all of its constituent nations. In the process, the United States may well have inadvertently convinced those plotting the August 1991 coup that their efforts to preserve the historical union would eventually be accepted by the West.

Time and again in recent years, the U.S. government has acted to strengthen Gorbachev's hand in confrontations with the forces of national separatism in the USSR. In essence, through diplomatic channels and public statements, the late Reagan and the Bush administrations made it clear that they were not prepared to move further in recognizing, de facto or de jure, national independence movements faster or in a more substantial way than was Gorbachev himself. In response to the various instances of Armenian-Azeri communal violence, the massacre of a score of Georgian citizens by Soviet security forces in the Georgian capital of Tbilisi in April 1989, and even the use of force by the Soviet authorities against the declarations of sovereignty by the three Baltic states—where in contrast to the rest of the the USSR the United States had certain political and legal obligations—the U.S. government made it plain that it considered these to be part of the internal affairs of the Soviet state and that it had no desire to turn the use of force by the Soviet government in defense of its integrity as a state into an impediment to the improvement of U.S.-Soviet relations.[8] President Bush's warning to the Ukrainian parliament on August 1, 1991, against what he called "suicidal nationalism" was only the most candid and public of recent statements of official U.S. reserve toward the movements for national independence in the USSR.[9]

Indeed, the U.S. government made explicit its support for Gorbachev, and thus of *his* concept of the union, as the basis of policy toward the Soviet Union. One critical consequence of reducing U.S. policy toward a great state to one man's internal policies is that, intentionally or not, the U.S. government in effect accepted the *Soviet* agenda for future relations between the central Soviet authorities and the various nations of the

USSR. This is, as we have seen, broadly in line with the pattern of U.S. relations with the USSR over the past sixty years, as the United States has since 1933 based its relations with Soviet Russia on the assumption of the political and territorial integrity of the Soviet state, as defined by those who effectively rule, or at least control, that state. That is standard diplomatic practice, and in itself should come as little surprise, Gorbachev or no.

U.S. Hesitations on Baltic Independence

The true measure of the broader sea change that set in in U.S.-Soviet relations since the late 1980s is seen in the painstaking efforts that the Bush administration made to disassociate itself de facto from the traditional U.S. policy of refusing to recognize the forcible incorporation of Lithuania, Latvia, and Estonia into the USSR in 1940. Certainly, the Bush administration went to some lengths to affirm that its formal policy of nonrecognition never changed. But in practice, the U.S. government, from the beginning of the Baltic sovereignty crisis in early 1990 until even after the defeat of the coup d'etat on August 21, 1991, consistently refused to permit considerations about the political status of the Baltic states to interfere with its broader, Gorbachev-centered policy toward the Soviet Union. President Bush's refusal to visit the Baltic states during his July–August 1991 summit visit to the USSR gave visible and dramatic expression to this point.

This sensitivity on the part of the Bush administration toward Gorbachev's concerns did not go unappreciated, either in Moscow or in the three Baltic capitals. Indeed, the reference by coup "leader" Gennady Yanaev on the first day of the coup (August 19, 1991) to the need to preserve "stability" in a "nuclear superpower" strongly suggests that party reactionaries concluded that the West would prefer the preservation (in effect restoration) of the historical union—whatever its political coloration—to the uncertainties associated with a more plural (and democratic) confederation.[10] At the height of the Lithuanian sovereignty crisis in April 1990, the Soviet government newspaper *Izvestiya* editorialized, "The [Bush] administration's initial approach toward this question cannot be said to lack a laudable restraint."[11] Earlier that month, a senior Soviet foreign ministry official, Boris Krasulin, noted that the United Nations and the Western world, including the United States, had assumed a "correct position" on the Lithuanian issue. "The West," he concluded, "understands Moscow's position well."[12]

Further along these lines, Gennady Gerasimov, at the time spokesman for the Soviet Foreign Ministry, in an April 1990 press conference commended the United States as well as the Scandinavian countries (in spite of their official nonrecognition policies) for having refrained from what he termed "any kind of advice and direct interference in this situation." Gerasimov, with his characteristic sense of ironic insight, noted that the Lithuanian declaration of sovereignty had indeed presented Western countries "with a very unpleasant judicial problem. . . . I do not think that they are very happy with that," he closed. Finally, and to close this sketch of Soviet appreciations, one *Moscow News* correspondent expressed puzzlement as to U.S. aloofness on the Baltic question, because, as she noted, "for the Americans the problem does not exist as such."[13] In this view, the recent Soviet condemnation of the secret protocol affixed to the Nazi-Soviet Nonaggression Treaty of August 1939—the very basis for the Soviet takeover of the Baltic states the following year—as well as the exemplary political conduct of the Baltic peoples themselves in their march toward independence, would seem to have justified Washington's long-standing policy of nonrecognition. Yet, the perplexed correspondent correctly noted that the Bush administration was in no hurry to recognize Lithuania as an independent nation. Indeed, even after the Soviet government had officially consented to Baltic independence after the failure of the August 19–21 coup, the United States, concerned not to embarrass Gorbachev, was one of the last of the Western democracies to accord formal recognition of the three Baltic states' new status.

President Bush made explicit the U.S. standard for reacting to the Baltic efforts to regain their independence. On March 13, 1990, at the outset of the crisis over the Lithuanian declaration of sovereignty, the president stated, "In terms of recognition, there is a standard of control of one's territory that I've been advised should guide this."[14] Given the fact that the Soviet army is practically as large as the combined native populations of the three Baltic states, it was obvious that the central Soviet government could exercise significant "control" over the Baltic states, as long as a Soviet state with the will to do so existed. Presidential spokesman Marlin Fitzwater expanded on this concept in October 1990 when he stated that the United States could not support the attempts of the Baltic states to join the Conference on Security and Cooperation in Europe (CSCE) until "effective" independence was first achieved.[15] Use of this criterion for recognition made the prospects for U.S. recognition of Baltic independence hinge on the central Soviet government's determination of what is permissible sovereignty for the nations of the USSR. Had the August 1991 coup succeeded, such a standard of recognition would have found the United States quickly accommodating itself to the new rulers of the USSR.

In truth, the United States has hardly been alone in its reluctance to upset what it has seen as the Gorbachev "apple cart" in the USSR. The Norwegian government, which in the fall of 1990 helped sponsor a

Lithuanian Information Office in Oslo (and which immediately after the August 1991 coup did extend diplomatic recognition to the Baltic states), stated at the same time that it could not grant such an office diplomatic status because "diplomatic realities dictate that the USSR first recognize Lithuania as an independent state." Along similar lines the Italian government in September 1990 observed that Baltic participation in the CSCE would be legally impossible, as only fully sovereign states are admitted and the unanimous agreement of all CSCE states, i.e., including the USSR, would be required for Baltic entry. This was identical to the official Soviet position on the question of CSCE participation.[16]

The first practical test of the broader Western attitude toward Baltic independence came during the November 1990 session of the CSCE in Paris, where Baltic representatives had in fact been issued guest status by the French government. At Soviet insistence, the visiting Baltic delegations were expelled from the conference—without visible Western protestation. Indeed, according to the Latvian foreign minister, U.S. Secretary of State Baker told the Baltic delegations that the United States was unwilling to enter into a conflict with the USSR over the Baltic states, that such a conflict would prove "counterproductive" for all, and that the Baltic question could be resolved only through negotiations in Moscow.[17]

The precoup Western attitude toward the nations of the USSR was perhaps best and most forthrightly expressed to the press by British Foreign Secretary Douglas Hurd, after a speech in Kiev, the capital of the Ukraine (the USSR's second largest republic and comparable in size, population, and resources to France), on March 20, 1991. The British government (and by extension the West in general) is "not working for the disintegration of the Soviet Union," Hurd said. Intoning against nationalism, based on European rather than Soviet experience, Hurd continued, "Europe has learned the hard way in this century that crude nationalism of the old kind can turn pride into hatred and achievement into destruction." He declared forcefully, "We continue to support strongly the process of reform associated with Mr. Gorbachev and we will continue to wish that process every success." Finally: "We will want to cooperate with the Ukraine whatever its relationship with Moscow. That is a matter for you. We hope that Moscow will show respect for the aspirations of the Ukraine, Georgia and other republics. *But* [emphasis added] our cooperation will continue whatever happens."[18] Given that in reality Gorbachev's policies were by early 1991 no longer capable of preserving the historical union, those plotting that August's coup may be forgiven if they thought that they might have had at least tacit Western acquiescence in their effort to "save" the union from nationalist disintegration.

The desire to continue good relations with Gorbachev's USSR "whatever happens" is underscored by a remarkable press briefing that Marlin

Fitzwater gave in late March 1990 on the issue of Baltic sovereignty and its challenge to U.S. policy. Part of the dialogue is reproduced below. Those familiar with the British TV satire "Yes, Minister," will appreciate how political life can imitate art:

> *Q:* Marlin, you are constantly referring to the Government of Lithuania as if Lithuania were a foreign state. Is this how the United States sees the government of Lithuania?
>
> *A:* We have never recognized the incorporation of Lithuania in the Soviet Union . . .
>
> *Q:* But in the last few days you have not referred to them as the "Government of Lithuania."
>
> *A:* This does not mark a change in policy.
>
> *Q:* Does your policy consist of not recognizing the Government of Lithuania as part of the Soviet Union?
>
> *A:* There has been no change.
>
> *Q:* You have not formally recognized this government?
>
> *A:* There has been no change in policy.
>
> *Q:* So what does the Government of Lithuania represent as such?
>
> *A:* I do not undersand your question. . . .
>
> *Q:* This poses the question of de facto diplomatic recognition, am I not right?
>
> *A:* No, this is not de facto recognition. There has been no change in policy
> . . .
>
> *Q:* You have said that a more complex situation may arise as a result of intimidation and heightened tension. Do you consider that an atmosphere of intimidation already exists or that it could arise?
>
> *A:* No, we used the subjunctive in our statement. That means that should that happen, we would view it in precisely that context, but we have deemed it necessary not to draw any conclusions.
>
> *Q:* If the Soviet Union used force against Lithuania, what would the U.S. reaction be?
>
> *A:* We do not make assumptions on hypothetical situations . . .
>
> *Q:* . . . would the use of force against Lithuania affect U.S.-Soviet relations . . . ?
>
> *A:* I cannot comment on this, I do not know.
>
> *Q:* . . . Do you no longer regard this as an internal affair of Gorbachev's?
>
> *A:* Our policy has undergone no change.[19]

I have dwelt on the Baltic aspect of the national transformation of the USSR precisely because of its exceptional quality. The Baltic states, of all the nations of the USSR, presented the case that should have found the United States maximally prepared to cultivate a relationship parallel to, if not independent of, its overall ties with the Soviet government. That the Bush administration chose not to permit the niceties of its formal commitment to Baltic sovereignty to mix with its broader Soviet policy speaks eloquently about its broader indifference to the concerns of the other nations of the USSR, which unlike the Baltic states had no legal or political claims to advance upon the United States. Again, the coup junta could easily have drawn the conclusion—and the language of its early communiques suggest that it did—that the U.S. government might well tolerate its attempt to keep the old union intact.

Republican Sovereignty and U.S. Policy

Until events forced its hand after the failure of the August coup, the U.S. government consistently chose not to be an active participant in the national transformation of the Soviet Union, a process that, as was suggested at the outset of this chapter, can hardly help affecting important U.S. interests. It would seem that the Bush administration did sense the importance of the issues at stake; hence its desperate clinging to Gorbachev in the hopes that somehow enough Western support for the Soviet leader would make the problem disappear. But the U.S. and other Western governments, even if they sensed the gravity of the contest for sovereignty between the Soviet authorities and the constituent republics, do not even now seem to have an adequate concept for understanding the dynamic forces that have been set in motion. Sooner rather than later the Western governments will have to make choices that their previous pro-Gorbachev policies were intended to avoid.

By way of example, the parliament of Belorussia, the republic that has been widely considered the *most* assimilated into the Soviet Russian system outside of Russia itself (both assumptions having now been effectively disproven), as early as July 27, 1990, passed a declaration of sovereignty that, among other items:

1. Contained no reference to USSR citizenship
2. Called for an independent system of foreign relations for Belorussia
3. Demanded the right to maintain army and security forces independent of the union
4. Declared that in the future Belorussia will be a nonnuclear weapons zone and a neutral state[20]

These items are comparable to those passed in the Ukrainian declaration of sovereignty of the same month, which formed the basis of the parallel Ukrainian vote to the Gorbachev referendum of March 17, 1991, to continue in a union relationship. In greater or lesser degree, the same determination to uphold an independent international profile—even if certain powers remain delegated to a central federal authority—may be found in every union republic of the USSR. Thus, even if some kind of union of the Soviet republics can be reconstructed, it will almost certainly be on a basis that will permit its constituent parts a quite different kind of participation in international relations than they have hitherto exercised. It should be recalled that every union republic possessed a foreign ministry under the Soviet constitution. Furthermore, Belorussia and the Ukraine (though not, ironically, Russia itself) had full representation in the United Nations, and so were already juridically competent to conduct the entire range of international relationships.

Like it or not, the United States will soon be facing an increasing array of situations arising out of the union republics' desire for a greater international presence. These challenges will compel Washington to come to terms with sovereign nationalisms within the existing USSR. We have already noted the specific challenge that the Baltic states posed to the West by asking in fall 1990 for simple observer status in the CSCE. Even before its declaration of independence of April 1991, the Georgian Republic had established separate economic departments in its own, Georgian, foreign ministry to oversee foreign trade, independent of the all-union central ministries. Also in April 1991, the ethnic Romanian Soviet republic of Moldavia signed a series of important political, economic, and cultural agreements with Romania, without reference to the central Soviet government.[21] In a similar vein, the republic of Russia not only signed its own political and economic treaties with the Baltic states and the Ukraine, again without reference to the central Soviet authorities, but also began a set of treaty relationships with Poland and the countries of East-Central Europe. In July 1991, Lithuania and Georgia extended full diplomatic recognition to Slovenia. (Interestingly, the U.S. Articles of Confederation, criticized for leaving too much power in the hands of the constituent states, explicitly prohibited the states from signing treaties with foreign countries. This underscores the extent to which the Soviet republics had already before the coup shattered traditional political concepts in their search for the sovereign expression of their national interests.)

The parliament of the Central Asian republic of Kazakhstan, in October 1990, passed a bill "banning" all nuclear weapons tests at the main Soviet testing site of Semipalatinsk, located within the republic. By October 1991, the Soviet military reconciled itself to Kazakh wishes on this point and began the dismantling of its nuclear test sites in the republic. For his part, Boris Yeltsin had at one time or another before the August 1991 coup claimed Soviet agreement to a Russian foreign trade bank, backed by Soviet gold. Furthermore, he asserted that all Soviet borrowings abroad would first have to be cleared with the Russian government. Yeltsin even declared that if representatives of the Russian government were not included in key diplomatic negotiations affecting the interests of Russia, then the Russian government would not be bound by any agreements that the central Soviet government might thereby reach (such as one concerning the territorial dispute surrounding four islands north of Hokkaido that the Soviet Union occupied after World War II.) These concerns were reflected in the negotiations on a new union treaty. The dramatic increase in Yeltsin's power as Russian president after his role in the defeat of the August 1991 coup and the subsequent collapse of the Soviet state means that the Russian Republic has assumed the authority of the Soviet state in international as well as internal affairs, as Russia's accession to the USSR's U.N. Security Council seat in early 1992 demonstrates. In a forceful display of Russian authority, Yeltsin, on November 29, 1991, established temporary custody over the Soviet Foreign Ministry, which was about to become defunct owing to the bankruptcy of the Soviet treasury.

Another sign of things to come may be seen in the vigorous campaign that the Belorussian foreign minister, Piotr Krauchanko, waged in the October 1990 United Nations General Assembly on behalf of the victims of the Chernobyl accident in Belorussia. In brief, Krauchanko urged the internationalization of the Chernobyl issue, arguing the incompetence (technical and, by extension, political) of the central Soviet authorities in addressing the concerns of Belorussia, which had lost the use of about 10 percent of its territory and up to 20 percent of its arable land due to the irradiation of Chernobyl.

These instances of increasing national autonomy, if not outright independence, in the sphere of international politics are the cornerstones of an entirely new and still inchoate pattern of international relationships emanating from the territory of the Soviet Union. They reflect what University of Michigan scholar Roman Szporluk has called the process by which interethnic relations have become genuinely international relations and challenge the very concept of "Soviet" foreign policy that we have used, unconsciously, in thinking about the international behavior of the multinational Soviet Russian state.[22] If only for the mundane reason that each of the union republics can initiate diplomatic contacts through its existing foreign ministry (and increasingly through UN representation), the U.S. and other Western governments would be wise to think through the implications of responding, or not, to the feelers that will inevitably come. As a first step, they will have to take seriously the force of nationalism in the contemporary USSR and develop an adequate concept for relating to the new country and set of countries that have in effect already come into existence.

Guidelines of Future U.S. Policy

What will be the likely U.S. reaction to the proliferation of claims to independence, including independent foreign policies, that are now flowing from the nations of the Soviet Union? If these nations, including the Russians, may be considered the inner empire of the Soviet state, then the history of U.S. policy toward the outer empire, that is, Eastern Europe, through the postwar period until 1989, may prove instructive in gauging the future contours of U.S. policy. As Chapter 3 has shown, U.S. relations with Eastern Europe from 1945 to 1989 were usually a secondary consideration in U.S. foreign policy. Except for momentary periods of acute crisis, such as the Soviet invasion of Hungary in 1956 and the Warsaw Pact invasion of Czechoslvakia in 1968, developments in Eastern Europe have never preoccupied Washington the way that those in Western Europe, East Asia, and the Soviet Union itself have, in the sense of justifying a major claim upon U.S. attention and resources. Furthermore, U.S. relations with Eastern Europe were always, perhaps especially in those moments of crisis, seen in light of overall U.S. foreign policy toward the Soviet Union.

The rhetoric of "rollback," and the policies of "bridge building," "differentiation," and so on, were aimed at Eastern Europe insofar as change within that region might affect the problem of Soviet power in Europe, which was expressed largely through the hegemonic Soviet power position in the region. This proved true whether U.S.-Soviet relations were good or bad: When bad, Eastern Europe was seen as a lever to be used against Moscow; when good, Washington was reluctant to press its presence in ways that might incur Moscow's displeasure over a region that the United States had long conceded to be an area of vital Soviet security interest. Washington did not want to jeopardize superior U.S. interests at stake in its relations with the other superpower, such as arms control or political detente. The United States thus never developed an independent concept for Eastern Europe, one that responded directly to the problems and concerns of the region as such, as opposed to the ways in which regional problems related to the broader question of dealing with Soviet power in Europe.

Given the fact that the United States has not begun seriously to develop a policy concept for the Soviet republics that is even loosely comparable to the policy of "differentiation" toward Eastern Europe, and given the determined wager on Gorbachev and the survival of the central Soviet state that had been made by the Bush administration, it will be some time before the United States will be in a position to take the lead in formulating a concept or policy that could help guide it in responding to the disintegration of the USSR. At best, the United States seems to have been prepared to follow Gorbachev's lead in developing ties with the union republics. Gorbachev's eclipse by Yeltsin in August 1991 means that the republics will have an increasingly free hand in determining the character of their international policies.

What *are* the U.S. interests that might be affected by the disintegration of the USSR, whether that disintegration be violent or peaceful, whether it result in a stable reconfiguration of ties among the existing Soviet republics or a more chaotic set of political associations? The geopolitical interests at play have to be seen in light of the broader U.S. stake in world politics. Apart from the question of survival as a nation, which because of the U.S. ideology transcends physical survival or territorial integrity to embrace the nature of the U.S. political system, the primary U.S. interest in international politics is that there be a plural and if possible, a stable, distribution of global power. The prosperity, security, and political health of the United States depend not on the reproduction of the U.S. system worldwide, or even upon U.S. predominance in world affairs. It is sufficient for the protection and promotion of U.S. interests only that such predominance be denied to any single state or agglomeration of states. When the rhetoric of democratic idealism is put aside, such was the motivation for U.S. intervention in the two world wars and for the policy of containment of the Soviet Union following 1947.[23]

The consequence of the global deployment of U.S. power after 1945 has been the reestablishment of strong societies and political systems in Western Europe and Japan, the foundations of resistance to any prospective Soviet bid for hegemony over Eurasia, and thus the world. As I suggested in Chapter 1, this stable anchoring of the balance of power came into being long before the collapse of Soviet power in Europe in 1989. That collapse only serves to emphasize the conducive nature of the contemporary international system to U.S. interests. (That the United States could send half a million troops to Iraq, a country 200 miles from the Soviet frontier, and conduct a smashing military campaign with Soviet acquiescence is a striking testimony to the radically receptive character of the international system today to U.S. power.)

This analysis suggests that it will be the international, as opposed to internal, conduct of states, including those of the former USSR, that will prove decisive in framing U.S. foreign policy choices on issues of vital interest to the United States. Part of the problem is that it is becoming increasingly difficult to disentangle internal from international conduct in the case of the Soviet region today. The international behavior of the "sovereign" republics has fast overtaken the ability of any central authority to regulate it. This is what is meant by the end of Soviet foreign policy, as we have known it since 1917.

Yet, whereas the disintegration of the USSR will continue to spawn new international relationships, the collapse of the Soviet position in East Central Europe since 1989—the foundation, in fact, of the USSR's entire global standing as a superpower—means that for the United States (Europe is a separate matter) developments within the former USSR no longer have the significance that they had when it stood astride Central Europe as the world's second superpower. The existence of a strong Western Europe, based on a powerful and unified Germany, on the one hand, and of a stable East Asia, based on a unified China and an economically (and potentially militarily) powerful Japan, on the other, provides effective "shock absorbers" against the spread of social, economic, and political instability across formerly Soviet borders in the event of a violent denouement in the Soviet area. Within that context, there is very little that could happen in a geopolitical sense as a result of the disintegration of the USSR that could affect truly vital U.S. security interests, as they have been traditionally conceived.

The Promise of Russian Nationalism

This does not mean that there will not be serious consequences as a result of the end of the USSR. There will be such consequences, although they may just as easily be positive in character as negative. This is certainly true as far as the political forces represented by Boris Yeltsin are concerned. Contrary to widespread consensus, the Russian nationalism expressed by Yeltsin is thoroughly healthy in nature. Indeed, it is the first genuine expression of political nationalism in the history of Russia, i.e., the idea that the historical mission of Russia is restricted to an essentially ethnically Russian state (the Russian Federation, of which Yeltsin is president) as opposed to a multinational empire in which the Russians have never been more than a bare majority. If this political concept can be institutionalized, it would provide a sound foundation, much sounder than anything that Gorbachev has proposed, for a democratic Russia. Shorn of the need to keep a multitude of fractious nations in tow, Russia could then dispense with the autocracy that has always been held indispensable to the preservation of the Russian interest at home and abroad.

A vigorous nationalist concept, which Russia has always been denied, could actually provide the political basis for the acceptance of difficult economic reforms that could lead to a market economic system. Such a market, if successful, could actually provide for a much more tightly integrated set of economic relationships among the nations that have made up the USSR than was possible for the essentially mercantilist system of centralized economic planning, which severely retarded the economic integration of the region. It is market forces, as evidenced most dramatically by Western Europe (and the United States itself) that are the most effective agents of economic and eventually political integration. Thus, there may not be a need for an "antidote" to Russian "nationalism," as many have thought. A healthy Russian nationalism, as defined by a vigorous, nonimperial nationalist like Boris Yeltsin, offers the best possibility of containing the ugly xenophobic and anti-Semitic forces (such as the Pamyat' organization). Those forces clothe themselves in the mantle of Russian nationalism but have proved incapable of attracting the sympathy of Russian voters in a series of elections held since 1989.

The reconstruction of the USSR along decentralized lines that is currently being attempted is in fact the best chance of avoiding the cataclysms that preoccupy Soviet citizens and the outside world. At issue has been not the distribution of powers between the central Soviet authorities and the constituent republics but rather the locus of sovereignty in the political system. And sovereignty—the ultimate source of power and legitimacy, the authority to decide upon the strategic directions of a country—is not an item that can be shared. In fact, Gorbachev had been constrained, even before August 1991, to capitulate on the ceding of sovereignty to the republics. A stable agreement on sovereignty—such as that embodied in the declaration of the Commonwealth of Independent States—is essential to overcoming the present political and economic impasse in the region; its absence would make certain the slide of the country into obscurity. Moreover, a prolonged impasse on the locus and terms of sovereignty would lead to the collapse of all recognized authority and a degeneration into one of two possible situations. The Commonwealth area could be balkanized, with the constituent parts seeking a mythic self-sufficiency as protection against the collapse of the general political system, or there could be a desperate effort by those who retain control over the means of coercion, whether civilian or military, to force the union to stay intact (as in August 1991). The results of the latter would be indistinguishable from the chaotic fragmentation of the country, as it would extinguish all possibilities for creative reform.

With such enormous stakes at risk, the international community, in particular, the United States, actually has precious little to say about the prospects for a stable transition to a new political order within the former USSR. Certainly, an unstable disintegration would create considerable costs, mainly economic and social (refugees) for countries along the Soviet borderlands, especially in Eastern Europe. Yet here it is primarily Western Europe, especially Germany, and together with them the framework of the Conference on Security and Cooperation in Europe (CSCE, which includes the United States and Canada as well), that are the appropriate vehicles as the directly affected parties for containing the damages that the shattering of the USSR would cause abroad. In fact, given the smaller scale of the problems of Poland, Czechoslovakia, and Hungary; their demonstrably greater commitment and progress toward democratic reform; and the degree of technical competence to date exhibited, efforts to insulate the international system from the possible shocks of Soviet instability might best be focused on guaranteeing reform in those three countries, beginning with Poland, and moving on to Czechoslovakia, with Hungary last. The United States would, and probably should, be a bystander and restrain its natural enthusiasm to "engineer" a "solution" to a problem that is not susceptible to its influence and that, especially after 1989, is of only secondary interest to it. In any event, between September 1990 and December 1991, the international community committed $80 billion in various forms of official aid to the USSR. This does not include additional billions in private gifts and debt relief. Clearly, it will take years for the Russian and other Commonwealth governments to absorb just this amount—comparable to the Marshall Plan and Soviet Lend-Lease programs—effectively. Interestingly, over 57 percent of such aid has been provided by one country: Germany.[24]

Indeed, the unfortunate record of U.S. "support" of Gorbachev, which actually seems to have bolstered the confidence of the coup junta that their efforts would be at least tacitly tolerated, argues strongly in favor of U.S. restraint. What the United States, and Americans, can do in order to understand and respond helpfully to the current crisis in the USSR is, first, to rid themselves of their stereotypes about Russian nationalism and of their preoccupation with any single political personality, such as Gorbachev or Yeltsin. They need to cast their vision of the Commonwealth and the issues confronting it much more widely than the central "authorities." At a minimum, the United States should take care not to make its political and economic engagements with the region a retardant to the positive disintegration that is required if a long-term stable set of political relationships is to be established on the terrritory of the former USSR.

In truth, there is another issue that is deeply affected by the political and nationalist convulsion of the USSR and that, for the United States, far outweighs the question of the success or failure of Soviet political and economic reform. That concerns the nuclear future of the nations currently making up the Commonwealth. Even during the height of the cold war, as indicated in Chapter 2, the logic of the nuclear age had imposed certain patterns of strategic collaboration between the USSR and the United States, including arms control, confidence-building measures, strategic signaling, and the sharing of information necessary for the effective control of nuclear weapons. The prospect of an unstable disintegration of a USSR bristling with 27,000 nuclear weapons throughout its various now independent republics is sure to reinforce the exclusively bilateral, Moscow-focused direction of past U.S.-Soviet relations, and for very good reasons: Nuclear weapons are the only conceivable threat to vital U.S. interests emanating from the former USSR today.

When the nuclear relationship is stripped of its strategic, geopolitical aspect, its management, which had served the USSR so well in establishing and maintaining its otherwise ill-deserved parity with the United States, will continue to bind the U.S. government to those within the USSR or its equivalent who control the instruments of mass destruction. The Soviet General Staff has already taken note of this problem, which was brought dramatically to light in 1990 by the development of an arms race within the USSR itself, as contending nationalist forces resorted to raiding Soviet military arsenals in support of their own causes. Upwards of 500,000 weapons, primarily small arms but including several surface-to-air missiles, tanks, helicopters, and other armored vehicles, were stolen from the Soviet military in 1990. In early 1990, a Soviet military base containing nuclear weapons in Azerbaijan also came under attack. It is in this context that Marshal Mikhail Moiseyev, who was then chief of the General Staff, declared in late September 1990 that it had begun the task of moving Soviet nuclear weapons based in non-Russian territories back to Russia. (This still begs the question of the political intentions of a Yeltsin Russian government toward nuclear weapons and the military, as well as that of the possible disintegration of Russia itself, which cannot be excluded.) Former defense minister Dmitri Yazov, on October 20, 1990, declared that all intercontinental nuclear-charged missiles, that is, those capable of striking the United States, were based in the Slavic republics of the USSR. (His statement seemed designed to provide political reassurances: The Slavic republics of Belorussia and Ukraine, in addition to demanding their own armies, have stated their intention of becoming nonnuclear states.) Later that October, then–CIA chief William Webster noted that there still exists tight central control over Soviet nuclear weapons.[25]

As of early 1992 this situation holds, although since the failure of the August 1991 coup those non-Russian republics on whose territory nuclear weapons are based, especially the Ukraine, have demanded an equal voice with Russia and the union authorities in decisions affecting the disposition of nuclear weapons on their national territories. In the Ukrainian view, decisions to relocate or destroy Ukrainian-based nuclear weapons may not be taken without the consent of the Ukrainian government. The central authorities, mainly the Soviet military, continue to exert physical custody over Soviet nuclear weapons.

As in the case of the Soviet military statements, however, the question is, who is the center? The Communist Party, which has collapsed; the newly formed State Council, representing the republics and what remains of a central government; the military and intelligence agencies themselves? This is all extremely doubtful at the moment. Indeed, it is difficult to identify any agency of civilian control over the Soviet military's nuclear establishment other than the person of Boris Yeltsin himself.[26] In the aftermath of the August 1991 coup, during which Gorbachev's codes for the release of nuclear weapons had been forcibly removed from his control, even this can no longer be taken for granted. Certainly, it is difficult to discern any agency of civilian "governance" worthy of confidence about its general organizational competence or its ability to discipline the Soviet military's nuclear authorities. Indeed, in its annual review of Soviet foreign policy, the Soviet Foreign Ministry in early 1991 counted among the security threats facing the USSR "the continuing risk of an accidental or unsanctioned use of arms. (This risk might increase in the event of internal disturbances in regions where strategic facilities are located.)"[27]

Outside of Yeltsin, it would seem that the command and control of the Soviet strategic nuclear system are shared by the Soviet strategic military command, which control the strategic nuclear weapons themselves, and the intelligence service, which holds the codes for the activation of the nuclear warheads. Those who can demonstrate effective control over Soviet nuclear weapons will be able to determine the basic framework of future U.S. relations with the region. The postwar history of those relations has conclusively demonstrated that the two powers' nuclear bond overshadows every other aspect of their policies toward each other. This can be expected to continue in the future, even if it means that the United States must choose between the Soviet military and the forces for reform. As William Webster said, in the event that the USSR should "disintegrate . . . then we would have to see who are the people moving to take control over those particular weapons."[28] In short, and in confirmation of my broader theme, relations with the forces that assert control over the central arsenal of mass destruction—be it Yeltsin and the Commonwealth, as now; the military, as might be; or the "sovereign" republics, as is also possible—will continue to be the prism by which all other aspects of the U.S. relationship with the post-Soviet region are refracted.

Webster has raised a key point, which has hardly been examined in the political or academic communities in the United States: the relationship between domestic political order and nuclear weapons. The collapse of the USSR challenges the unstated assumption of nuclear deterrence and arms control that the major nuclear powers are also stable states. It is therefore not enough to develop arms control, no matter how broad in scope, on a purely state-to-state basis. It is now essential that the approach to controlling nuclear weapons take into account the character of the political systems of the nuclear states themselves. This represents a profound challenge to the way we have thought about nuclear arms control, for it implies the progressive divorce of nuclear arsenals from national control.

The question is whether an internationalized approach to nuclear arms control can be developed, after the fashion of the International Atomic Energy Agency in the civilian application of nuclear energy. Perhaps one way to start conceptualizing this process is to return to the dawn of the nuclear age. In 1946 the internationalized approach to nuclear energy was universally accepted as the only legitimate one. Some combination of national and international oversight of national nuclear weapons establishments seems necessary in order to insulate the management of nuclear weapons, an intrinsically global affair, from the by comparison parochial vicissitudes of national politics. What that combination might be is at this stage unclear. Perhaps the extension of the Nuclear Nonproliferation Treaty to include the union republics, which are institutionally fully competent to make such an undertaking, might be a first step in this direction. This might be linked to an international research and verification agency, which could employ nuclear specialists from East and West, in part to stem any flow of scientific talent from contributing to nuclear weapons programs of unstable states. It is clear that citizens of East and West must reexamine approaches to deterrence and arms control. The current situation makes security a hostage not merely to allegedly rational political actors but also to potentially explosive and irrational political, and economic, forces.

Notes

1. The language of Gorbachev's referendum item was, "Do you consider it necessary to preserve the Union of Soviet Socialist Republics as a renewed federation of equal sovereign republics, in which human rights and the freedom of people of all nationalities will be fully guaranteed?" Of the 80 percent of the 185 million eligible voters casting ballots, about 76 percent—or 58 percent of the eligible voters—voted yes. This must be qualified by the following facts: Of the fifteen union republics, six—Armenia, Georgia, Moldavia, Lithuania, Latvia, and Estonia—representing about 10 percent of the total Soviet population, abstained from the voting altogether. Only four—Belorussia, Kirghizia, Tadzhikistan, and Turkmenistan—accepted the referendum as proposed, whereas in the Ukraine, 70 percent of the voters approved a parallel referendum item reaffirming its 1990 Declaration of Sovereignty, which asserts independent nation-state status for the Ukraine. In Russia proper, 70 percent of those voting approved a parallel refer-

endum item calling for the direct election of the Russian president, in effect an endorsement of Boris Yeltsin, Gorbachev's leading opponent. For the language of the various referenda, see *New York Times,* March 17, 1991, p. 10; for voting results, see RFE/RL Research Institute, *Report on the USSR,* April 5, 1991, p. 31; and March 29, 1991, pp. 21–22 and passim.

2. *Financial Times,* June 8–9, 1991, p. 2.

3. Ibid.

4. Ibid., July 30, 1991, p. 2, and *RFE/RL Daily Report,* July 30, 1991, p. 1.

5. According to Matthew Sagers, director of the energy services section of Planecon, *RFE/RL Daily Report,* August 6, 1991, p. 3. Sagers maintained that the export figures reported by Moscow do not square with the totals of oil imports registered in Western countries and in Eastern Europe.

6. Vera Micheles Dean, *The United States and Russia* (Cambridge: Harvard University Press, 1948), p. 23.

7. Only indirect and circumstantial corroboration in writing can be found on this point. See Desmond Ball, "The Development of the SIOP, 1960–1983," in Desmond Ball and Jeffrey Richelson, eds., *Strategic Nuclear Targeting* (Ithaca, N.Y.: Cornell University Press, 1986), pp. 76–77; David T. Coltell and George Quester, "Ethnic Targeting: Some Bad Ideas," in ibid., pp. 267–284; Zbigniew Brzezinski, *Power and Principle, Memoirs of the National Security Advisor, 1977–1981* (New York: Farrar, Straus, Giroux, 1983), pp. 454–459; and Raymond Garthoff, *Detente and Confrontation: American-Soviet Relations from Nixon to Reagan* (Washington, D.C.: Brookings Institution, 1985), pp. 789–790.

8. The State Department has consistently refused to oppose the use of force by the central Soviet authorities in dealing with intercommunal and other tensions in the Soviet Caucasus. In response to raids by the Soviet army against Armenian villages in the disputed territory of Nagorno-Karabakh in early May 1991, the State Department urged that only a "minimum" of force be used to end Armenian-Azerbaijani unrest. As reported in *New York Times,* May 10, 1991, p. A11.

9. For the text of Bush's speech, see *New York Times,* August 2, 1991, p. A10.

10. As monitored by the Harriman Institute Soviet TV Project, August 19, 1991.

11. *Izvestiya,* April 22, 1990.

12. *Narodnaya Armiya* (Sofia), April 6, 1990.

13. *Moscow News,* May 1–7, 1990.

14. *RFE/RL Daily Report,* March 14, 1990.

15. *RFE/RL Daily Report,* October 15, 1990. The Fitzwater statement was made on October 12, 1990.

16. *RFE/RL Daily Report,* September 27 and October 8, 1990.

17. *RFE/RL Daily Report,* November 20, 1990.

18. *Financial Times* (London), March 21, 1991. For a ringing French endorsement of Gorbachev, see the account of French President François Mitterrand's Moscow May 1991 meeting with the Soviet leader in *Le Monde,* May 8, 1990.

19. The news conference took place on March 20, 1990. The U.S. government has published only excerpts from the formal statement made at the outset by Marlin Fitzwater. See *Weekly Compilation of Presidential Documents,* March 26,

1990, p. 444. See ibid., March 19, 1990, for a formal statement on U.S. policy toward the Baltic states. The dialogue is taken from *Rabochaya Tribuna,* March 25, 1990, as translated in Foreign Broadcast Information Service, *Daily Report. Soviet Union,* March 26, 1990.

20. Kathleen Mihalisko, "Belorussia as a Sovereign State: An Interview with Henady Hrushavy," in Radio Liberty, *Report on the USSR,* August 31, 1990, pp. 11–16. For a discussion of the Ukrainian declaration of sovereignty, see Mihalisko, "Ukraine's Declaration of Sovereignty," ibid., July 27, 1990, pp. 17–19. For the text of the Belorussian declaration, see *Sovetskaya Belorussiya,* July 28, 1990.

21. *Financial Times,* April 10, 1991.

22. See the op-ed piece by Roman Szporluk in the *New York Times,* January 23, 1991, p. A19.

23. David F. Trask, *Victory Without Peace* (New York: Wiley, 1968).

24. European Community data, as cited in *The New York Times,* January 23, 1992, p. A8.

25. As reported by Reuters, October 25, 1990; see the *Washington Post,* October 20, 1990, for a statement by Soviet Defense Minister Yazov on the location of Soviet strategic nuclear missiles; RFE/RL Research Institute, *Report on the USSR,* October 12, 1990, p. 35; and Alexander Rahr and R. Alex Bryan, "Concern Over Security of Soviet Nuclear Arms," ibid., pp. 6–7; and *Washington Post,* September 28, 1990.

26. As reported in *New York Times,* August 24, 1991, p. 9.

27. "Vneshnepoliticheskaya i diplomaticheskaya deyatel'nost' SSSR," *Mezhdunarodonaya Zhizn',* no. 3 (March 1991), p. 16.

28. As reported by Reuters, October 25, 1990.

9

Prospects

Before turning to the political implications of this reconsideration of East-West and U.S.-Soviet relations, past, present, and future, let us briefly summarize the main findings of this book. They are:

1. The revolutions in Soviet foreign policy since 1985 and in East-Central Europe since 1989 have shattered not the cold war order in East-West relations but rather the post–cold war order that had been established by the early 1970s on the basis of the division of Germany and the division of Europe. As a result, although remarkable progress has been made in demilitarizing the remnants of the East-West political-military confrontation in the past several years, governments in East and West find themselves confronted with problems—such as the unification of Germany and the open expression of nationalist aspirations in Eastern Europe and the "post"-Soviet Union—that defy the long-established patterns of interbloc (and intrabloc) political management.

2. Parallel with this heritage of geopolitical collaboration in the name of "stability," one can identify an even more intense framework of strategic collaboration between the Soviet Union and the United States in managing their potentially deadly nuclear relationship. This can be expected to continue, irrespective of the political fluctuations that have been endemic to U.S.-Soviet relations even in periods of relaxed tensions.

3. The history of U.S. relations with Eastern Europe from 1945 to 1989 demonstrates that the United States has viewed its policies toward this region in strict subordination to its broader Soviet policy. In part, this has reflected U.S. sensitivity to the implications of a possible confrontation with the USSR in a region deemed vital to Soviet security interests. It has also reflected the fact that as long as Soviet hegemony

was effectively denied to the western half of Europe, the political fate of Eastern Europe did not directly intersect the vital security interests of the United States. If Eastern Europe during that period is viewed as constituting the USSR's "outer empire," then the postwar history of U.S. policy toward the region can serve as a test case of likely U.S. policy toward a disintegrating USSR. The historical record strongly suggests that the United States will, as it did in Eastern Europe, view its policies toward the post-Soviet republics in subordination to its relations to the Russian government, as long as that government retains effective command and control of Soviet nuclear weapons.

4. The unintended consequences of Mikhail Gorbachev's political reforms, bold as they have been, have unleashed political, and in particular nationalist, forces beyond his initial comprehension. The disintegration of the Soviet political system and thereby of the bipolar assumption in world politics has resulted. Gorbachev had moved so rapidly since the spring of 1991 to accommodate these newly dominant political forces that the West (which remains confused by Soviet nationalisms) found itself attempting to support a Gorbachev that Gorbachev himself had already abandoned.

5. There is an impressive body of Soviet policy-analytical work, much of it predating the Gorbachev period, which provides important context to the foreign policy changes over which Gorbachev has presided. This literature, and the influential positions that many of its authors now hold in the Russian foreign policy establishment, demonstrate that the Gorbachev foreign policy has not been a set of tactical maneuvers, however brilliant, but rather reflects a serious reexamination of the USSR's relationship to its international environment.

6. By 1990, the virtual collapse of Soviet foreign policy had occurred. A series of deeply rooted factors, both internal and international, practically prohibit any of the USSR's constituent parts from entertaining hegemonic ambitions for the foreseeable future. The eclipse of Mikhail Gorbachev implies that the West will have to shed itself of its past preoccupation with the Soviet leader if it is to think creatively about its future ties with the Soviet successor states.

7. The Soviet ideology of Marxism-Leninism will retain specific importance for the direction of post-Soviet internal and international policy for some time to come. The intellectual categories of Soviet ideology retain their hold on many of those operating within a post-Soviet political system. Whereas the content of the ideology has changed in many critical ways, the presentation of ideology is still seen as an important weapon in the struggle for power. Soviet ideology will thus continue to affect the manner of adjustment to the international environment, although in the long run its impact will surely decline

as nationalist forces fill the void of the central Soviet government and new generations come to power.

8. The USSR has disintegrated as a functioning political unit. The United States cannot avoid being affected by this basic political fact. At the same time, Soviet collapse will actually tend to reinforce the pattern of nuclear collaboration between the United States and those who maintain control over nuclear weapons on post-Soviet territory. Yet the historic inability of the United States to come to terms with nationalism in the USSR finds the former ill prepared to react to a wholly new issue in world politics: the relationship of the internal political order of unstable nuclear states to nuclear arms control.

So, what does it all mean? What can be said on the basis of this analysis about the likely tendencies in East-West relations and their implications for the United States? One should be cautious here about raising false expectations, especially as I have argued, at my peril, that part of the explanation for the haphazard progress in the study of Soviet foreign policy over the past two decades lies in the pervasive policy orientation of the field. By that I mean that scholars of the Soviet Union's international relationships have been almost universally absorbed with contemporary Soviet policy and, less explicitly but more troublesome, with its alleged implications for U.S. foreign policy.[1] Given the U.S. culture's propensity for clear and quick answers to problems of public policy (as if any "solution" in social life does not entail its own specific problems), scholars are expected to provide wisdom of a kind that is usually beyond the bounds of the scholarly vocation. William Zimmerman, a social scientist specializing on Soviet foreign policy, has made the following observation on this situation in his field:

> There is much that we do not know. Some of it we cannot know. One of the problems that persists in relations between policymakers and academics is that policymakers [and journalists and the public] want to know the answers to single-shot questions. Will the Soviet Union, for instance, intervene in Poland in the next several weeks? Academics do not know the answer to that and ought not to claim that they can know the answer. This is not the kind of scientific knowledge which can be achieved. . . . There is very little that we can know about Soviet foreign policy in the future except to specify limits or ranges.[2]

Adam Ulam added the cautionary note that the first obligation of the student of Soviet affairs is "to be neither hopeful nor pessimistic, but simply to state the facts and tendencies of Russian politics. It is when he begins to see in certain political trends the inevitabilities of the future and when he superimposes upon them his own conclusions about the desirable policies of America toward the USSR that he is courting trouble."[3]

Consequently, what this concluding chapter can offer is my understanding of how the evolution of East-West relations has shaped their present structure and, furthermore, what that structure might imply for the range of choice in future U.S. policy after the collapse of the post–cold war order. It would be presumptuous to provide a set of policy prescriptions. In the final analysis the choice of policies depends on one's political values, not on a particular political analysis. Such analysis can clarify the opportunity costs involved in a given political situation, but it cannot as a practical matter substitute for the specific values that individuals, social classes, political groups, and parties bring to matters of social choice. Nor should it, as a matter of democratic justice. It is therefore best to distinguish as rigorously as possible the practice of politics from its study.

There are five areas where our reconsideration of the character of the East-West relationship, and in particular of its U.S.-Soviet component, warrants a reexamination of U.S. foreign policies: the consequences of the current balance of international power for the overall world role of the United States; U.S. policy toward the Soviet successor states; the control of nuclear weapons; the possibilities of establishing effective institutions of multilateral security; and the opportunity costs for the United States itself of the international choices that now lie, perceived or not, before it.

The New Balance of Power and the U.S. World Role

The collapse of communism in East-Central Europe and the subsequent expulsion of the USSR as a political-military presence in the heart of Europe only emphasizes the profoundly receptive nature of the contemporary international political system to the national interests of the United States. As I argued in earlier chapters, the two superpowers by the early 1970s had been able to remove Europe, the very centerpiece of the cold war, as a bone of contention in their relationship. The dismantling of the Soviet military infrastructure in Eastern Europe, and now the collapse of the Communist Party's authority within the USSR itself, have removed even the theoretical possibility, regardless of intentions, of any early aggression against Europe. Indeed, the reformation of the USSR along decentralized lines is beginning to erect internal barriers in the form of more pluralistic political systems. Those will themselves act as a check against the recrudescence of expansionist tendencies.

The European Community, anchored on a strong, united, prosperous, and democratic Germany, is fully capable of constituting on its own that pole of stability that has always been the aim of postwar U.S. foreign policy. Although it may be preferable to maintain the reassurance afforded by the North Atlantic Treaty, as well as a symbolic commitment of U.S. military forces in Europe, a major U.S. military presence there is no longer needed to discourage a potential hostile hegemonic enterprise. That was the justification for U.S. intervention against Germany in two world wars and again against the spread of Soviet power after World War II.

Turning to Asia, any danger of future Soviet or Russian aggression, which seems daily more hypothetical, is adequately taken into account by the simple existence of a strong, unified PRC and an economically powerful Japan. Here the United States has long played a more indirect role in reinforcing the balance of power: Apart from the presence of a relatively limited number of troops in Japan and Korea, the U.S. role has entailed maintaining normal relations with China, which has its own national interest in containing the expansion of Soviet and/or Russian power. The European role of the United States might come to resemble its secondary part in East Asian security. The macrostability of the contemporary Eurasian balance of power strongly suggests that this can be prudently managed.

The truth of the matter is that for many decades the United States itself has not had to be the main pillar of the global balance of power. What the collapse of Soviet foreign policy since 1989 has done is to make that recognition palatable in terms of U.S. domestic politics. As George Kennan recognized in formulating the policy of containment in the late 1940s, the vital interests of the United States, i.e., the preservation of the political system and way of life, did not require that the U.S. system be emulated throughout the world but only that a hostile concentration of international power be prevented. In the political context of the time, with the onset of what would become known as McCarthyism, the limited foreign policy thereby implied proved impossible to implement, and Kennan soon resigned from the State Department's Policy Planning Staff.

It is interesting that all three specific objectives that Kennan established as the goal of containment policy, which itself continues to undergird the global political-military presence of the United States, have now been achieved. These were (1) the restoration of self-confidence in the nations then threatened by the Soviet Union; (2) a significant reduction in Soviet ability to project its influence abroad; and (3) a modification in the Soviet concept of international relations, so as to facilitate the settlement of outstanding differences between East and West.[4] Considering that roughly half of the annual U.S. defense budget has in recent decades been devoted to the problem of European defense—about $150 billion per year in current dollars—the time may have arrived to consider whether this is the most cost-effective way to achieve its purpose, i.e., to secure the U.S. political system and way of life.

There are certain implications of such a modest view of the global role of the United States. One of them is certainly the relative increase in the geopolitical influence that a more unified European Community, and within it Germany, will have on European, East European, and world affairs. Yet, as we have seen in the extraordinary progress toward a common European economic space by 1992 and the still more startling unification of Germany in 1990, the increase in Europe's specific political weight is inevitable. Moreover, in the final analysis, the ability of Europe, especially Germany, to anchor the East European states and eventually the Soviet successor states in a strong European economic and political framework represents the best hope for long-term stability in that region. As the historian Dominic Lieven has forcefully argued, "The German economic, moral, and political miracles since the Second World War are the foundations for whatever optimism we may have about the future Europe."[5] A democratic Germany—nurtured by the United States—tightly integrated into a broader European political and economic environment may now assume the political role for which its economic position destines it.

The specifics of the European response to this challenge, that is, how they propose to assume the political and security burdens so long borne by the United States, is a matter primarily for the Europeans themselves to resolve. Their choice, whatever it is, will affect only the relative distribution of political and economic power within Europe, i.e., how strong Germany will be permitted to become; it cannot change the fact that there now is a stable core of strong European states that themselves can maintain the balance of power in western Eurasia. There is a sum—impossible to identify with precision but certainly far lower than existing spending levels—beyond which U.S. resources spent on reinforcing a Europe that can independently contain European threats to U.S. "security," defined in terms of the health of U.S. domestic institutions, can only serve to diminish that security.[6]

U.S. Policy Toward the Post-Soviet Region

The first point to make about U.S. policy toward the USSR is that, both objectively and subjectively, the "Soviet threat" of the past is no more. The removal of the Soviet army from Europe has undercut the technical possibilities for any rapid Soviet military advance into Europe and at the same time made implausible the Soviet Union's postwar claim to global political parity with the United States. The collapse of the Soviet Communist Party at home after the failed coup of August 1991 has removed the political foundation for any such scenario as well. Furthermore, the evolution of U.S.-Soviet relations since Gorbachev's accession to power has effectively removed the issue of detente as an item on the U.S. political agenda. Ronald Reagan's signature on the INF treaty meant that no longer would detente be debated in U.S. politics: Henceforth, only the level of that detente, and not its desirability (as in the 1970s), would be discussed. In sum, not only has there been a revolution in U.S. perceptions of Soviet intentions—which were argued to be ambiguous and subject to rapid change—but key Soviet capabilities to harm U.S. interests have declined as well. The establishment of Boris Yeltsin's Russian government as the successor to the USSR, and its commitment to view the United States as an "ally," further reinforces the point.

The second point is that in light of the redrawing of power by the Soviet republics, the United States will have to develop a multilevel set of policies toward the new USSR. Such policies must take into account the reality of sovereign republican power, in international as well as internal affairs, if they are to respond adequately to the prospects for reform and a maximally stable "new world order." Americans will need to ask themselves, as they contemplate the question of "supporting" reform: What, and more specifically, whom, are they supporting? With the momentum for reform now coming directly from the republics, as Chapters 4 and 8 have shown, the attempt to provide assistance, whether in the form of capital or rhetoric, to a central authority is likely to prove irrelevant, if not counterproductive, to U.S. intentions.

There is, in addition, the question of whether the United States can have a constructive impact on such internal processes. Aside from the enormous scale of the problem—a region with eleven time zones and nearly 300 million people—there is so much that we do not know about Russian, as distinct from Soviet, politics, that it seems fantastic that serious people speak about what amounts to surgical political-economic intervention in an unprecedented political upheaval. Actually, events have been proceeding in a hopeful direction. The delicate post-coup political balance between Gorbachev and Yeltsin, which before August 1991 found each both too powerful and too weak to act in isolation from the other, served the interests of the Soviet peoples and the international community in devising new political principles for relations among the nations making up the USSR. The outside world should take great care before making itself a player in such processes; by bringing its considerable moral and material weight to bear, the West may upset the process of mutual accommodation or may achieve its alleged goals of sustaining reform. In truth, we do not, and cannot, know which will be the likely effect. As outsiders to the process, with an unenviable analytical record in the past, we might best learn how to restrain ourselves. The inadvertent Western role in encouraging the coup junta—by making it appear that the West would support almost any effort to preserve the historical USSR—should serve as an important cautionary note about U.S. ability to communicate intelligently with foreign cultures. (As noted earlier, the USSR had already received $80 billion in outside aid commitments just between September 1990 and December 1991; it will take years to absorb such sums effectively.)

Policy on Nuclear Arms Control

The signature of the Strategic Arms Reduction (START) Treaty by the United States and the Soviet Union at the Moscow summit meeting in late July 1991 presents an opportunity to move rapidly toward effective, if not complete, disarmament in the field of nuclear weapons. Cynics pointed out that the treaty reduces Soviet and U.S. strategic nuclear weapons only to the excessive levels each side possessed when the negotiations began in 1982. Yet this is the first agreement that codifies the principle of reducing, rather than simply ratifying, existing levels of strategic nuclear weapons. Moreover, the treaty incorporates agreed principles for counting existing weapons systems, for reducing those systems, and for mandatory on-site verification to ensure that its terms are being faithfully executed. The additional impulse given nuclear arms control in September 1991 by U.S. and Soviet agreement unilaterally to eliminate all tactical nuclear weapons, stand down strategic nuclear bombers from alert status, and aim for further early reductions in strategic nuclear weapons opens up even broader prospects for denuclearizing the U.S.-Soviet relationship. Boris Yeltsin has since committed the Russian government to a comprehensive denuclearization of the Russian-American relationship.

The challenge for the future will be how to build on these precedents so as to achieve further significant reductions in the most stable possible way. This entails at least three kinds of steps, each of varying complexity. First, the progress registered by the START treaty, combined with the collapse of even a hypothetical threat by the Soviet army, means that it is now feasible to begin to break the link between nuclear weapons and both Soviet and U.S. foreign policies. The withdrawal of the Soviet army from Europe means that the United States no longer needs to rely upon nuclear weapons in Europe to deter the USSR. The thousands of "tactical" nuclear weapons based in and around Europe that give credibility to U.S.

promises to "defend" Europe have lost their function. The obsolescence of such "extended deterrence" means that the political pressures to integrate nuclear weapons into overall U.S. security policy, i.e., to view nuclear weapons as actual tools of policy rather than as the ultimate guarantee of national survival, can now in principle be overcome. President Bush's unilateral commitment in September 1991 to eliminate all tactical nuclear weapons reflects recognition of this insight.

Second, shorn of the need to extract political capital from intrinsically unusable nuclear weapons, the United States is now free to examine seriously the requirements for minimal nuclear deterrence. That is, what is the minimum number and disposition of nuclear weapons needed to deter attack upon the United States? A radically reduced nuclear force would emphasize the progressive divorce of nuclear weapons from foreign and security policies; it would therefore complicate efforts to "renuclearize" foreign policies, with its attendant risks. A smaller force would also be easier to control, as it would be more secure against terrorist attack and the kind of political instability that has engulfed the USSR. Such reduced forces would also lend themselves more easily to internationalized control, should that someday prove feasible. In addition, and not the least important, a radically reduced nuclear force would in the long run be much less expensive to maintain, given that currently about $60 billion annually is spent by the United States on its nuclear arsenal. (The USSR, which had been examining the idea for several years, submitted to the UN secretary general in July 1991 a proposal for the five nuclear powers on the Security Council to adopt a military doctrine of "minimal nuclear deterrence," with "corresponding reductions in nuclear forces and changes in their role in foreign policy.")[7]

Third, it is also true that smaller need not be better. In theory, a set of very small nuclear forces (say, in the dozens, as opposed to the thousands at the disposal of the two nuclear superpowers today) could be vulnerable to surprise attack and thus susceptible to preemptive use in a crisis. Great care should be taken, then, in deciding how nuclear forces are to be reduced. In the best case, weapons (especially missiles) with multiple nuclear warheads should be phased out. If every nuclear weapon carried only one warhead, it would be theoretically impossible for a rationally calculated nuclear aggression to take place. Because, given the uncertainties involved—these systems never having actually been used—planners have to assign at least two warheads to each target, an aggressor would have to use his entire nuclear force to destroy at most half of an adversary's, ceteris paribus. Adding mobility to the remaining forces, as is done today with missile-bearing submarines and movable missiles, would increase a potential aggressor's uncertainties and hence reinforce stability. In this strategic context, an antiballistic missile system—although costly and perhaps impracticable—need not prove destabilizing, as the limits on the numbers, kinds, and deployments of offensive forces would preclude a decapitating first strike. There would thus be no way in which an offensive force could hide behind a defensive shield for offensive purposes, as the offensive forces would be incapable of sufficiently damaging a counterpart's forces. It would be even theoretically impossible to use nuclear weapons to secure strategic advantage. The joint Yeltsin-Bush press conference of February 1, 1992, suggests considerable movement in this direction.

At the same time, Americans might begin thinking about whether they need nuclear weapons at all. It is only nuclear weapons, in the final analysis, that have proved capable of jeopardizing the territorial integrity and survival of the United States. Unlike the Soviet Union, which was threatened with national extinction in the prenuclear age (i.e., by the Nazis), nuclear weapons per se do not provide any margin of security for the United States. Although the post-1945 proliferation of nuclear knowledge and technologies and the irreducible Russian interest in some nuclear deterrent guarantees that the nuclear genie cannot be put back in the bottle, serious thought might be given to internationalizing the military applications of nuclear energy. The receptivity of the USSR to on-site inspection, as proven in a series of nuclear and conventional arms control agreements since 1986, indicates that a latter day Baruch Plan for the control of nuclear energy worldwide may now be feasible. Such a scheme, should it prove practicable, would have the distinct advantage of providing a mechanism for addressing the question of political instability in nuclear states, thus dissociating the control of nuclear weapons from domestic political instabilities. It could also provide an agency for employing ex-Soviet nuclear scientists, thereby reinforcing the nuclear nonproliferation regime.

A first step in this direction, which could be concluded rapidly judging from the Soviet republics' political views, could be to extend the Nuclear Nonproliferation Treaty to include the fifteen union republics of the USSR. Such a measure would not only have a confidence-inducing effect within and without the region, it would also provide a precedent for applying a joint international/national approach for the control of nuclear weapons.

Toward Multilateral Security

The case for extending the Nuclear Nonproliferation Treaty to the USSR's union republics also highlights the opportunity to build a more effective framework of multilateral security in the "new world order."

Russia is prepared for such a demarche; consistent Soviet support for U.S. policy in the United Nations on isolating and then defeating Saddam Hussein's Iraq—itself a long-time Soviet ally—affords convincing proof of this. The Gulf War also demonstrated that the United Nations can be a cost-effective mechanism for maintaining the plural and stable distribution of international power that is the irreducible U.S. interest in world politics.

The question is whether Americans, politicians and people alike, are willing to accept a cession of sovereignty and a diminution of influence in specific situations in exchange for rooting generally applicable principles of conflict resolution in international relations. They will first have to confront, on the political as well as on the social level, the deeply rooted ambivalence in U.S. society about the U.S. world vocation: In short, need compromise with the outside world compromise U.S. values?

The Opportunity and the Opportunity Costs That Beckon

The United States in 1992 is confronting in its foreign policy what the philosophers deem to be one of the two sources of frustration in life: It has succeeded. It is now politically impossible to deny what I have argued in this book happened long ago: that the cold war is over (again). The Soviet threat has disappeared. A stable balance of power has become firmly established in Eurasia; furthermore, that balance can now be largely maintained independent of U.S. efforts. An enormous opportunity thus presents itself to Americans, one of which the impoverished Soviet peoples can only dream, i.e., to initiate a substantial and effective reallocation of its resources from the military to the civilian sphere and to rethink the nature of its engagements with the wider world. How substantial that reallocation should be and what its character should be are beyond my competence to judge. What is not at dispute is that the revolution in East-West relations engendered by the collapse of the post–cold war order presents to the United States the most unthreatening political-military environment in world politics since World War II.

Beneath the opportunity also lies an opportunity cost. The indices of social decay throughout the United States are so dramatic that a refusal to exploit the opportunity will very likely serve to undermine the values of the United States that were presumably being defended on the front lines of the cold war. Sovietologists have pointed out that a handful of social indicators were enough to show the pathological crisis into which Soviet society had fallen: the drop in male life expectancy in the 1970s, the dramatic increases in infant mortality rates, and the quantum jump in female alcoholism. When nearly one-fourth of U.S. children entering the first grade in the late 1980s were living below the poverty line; when nearly half of the children in high school have taken illegal drugs; when a male in East Harlem is less likely to survive to the age of forty than the average citizen of Bangladesh, and life expectancy for the U.S. black male population as a whole has been declining every year since 1985; when the chances of an urban black male between the ages of fifteen and twenty-four being killed are about one in thirty, that is, higher than those of U.S. soldiers in World War II—all of this suggests, as conclusively as did comparable Soviet indicators in the 1970s, that the United States is losing control over a large part of its patrimony.[8]

Several years ago, an interesting national discussion arose over a work of comparative history by historian Paul Kennedy entitled, *The Rise and Fall of the Great Powers*.[9] What aroused the U.S. sense of self-conscious angst was Kennedy's apparent suggestion that the United States was destined soon to follow the declining path of all great powers, by virtue of a fatal imbalance in the expenditure of resources on defense, as compared to domestic civilian investment. In fact, the remarkable aspect of Kennedy's book was the astonishingly precise portrayal of how such an imbalance in public expenditure had already come to eviscerate the Soviet system from within, thereby anticipating the implosion of the system that has now come to pass. In reality, and contrary to the public interpretation of Kennedy's message, his book offers a hopeful vision of the U.S. future: Unlike the USSR, the United States—among the least heavily taxed of the advanced industrial nations—can still choose its fate.[10]

Notes

1. My presentation to the Social Science Research Council, January 12, 1989. William Zimmerman, one of the nation's foremost social scientists specializing in Soviet international behavior, wrote in the mid-1980s in this regard: "It distresses me that so little by way of basic knowledge has accumulated, and there is genuine reason to worry who will constitute the cadres to undertake future research." See his article, "What Do Scholars Know About Soviet Foreign Policy?" in Robbin F. Laird and Erik Hoffmann, eds., *Soviet Foreign Policy in a Changing World* (New York: Aldine, 1986), p. 97.

2. Ibid.

3. Adam Ulam, "Anatomy of Policymaking," in ibid., p. 111.

4. For an analysis and supporting documentation, see John Lewis Gaddis and Thomas H. Etzold, eds., *Containment: Documents on American Policy and Strategy* (New York: Columbia University Press, 1978), pp. 25–37 and passim.

5. "Should There Be a Soviet Union? A Conversation Between George Urban and Dominic Lieven, Parts 3 & 4," RFE/RL Research Institute, *Report on the USSR,* July 26, 1991, p. 19.

6. See William W. Kaufmann, *Glasnost, Perestroika, and U.S. Defense Spending* (Washington, D.C.: Brookings Institution, 1990).

7. Ibid., and *Suddeutsche Zeitung* (Munich), July 22, 1991.

8. Murder rates for American black men are provided by the U.S. Department of Justice, as reported by *New York Times,* March 9, 1987, p. A13, and by the Federal Center for Disease Control, as reported in *New York Times,* December 7, 1990, p. A26; information on American black life expectancy is provided by the National Center for Health Statistics, as reported in *New York Times,* November 28, 1990, p. A1; data on children living in poverty is given by the Children's Defense Fund, *A Call For Action To Make Our Nation Safe For Children: A Briefing Book On The Status Of American Children In 1988* (Washington, D.C.: 1988). See also *Economist,* March 30, 1991, pp. 11–12, 17–21, for a sobering account of what it calls "America's wasted blacks."

9. Paul Kennedy, *The Rise and Fall of the Great Powers: Economic Change and Military Conflict from 1500 to 2000* (New York: Random House, 1987).

10. Americans pay in taxes slightly more than half of the taxes of the typical West European. The difference in social environment is telling. According to data gathered by the Center for Community Change, total U.S. federal taxes as a percentage of gross national product are lower than in twenty other industrialized nations. As reported in Tom Wicker, "America's Real Deficit," *New York Times,* November 7, 1990, p. A31.

Documents

Four-Power Agreement on Berlin

On September 3, 1971, the United States, the USSR, Great Britain and France, as the legal occupying powers in Berlin, signed an agreement guaranteeing unimpeded Western access to Berlin, a distinct status for West Berlin vis-à-vis West Germany, and a general improvement in contacts between West Berlin and East Germany. They thereby removed the single most troublesome item from the East-West agenda: twice—in 1948–1949 and in 1961—Soviet-Western confrontation over divided Berlin had brought the world to the edge of war.

PART II. Provisions Relating to the Western Sectors of Berlin.

A. The Government of the Union of Soviet Socialist Republics declares that transit traffic by road, rail and waterways through the territory of the German Democratic Republic [i.e., East Germany] of civilian persons and goods between the Western Sectors of Berlin and the Federal Republic of Germany [i.e., West Germany] will be unimpeded; that such traffic will be facilitated so as to take place in the most simple and expeditious manner; and that it will receive preferential treatment. . . .

B. The Governments of the French Republic, the United Kingdom and the United States of America declare that the ties between the Western Sectors of Berlin and the Federal Republic of Germany will be maintained and developed, taking into account that these sectors continue not to be a constituent part of the Federal Republic of Germany and not to be governed by it. . . .

C. The Government of the Union of Soviet Socialist Republics declares that communications between the Western Sectors of Berlin and areas bordering on these Sectors and those areas of the German Democratic Republic which do not border on these Sectors will be improved. Permanent residents of the Western Sectors of Berlin will be able to travel to and visit such areas for compassionate, family, religious, cultural or commercial reasons, or as tourists, under conditions comparable to those applying to other persons entering these areas. . . .

Source: The Department of State Bulletin *65, no. 1683, September 27, 1971, pp. 318–325.*

U.S.-Soviet Agreement to Reduce the Risk of Nuclear War

On September 30, 1971, the USSR and the United States signed an agreement designed to minimize the risk of nuclear war and confrontation in their mutual relations. It reflects both countries' determination to prevent their broader political competition's leading to a nuclear crisis.

The United States of America and the Union of Soviet Socialist Republics, hereinafter referred to as the Parties:

Taking into account the devastating consequences that nuclear war would have for all mankind, and recognizing the need to exert every effort to avert the risk of outbreak of such a war, including measures to guard against accidental or unauthorized use of nuclear weapons,

Believing that agreement on measures for reducing the risk of outbreak of nuclear war serves the interests of strengthening international peace and security, and is in no way contrary to the interests of any other country,

Bearing in mind that continued efforts are also needed in the future to seek ways of reducing the risk of outbreak of nuclear war,

Have agreed as follows:

Article 1

Each Party undertakes to maintain and to improve, as it deems necessary, its existing organizational and technical arrangements to guard against the accidental or unauthorized use of nuclear weapons under its control.

Article 2

The Parties undertake to notify each other immediately in the event of an accidental, unauthorized or any other unexplained incident involving a possible detonation of a nuclear weapon which could create a risk of possible outbreak of nuclear war. In the event of such an incident, the Party whose nuclear weapon is involved will immediately make every effort to take necessary measures to render harmless or destroy such weapon without its causing damage.

Article 3

The Parties undertake to notify each other immediately in the event of detection by missile warning systems of unidentified objects, or in the event of signs of interference with these systems or with related communications facilities, if such occurrences could create a risk of outbreak of nuclear war between the two countries.

Article 4

Each Party undertakes to notify the other Party in advance of any planned missile launches if such launches will extend beyond its national territory in the direction of the other Party.

Article 5

Each Party, in other situations involving unexplained nuclear incidents, undertakes to act in such a manner as to reduce the possibility of its actions being misinterpreted by the other Party. In any such situation, each Party may inform the other Party or request information when, in its view, this is warranted by the interests of averting the risk of outbreak of nuclear war.

Article 6

For transmission of urgent information, notifications and requests for information in situations requiring prompt clarification, the Parties shall make primary use of the Direct Communications Link [i.e., the "Hotline"] between the Governments of the United States of America and the Union of Soviet Socialist Republics.

For transmission of other information, notifications and requests for information, the Parties, at their own discretion, may use any communications facilities, including diplomatic channels, depending on the degree of urgency.

Article 7

The Parties undertake to hold consultations, as mutually agreed, to consider questions relating to implementation of the provisions of this Agreement, as well as to discuss possible amendments thereto aimed at further implementation of the purposes of this Agreement.

Article 8

This Agreement shall be of unlimited duration. . . .

Source: Documents on Disarmament, 1971 *(Washington, D.C.: U.S. Government Printing Office, 1972), pp. 634–635.*

U.S.-Soviet Declaration on Basic Principles of Relations

During the first Nixon-Brezhnev "detente" summit in late May 1972, the nuclear superpowers signed a statement of general principles to guide future U.S.-Soviet relations. Hidden conceptual differences over terms, such as "peaceful coexistence," as well as the later collapse of U.S. presidential authority as a result of the

Watergate scandal, were to sidetrack the detente that this declaration was intended to codify. Nevertheless, it may be taken as a reflection of the extent to which both countries wished to move their relations forward at the time. Key excerpts are included below.

First. [The USA and USSR] will proceed from the common determination that in the nuclear age there is no alternative to conducting their relations on the basis of peaceful coexistence. Differences in ideology and in the social systems of the USA and the USSR are not obstacles to the bilateral development of normal relations based on the principles of sovereignty, equality, non-interference in internal affairs and mutual advantage.

Second. The USA and USSR attach major importance to preventing the development of situations capable of causing a dangerous exacerbation of their relations. Therefore, they will do their utmost to avoid military confrontations and to prevent the outbreak of nuclear war. They will always exercise restraint in their mutual relations, and will be prepared to negotiate and settle differences by peaceful means. Discussions and negotiations on outstanding issues will be conducted in a spirit of reciprocity, mutual accommodation and mutual benefit.

Both sides recognize that efforts to obtain unilateral advantage at the expense of the other, directly or indirectly, are inconsistent with these objectives. The prerequisites for maintaining and strengthening peaceful relations between the USA and the USSR are the recognition of the security interests of the Parties based on the principle of equality and the renunciation of the use or threat of force.

Third. The USA and the USSR have a special responsibility, as do other countries which are permanent members of the United Nations Security Council, to do everything in their power so that conflicts or situations will not arise which would serve to increase international tensions. Accordingly, they will seek to promote conditions in which all countries will live in peace and security and will not be subject to outside interference in their internal affairs. . . .

Fifth. The USA and the USSR reaffirm their readiness to continue the practice of exchanging views on problems of mutual interests and, when necessary, to conduct such exchanges at the highest level, including meetings between leaders of the two countries.

The two governments welcome and will facilitate an increase in productive contacts between representatives of the legislative bodies of the two countries.

Sixth. The Parties will continue their efforts to limit armaments on a bilateral as well as on a multilateral basis. They will continue to make special efforts to limit strategic armaments. Whenever possible, they will conclude concrete agreements aimed at achieving these purposes.

The USA and the USSR regard as the ultimate objective of their efforts the achievement of complete and general disarmament and the establishment of an effective system of international security in accordance with the purposes and principles of the United Nations. . . .

Eleventh. The USA and the USSR make no claim for themselves and would not recognize the claims of anyone else to any special rights or advantages in world affairs. They recognize the sovereign equality of all states.

The development of U.S.-Soviet relations is not directed against third countries and their interests.

Twelfth. The basic principles set forth in this document do not affect any obligations with respect to other countries earlier assumed by the USA and the USSR. . . .

Source: Weekly Compilation of Presidential Documents, *June 5, 1972, pp. 943–944.*

Political and Military Provisions of the Helsinki Final Act

The human rights provisions ("Basket Three") of the Helsinki Final Act, signed on August 1, 1975, by thirty-three European states and the United States and Canada, are well known and do not require reproduction here. Less remembered are the political provisions of the act. These passages essentially codified the political-territorial division of Germany and of Europe and thus served as the de facto substitute for the peace treaty that was to have formally signified the end of the Second World War but that—because of the cold war—was never signed. They included: "sovereign equality, respect for the rights inherent in sovereignty . . . ; refraining from the threat or use of force . . . ; inviolability of frontiers . . . ; territorial integrity of states . . . ; peaceful settlement of disputes . . . ; and non-intervention in internal affairs." In other words, the Communist status quo in Eastern Europe would not be challenged as a matter of state policy by the West.

Still less publicized were the military provisions of the Final Act, which envisaged the prior notification of major military maneuvers, the exchange of observers at such maneuvers, and other military confidence-building measures. The relevant sections are reproduced below, by way of demonstrating the concerted effort as early as 1975 to minimize the chance of military miscalculation in the heart of Europe. (The provisions on prenotification of maneuvers and on the sending of foreign observers were significantly strengthened in the 1986 follow-up agreement signed in Stockholm at the Conference on Confidence-and Security-Building Measures and Disarmament in Europe.)

2.I Prior Notification of Major Military Manoeuvres

They [the Parties] will notify their major military manoeuvres to all other participating States through usual diplomatic channels in accordance with the following provisions:

Notification will be given of major military manoeuvres exceeding a total of 25,000 troops, independently or combined with any possible air or naval components (in this context the word "troops" includes amphibious and airborne troops). . . .

Notification will be given of major military manoeuvres which take place on the territory, in Europe, of any participating State as well as, if applicable, in the adjoining sea area and air space.

In the case of a participating State whose territory extends beyond Europe [i.e., the USSR and Turkey], prior notification need be given only of manoeuvres which take place in an area within 250 kilometres from its frontier facing or shared with any other European participating State. . . .

Notification will be given 21 days or more in advance of the start of the manoeuvre or in the case of a manoeuvre arranged at shorter notice at the earliest possible opportunity prior to its starting date.

Notification will contain information of the designation, if any, the general purpose of and the States involved in the manoeuvre, the type or types and numerical strength of the forces engaged, the area and estimated time-frame of its conduct. The participating States will also, if possible, provide additional relevant information, particularly that related to the components of the forces engaged and the period of involvement of these forces. . . .

Exchange of Observers

The participating States will invite other participating States, voluntarily and on a bilateral basis, in a spirit of reciprocity and goodwill towards all participating States, to send observers to attend military manoeuvres.

The inviting State will determine in each case the number of observers, the procedures and conditions of their participation, and give other information which it may consider useful. It will provide appropriate facilities and hospitality.

The invitation will be given as far ahead as is conveniently possible through usual diplomatic channels. . . .

Source: U.S. Department of State, Bureau of Public Affairs, Office of Media Services, Conference on Security and Co-Operation in Europe: Final Act, Helsinki 1975 *(Washington, D.C.: U.S. Government Printing Office, 1975), Department of State Publication 8826.*

Gorbachev's 1984 Speech Anticipating Reform

Shortly before he burst into international prominence with his trip to London in mid-December 1984, when British Prime Minister Margaret Thatcher hailed him three months before his rise to power as a man with whom the West "can do business," Mikhail Gorbachev made a key domestic speech in which the outlines of his reform policies were discernible, if in muted form. Note in particular his comparison of the scale of the economic changes to come with that of the "industrialization of the country," i.e., Stalin's forced industrialization of the 1930s. Compare the tone of this speech, which assumes the salvageability of the existing system, with the text of the new Union treaty, excerpted below, which essentially ushers in a new, confederal political order.

Large-scale, complex tasks lie before us. . . . The conclusion that we are at the start of the historically prolonged stage of developed socialism was substantiated in depth. . . . The evaluations and conclusions that have been drawn up warn against running ahead too fast and confusing what is with what must be achieved.
. . .

Profound transformations must be carried out in the economy and in the entire system of social relations, and a qualitatively higher standard of living must be ensured for the Soviet people. As a result, socialism will rise to a new degree of maturity.

. . . [T]remendous potential for accelerating society's socioeconomic development lies in the combination of the masses' initiative and enterprise with a scientifically substantiated, creative approach toward the resolution of urgent problems.

. . . Let us turn to a vital and topical problem—that of the interaction between modern production forces and socialist production relations. Dogmatic ideas which sometimes do a disservice to our theory and practice have by no means been entirely overcome in the interpretation of this problem.

Life teaches us to examine with the greatest possible sense of responsibility the objective dialectic of the development of the production forces and production relations as a most important source of accelerating society's socioeconomic development. This makes it incumbent upon us to uncover the contradictions that arise here in good time and to resolve them.

. . . [W]e must think today about the prospects for the country's development. Life sets us a task of tremendous political significance—that of bringing the national economy up to a qualitatively new scientific, technical, organizational, and economic level and achieving decisive progress in the intensification of social production and in improving its efficiency.

The course of intensification is dictated by objective conditions and by the entire course of the country's development. There is no alternative. Only an intensive economy, developing on the latest scientific and technical basis, can serve as a reliable material base for increasing the working people's prosperity and ensure the strengthening of the country's positions in the international arena, enabling it to enter the new millennium fittingly, as a great and prosperous power.

. . . [T]he process of intensification of the economy must be given a truly nationwide character and must have the same political resonance as the industrialization of the country once had. . . .

Publicity (*glasnost'*) is an integral part of socialist democracy and a norm of all public life. Wide, prompt, and frank information is evidence of confidence in people and respect for their intelligence and feelings, and their ability to understand events for themselves. It enhances the working people's activeness. Publicity in the work of party and state organs is an effective means of combatting bureacratic distortions and obliges us to be more thoughtful in our approach to the adoption of decisions and the organization of monitoring their fulfillment and to the rectification of shortcomings and omissions. The extent to which propaganda is convincing, the effectiveness of education, and the guaranteeing of the unity of word and deed depend largely on this.

. . . [S]ocialism's main influence on world development was and is exercised through its economic policy and through successes in the socioeconomic sphere. . . . Socialist ideology incorporates the truly humanist ideals of social progress, the development of the human personality, and a world without weapons or war, without exploitation or oppression.

It is not we but capitalism that has to maneuver and disguise itself, resorting to wars, terror, falsifications, and subversion in order to ward off the implacable onslaught of time. The general crisis of capitalism is not only an exacerbation of its economic, social, and political contradictions; it is also a spiritual crisis, an ideological and moral crisis.

At the same time the ideological activity of the monopoly bourgeoisie has increased sharply in recent years. Our opponent has created a vast propaganda machine for ideological confrontation and uses sophisticated technical means and subversive and psychological methods. In its inventiveness, content, and methods, the "psychological warfare" being waged by imperialism today constitutes a special kind of aggression which flouts other countries' sovereignty.

In these conditions, adherence to party principles; a consistent class approach to the evaluation of current events and phenomena; political vigilance and intolerance of alien views; ideological work of a creative, offensive character; effectiveness; boldness; and persistence are more necessary than ever.

An offensive role on the part of our ideology does not just mean debunking bourgeois myths and stereotypes. It means, first and foremost, asserting our ideals, the socialist norms of public life, and genuine freedom and democracy, and propagandizing the historical achievements of real socialism.

An offensive role on the part of our ideology means the most active propagandizing of the peace-loving international policy of the CPSU, the Soviet state, and the community of socialist countries. . . .

[T]he ability, and sometimes the persistence, to organize matters in practice is not yet in plentiful supply everywhere, by a long way. The fierce enemy of lively thought and lively action was and is formalism, whose manifestations are multifarious. Its essence is incompetence, indifference, and the replacement of a party political approach with a bureaucratic approach, when importance is attached not to getting things done, but to looking good. . . . Our party will become still more cohesive and authoritative if we continue to rid ourselves of those who do not value party principles and party honor and get rid of moral degenerates, using the CPSU Rules, the laws, and public opinion to this end. . . .

Source: TASS account of Gorbachev speech of December 10, 1984, at a Moscow conference on ideology, as printed in Pravda, *December 11, 1984, p. 2. Translation by Foreign Broadcast Information Service,* Daily Report. Soviet Union, *December 11, 1984, pp. R2–R9.*

Leninism and the New Political Thinking

On November 2, 1987, the seventieth anniversary of the Russian Revolution, Mikhail Gorbachev made a speech, excerpted below, in which he raised funda-

*mental questions about the contemporary validity of Lenin's theory of imperial-
ism, by way of opening up the range of choice in both Soviet foreign and domestic
policy.*

. . . [W]hat grounds do we have for optimism and for considering that an all-
embracing security is indeed possible? . . . In this connection, we should first of
all, again from the standpoint of our Leninist teaching and making use of its
methodology, ask ourselves difficult questions. First—and this has to do with the
nature of imperialism, in which the main military threat is rooted, as is well
known—the nature of the social system cannot, of course, be changed by the
influence of external conditions. But is it possible at the present phase of world
development and at the new level of interdependence and integrality of the world
to have an influence on this nature that would block its most dangerous manifestations? In other words, is it possible to count on the natural logic of an integral
world, in which general human values are the main priority, being able to limit
the range of destructive actions of the egocentric, narrow, class-based features of
the capitalist system?

Here is the second question, and it is connected with the first. Is capitalism
able to free itself of militarism? Can it function economically and develop without
it? Concerning our invitation to the Western countries for programs to be prepared
and compared on the reconversion of economies—that is to say, their transfer to
a peaceful footing—is that not utopian?

The third question is: Can the capitalist system do without neocolonialism,
one of the sources for its present life support? In other words, is that system able
to function without its unequal exchange with the Third World, which is fraught
with unpredictable consequences?

Along with this, there is a further question: How realistic are the hopes that
an understanding of the catastrophic danger in which the world finds itself—and
we know that such an understanding is penetrating even the topmost echelons of
the ruling elite of the Western world—how realistic is it that this understanding
will be carried over into practical policy? . . .

These questions are far from idle. The answers to them will determine how
historical events in coming decades will unfold. . . .

So what are we counting on, knowing that we shall have to build a secure
world together with the capitalist countries? The postwar period has provided
evidence of a profound modification of contradictions which have determined
the main processes in the world economy and politics. I have in mind, first and
foremost, the fact that they have developed in a way that, in the past, inexorably
led to war, to world war between the capitalist states themselves. Now the
situation is different. Not only the lessons of the last war, but also the fear of
weakening itself in the face of socialism, which has become a world system, have
prevented capitalism from taking its internal contradictions to the extreme. They
have begun to involve themselves in a technology race against each other. They
have discharged with the aid of neocolonialism, and a unique kind of new
peaceful repartition of the world has taken place according to the same rule
about capital that Lenin revealed: Whoever is the richest and strongest at any
given moment gets the biggest share. A number of countries have begun easing

economic tension by pumping resources into the military-industrial complex under the pretext of the Soviet threat. The transformations taking place in the technological and organizational basis of the capitalist economy have also helped to reconcile contradictions and balance interests.

But that is not all. If in the past, faced with the fascist menace, an alliance of socialist and capitalist states became possible, does not a definite lesson follow from this for the present day, when the entire world has come face to face with the menace of a nuclear disaster and need to ensure the safety of nuclear power engineering and overcome the ecological danger? These are all completely real and acute problems, demanding not only that we be aware of them, but also that we seek practical solutions.

Further, is the capitalist economy capable of developing without militarization? Here one is reminded of the economic miracles in Japan, West Germany, and Italy. True, once the miracle was over they turned to militarism again. We must, however, establish to what extent this turn was determined by the essential laws of operation of contemporary monopolistic capital, and what role was played by transitory factors—the infectious example of the U.S. military-industrial complex, the cold war atmosphere, considerations of prestige, the need to have one's own military fist to talk to one's competitors in a language understood in that milieu, as well as the desire to reinforce one's economic invasion of the Third World by strong-arm policies. Whatever the case may be, a number of countries did go through a period of rapid development of the contemporary capitalist economy with minimal military expenditure, and this experience has remained a part of history. . . .

Source: Moscow Television Service, November 2, 1987, 0710 GMT, as translated by Foreign Broadcast Information Service, Soviet Union. Daily Report, November 3, 1987, pp. 38–61.

A General Protests Against the Gorbachev Foreign Policy

One of the earliest and most dramatic cries of opposition to the Gorbachev foreign and military policies came from Soviet Army General Albert M. Makashov during the first Russian Communist Party Conference in mid-June 1990. It is typical of much of the criticism of Foreign Minister Eduard Shevardnadze, who eventually resigned in December of that year (see the document following this one), and anticipates the logic of the abortive military coup of August 19–21, 1991.

Comrade communists! Russia is living in troubled times. The whole tragedy lies in the fact that we have created this situation ourselves. Like Shakespeare's King Lear, who gave away his state to his dissolute daughters, we, too, can find ourselves in a similar tragedy. In my opinion the CPSU is now the only party which has greater concern for other parties than it has for itself. [applause] Our Armed Forces are one of the nerves of perestroika that have been laid bare. Of all the structures in society the army and navy are, in their essence and in their form, the most vivid symbols of the state. Whoever wants to demolish the state to its foundations begins by defaming the armed forces, the Ministry of Internal Affairs and the KGB.

Citizen Arbatovs, Korotiches, Sobchaks, Gelmans, Yegor Yakovlevs [leading reformers], and company! Stand up and say it outright: We don't need the army. We can get by without the Armed Forces! [applause] Give a guarantee that there won't be any war, so that the people may know to whom it will be obliged for possible defeat in any conflict. And look carefully at history to see that conflicts or war are possible. Why, otherwise, should the NATO bloc be strengthening itself when the Warsaw Pact no longer exists? Germany is being reunited and will probably be a member of NATO. Japan is fast becoming the decisive force in the Far East. Only our own scientists-chaps twitter on about the fact that no one intends to attack us. [applause]

That formula is calculated to appeal to the feebleminded. [applause] Comrade communists! The army and navy will yet stand the Union and Russia in good stead.

In any state people are brought to book in all kinds of ways for undermining the fighting ability of their own armed forces. If this is not done by the government, then the people can stone the traitors. [applause]

The communists of the army and navy are indignant over the lack of activity by the Central Committee, the Politburo and the government with regard to those who defend them and with regard to those who trample on their own fighters and who stamp upon the concepts of patriotism and soldierly duty, concepts that are sacred for any people. Reducing your own Armed Forces unilaterally, using calculations and reasons unknown to the specialists, you do not have to spit on them first. Otherwise when the thunder rolls, appeals and party mobilizations will be of no avail. It takes centuries to cultivate patriotism, but it is destroyed by the yellow press and by television in a couple of years. [applause]

Only a blind person can fail to see this. [applause] The army is the least protected part of society, it is the most sacrificed part of it. It covered the death-dealing reactor of Chernobyl with the bodies of its own men, they died in the Hindu Kush and in Karabakh. Our Army never does anything of its own will. The army is led by politicians. . . . [O]nce in history Marshal Zhukov saved Khrushchev, and not from some paper Stalinism, but from the living Beria [i.e., the feared chief of Stalin's secret police]. For this Khrushchev thanked—in inverted commas—the man who saved him and sent him into disgrace. And we communists with the new thinking are still unable to rehabilitate the great military commander.

We Armed Forces are of one flesh with our people. The ideological opponent does everything to drive a wedge between the privates and the officers, between the officers and the generals, as though these generals, before putting on their trousers with generals' stripes, had not spent 20 years and more alongside the soldiers getting wet, getting frozen, or carrying out combat or training tasks in blistering heat. . . .

[A]ll attempts to depoliticize the Armed Forces should be opposed resolutely. And during these times, which are troubled ones for the Union and for Russia, when because of the victories—the so-called victories—of our diplomacy the Soviet Army is being driven without a fight out of countries which our fathers liberated from fascism, then the concern of the party and the people for the families of servicemen is essential.

Unfortunately, in some oblast party organizations such concern is shown only in words. Six autonomous republics and 10 oblasts upon which are the troops of the [respective] military district have failed to provide 31,500 square meters of housing under shared participation arrangements for which we have paid money; and more than 72,000 square meters under the decision of the CPSU Central Committee and Council of Ministers of September 8, 1984.

We understand that things are difficult for everyone. But believe me, the Armed Forces are not to blame for the fact that they are in such a difficult situation today. And in spite of everything we army communists cannot conceive of the Union without Russia or of Russia without the Union. And for this we are prepared to fight. [applause]

Source: Moscow Television Service, 2010 GMT, June 19, 1990, as translated by Foreign Broadcast Information Service, Daily Report. Soviet Union, June 21, 1991, pp. 92–93.

Shevardnadze's Resignation Speech

On December 20, 1990, Soviet Foreign Minister Eduard Shevardnadze stunned the world by announcing his resignation. Having endured six months of criticism of the sort exemplified by General Makashov's speech (see previous document), and sensing an impending political calamity, Shevardnadze took the opportunity of dramatizing the case for even-more-radical political reform. In the process, he predicted the failed coup d'etat of August 19–21, 1991.

Comrade deputies: I have perhaps the shortest and the most difficult speech in my life. . . .

The first part: Yesterday there were speeches by some comrades—they are our veterans—who raised the question of the need for a declaration to be adopted forbidding the president and the country's leadership from sending troops to the Persian Gulf. That was the approximate content, and this was not the first or the second occasion. There are many such notes and items in the press, on television, and so on.

These speeches yesterday, comrades, overfilled the cup of patience, to put it bluntly. What, after all, is happening in the Persian Gulf? On about 10 occasions both within the country and outside the country's borders I have had to speak and explain the atttude and the policy of the Soviet Union toward this conflict. This policy is serious, well considered, sensible, and in accordance with all standards, present standards, of civilized relations between states. We have friendly relations with the state of Iraq. They have been built up over years. These relations are being preserved, but we have no moral right to reconcile ourselves to aggression and the annexation of a small, defenseless country. In that case we would have had to strike through everything that has been done in recent years by all of us, by the whole country, and by the whole of our people in the field of asserting the principles of the new political thinking. This is the first thing.

Second, I have been repeatedly explaining—and Mikhail Sergeyevitch [Gorbachev] spoke of this in his speech at the Supreme Soviet—that the Soviet leadership does not have any plans—I do not know, maybe someone else has some plans, some group—but official bodies, the Defense Ministry—and they are now accusing the Foreign Ministry of having such a plan, a plan to land troops in the Persian Gulf, in that region. I have been explaining and saying that there are no plans like this, they do not exist in practice. Nobody is planning to send even one serviceman in a military uniform, even one representative of the Armed Forces of the Soviet Union. This was said. But someone needed to raise this issue, this problem again. I know what is happening in the corridors of the congress.
. . .

[P]ermit me to say a few words about the personal worth of the man, about his personal sufferings, because many people think that the ministers who sit there or the members of the government or the president or someone else are hired . . . and they can do what they like with them. I think this is impermissible. In this connection I remember the party congress. Was this really a chance phenomenon? Because at the congress a real struggle developed, a most acute struggle, between the reformers and—I will not say conservatives, I respect conservatives because they have their own views which are acceptable to society—but the reactionaries, precisely the reactionaries. [applause] Futhermore, this battle, it must be stated bluntly, was won with merit by the progressive section. . . . [I]t was against my will, without being consulted, that my name, I, my candidacy, was included for secret voting, and I had 800 against; 800 delegates voted against. What then: Is this random, or on purpose? Is the Foreign Ministry's policy not good enough? Or am I personally undesirable? . . . [T]his is not a random event. . . . At Comrade Lukyanov's [then the Soviet Vice President and Chair of the Party Congress] initiative, literally just before the start of the sitting, a serious matter was included on the agenda about the treaies with the German Democratic Republic. As it happened . . . the issue was a flop. I myself had to speak the following week. How did it turn out? Those same people . . . came out with serious accusations against the foreign minister, of unilateral concessions, of incompetence, lack of skills, and so on and so forth. Not one person could be found, including the person in the chair [i.e., Gorbachev], to reply and say simply that this was dishonorable, that this is not the way, not how things are done in civilized states. I find this deeply worrying.

Things went as far as personal insults. I endured that, too. Comrades, a hounding is taking place. I will not name the publications, all manner of publications, the Pamyat society [an extreme right-wing and anti-Semitic political organization]—I add the Pamyat society to these publications—what expressions: Down with the Gorbachev clique! They also add Shevardnadze and several other names. Who are they, the so-called reformers? I will put it bluntly, comrades: I was shaken; I was shaken by the events of the first day, the start of work of our congress. By the pressing of a button, the fate not only of the president but of perestroika and democratization was decided. Is that normal? Democrats, I will put it bluntly: comrade democrats, in the widest meaning of this word, you have scattered. The reformers have gone to seed. Dictatorship is coming; I state this with complete responsibility. No one knows what kind of dictatorship this will be and who will come—what kind of dictator—and what the regime will be like.

I want to make the following statement: I am resigning. Let this be—and do not respond, and do not curse me—let this be my contribution, if you like, my protest against the onset of dictatorship.

I express profound gratitude to Mikhail Sergeyevitch Gorbachev. I am his friend. I am a fellow thinker of his. I have always supported, and will support to the end of my days, the ideas of perestroika, the ideas of renewal, the ideas of democracy, of democratization. We have done great things in the international arena. But, I think that it is my duty, as a man, as a citizen, as a Communist; I cannot reconcile myself to the events taking place in our country and to the trials awaiting our people. I nevertheless believe, I believe that the dictatorship will not succeed, that the future belongs to democracy and freedom.

Thank you very much. [applause]

Source: Radio Moscow Domestic Service, 1200 GMT, December 20, 1990, as translated by Foreign Broacast Information Service, Daily Report. Soviet Union, December 20, 1990, pp. 11–12.

The Belorussian Declaration of Sovereignty

On July 27, 1990, the Belorussian Supreme Soviet, or parliament, issued a declaration of sovereignty. It is similar to one issued earlier that month by the Ukrainian parliament. The Preamble and Articles 10 and 11, excerpted below, underscore the lengths to which the Soviet republics—Belorussia had long been considered the most assimilated of all the Union republics into Soviet Russia— were determined to go in recasting the nature of the Soviet Union.

Preamble

The Supreme Soviet of the Belorussian Soviet Socialist Republic, expressing the will of the people of the Belorussian Soviet Socialist Republic, conscious of its responsibility for the future of the Belorussian nation, affirming its respect for the dignity and rights of the peoples of all nationalities resident in the Belorussian Soviet Socialist Republic . . . and respect for the sovereign rights of all peoples of the USSR . . . , regarding the republic as an independent member of the world community with full rights, acting in accordance with the principles of the Universal Declaration of Human Rights and the other universally recognized international legal acts, recognizing the necessity to build a law-based state, solemnly declares the full state sovereignty of the Belorussian Soviet Socialist Republic and the supremacy of the independence and totality of the state power of the republic within the limits of its territories, the legal validity of its laws, the independence of this republic in external relations, and declares its resolve to create a law-based state.

Article 10

The Belorussian Soviet Socialist Republic has the right to its own armed forces, internal troops, bodies of state and public security under the control of the Supreme Soviet of the Belorussian Soviet Socialist Republic. The Belorussian Soviet Socialist Republic has the sovereign right to decide the regime and conditions for military service in bodies of state and public security, to decide the presence and stationing of troops . . . on its territory. No military presence of foreign countries or military bases and facilities can be sited on the territory of the Belorussian Soviet Socialist Republic without the consent of its Supreme Soviet. The Belorussian Soviet Socialist Republic aims to transform its territory into a nuclear-free zone, and the republic into a neutral state.

Article 11

The Belorussian Soviet Socialist Republic independently exercises the right to voluntary unification with other states and free secession from the state Union. The Belorussian Soviet Socialist Republic proposes an immediate start on the elaboration of a treaty on a Union of sovereign socialist states.

Source: Radio Minsk Domestic Service, 0833 GMT, 0753 GMT, and 0718, respectively, July 27, 1990, as translated by Foreign Broadcast Information Service, Daily Report. Soviet Union, *July 30, 1991, pp. 79–80.*

The Precoup Treaty of Union

On June 27, 1991, Pravda *published the text of a "Draft Treaty on the Union of Sovereign States" to supersede the Treaty of Union of December 1922, which created the USSR as—in form—a multinational federation. The Basic Principles of the text, included below, show how far the republics had succeeded, before the failed coup d'etat of August 19–21, 1991, in recasting the union from what was in form a federation (though in practice a unitary party–state system) to a confederation, in which sovereignty reposes in the constituent states, which delegate power as they see fit to the central government. Article 9 on taxation is also included; this was soon supplemented by the separate agreement between the Gorbachev government and the republics in late July 1991 stipulating that all taxes would henceforth be levied by the republics alone, which would dispense 10 percent of revenues raised to the central government.*

I. Basic Principles

1. Each republic, which is a party to the treaty, is a sovereign state. The Union of Soviet Sovereign Republics (USSR) is a sovereign, federative, democratic state, formed as a result of the unification of equal republics and exercising state power within the bounds of the powers with which the parties to the treaty voluntarily vest in it.

2. The states comprising the Union retain the right to decide independently all issues of their development, while guaranteeing equal political rights and opportunities for social, economic, and cultural development to all peoples living on their territory. The parties to the treaty will operate on the basis of a combination of values common to all mankind and those belonging to individual nationalities and will resolutely oppose racism, chauvinism, nationalism, and any attempts to restrict the rights of peoples.

3. The states comprising the Union regard as a most important principle the preeminence of human rights, in accordance with the UN Universal Declaration of Human Rights and other generally recognized norms of international law. All citizens are guaranteed the opportunity to study and use their native language, unimpeded access to information, freedom of religion, and other political, social, economic, and personal rights and liberties.

4. The states comprising the Union see the shaping of a civil society as a most important condition for the liberty and prosperity of the people and each individual. They will seek to satisfy the people's needs based on the free choice of forms of ownership and methods of economic management, the development of a Union-wide market, and the realization of the principles of social justice and protection.

5. The states comprising the Union possess the full range of political power and autonomously determine their own national-state and administrative-territorial structure as well as the system of bodies of power and administration. They may delegate some of their powers to other states which participate in the treaty of which they are members.

Those participating in the treaty acknowledge democracy based on popular representation and direct expression of the will of the peoples as a general, fundamental principle, and strive for the creation of a rule-of-law state which would serve as a guarantor against any tendencies toward totalitarianism and arbitrariness.

6. The states comprising the Union consider one of their very important tasks the preservation and development of national traditions, state support for education, health, science, and culture. They will facilitate the intensive exchange of mutual enrichment of the peoples of the Union and of the whole world with humanist, spiritual values and achievements.

7. The Union of Soviet Sovereign Republics operates in international relations as a sovereign state and a subject of international law—the successor to the Union of Soviet Socialist Republics. Its main aims in the international arena are lasting peace, disarmament, the elimination of nuclear and other weapons of mass destruction, cooperation between states, and solidarity of the peoples in the resolution of the global problems of humanity.

The states comprising the Union are full members of the international community.

They have a right to establish direct diplomatic, consular, trade and other links with foreign states, to exchange authorized representatives with them, to conclude international treaties, and to participate in the activity of international organizations without encroaching upon the interests of each of the Union states and their common interests, and without violating the international responsibilities of the Union.

Article 9. Union Taxes and Levies.

In order to finance the Union's state budget and other expenditures associated with the exercise of its powers, Union taxes and levies are fixed at levels determined by agreement with the republics. Their percentage contributions to all-Union programs are also fixed. The level and designation of the latter are regulated by agreements between the Union and the republics with reference to their socioeconomic and development indices.

Source: Pravda, *June 27, 1991, p. 3, as translated by Foreign Broadcast Information Service,* Daily Report. Soviet Union, *June 27, 1991, pp. 26–32.*

The Revised Program of the Communist Party of the Soviet Union

On July 27, 1991, the independent newspaper Nezavisimaya Gazeta *published a version of the new draft program of the Communist Party of the Soviet Union, which Mikhail Gorbachev had pushed through against a reluctant plenary session of the party's Central Committee. The program, which jettisons the Leninist political heritage of the party, inclines toward a social-democratic political vocation and thus may be compared to the historic Bad Godesberg conference of the German Social Democratic Party of 1959, which rejected the party's revolutionary political tradition in favor of political compromise. The draft argues that "perestroika has opened the path to democratic reforms in all areas of society, but the process is developing with difficulty, in a context of social and political tensions, of economic crisis and great changes in social consciousness. . . . A radical renewal of the party, a new understanding of its role and place in society are indispensable." The basic principles of the program, rendered moot by the coup of August 1991, are listed below.*

The CPSU, through all of its intellectual and political means, will contribute:

- To the progress of society, in excluding any attempt to make people happy by imposing an illusory [social-political] formula. . . . No political entity may establish as a goal to impose change on society.
- To the affirmation of liberty in all of its forms—social, individual, economic, political, intellectual and moral. . . .
- To the free competition of producers of material and moral values. . . .
- To internationalism, to the free development of all peoples, large or small, to the renewal of the Union as a voluntary federal entity of sovereign republics.

The CPSU . . . is the party of democratic reforms, the party of economic and political liberty, the party of social justice and human values, the party which is in favor of consensus.

The October [1917] revolution has been one of the most important events of world history. It was a popular revolution, in which the people followed the party. . . . The worker and peasant masses believed in the possibility of creating a perfect and just society. . . . This was the meaning of life for generations of Soviet people.

The tragedy of our society is that the construction of socialism was deformed by the establishment of a totalitarian system. The creative energy of the people was placed in the jaw of state property, of the unlimited political power of the party and state bureaucracy, of the monopoly of a vulgarized Marxist ideology. Mass repression was the principal means used to preserve the regime's power.

The essential tasks are to prevent the destruction of the integrity of the economic mechanism and the structures of the multinational state . . . , the normalization of the political situation . . . , the strengthening of public order and respect for the law.

[The CPSU supports] the transition to a mixed economy, the equality in law of all forms of property: of state property, joint-stock property—private and cooperative . . . ; the redistribution of the land (including the right of transfer) . . . ; the free development of all collective or private forms of economy, to the exclusion of any form of constraint against the peasantry. . . .

Our party was created as the political organization of the working class. . . . We exclude any discrimination or preference based on social or professional status. The party views without prejudice the activity of all of the new levels of activity which have appeared in the area of private enterprise. . . . We categorically exclude any preference for any nationality and . . . any preference with respect to religion. The party respects the views of believers, and is in favor of the equality of all religions.

We have decided to act by legal political methods in the context of parliamentary democracy. . . . Our party is built on the attachment of its members to the values of an idea . . . , the idea of a humane, democratic socialism.

We understand that, if Marxism is one of the sources of modern social theory, there are also other humanist concepts in the world and in the Soviet Union.

Socialism, democracy and progress are the goals of the Communist Party of the Soviet Union. We are certain that these are the goals which correspond to the interests of the people.

Source: Nezavisimaya Gazeta, *July 27, 1991.*

Bibliography

Acheson, Dean. *Present at the Creation: My Years in the State Department.* New York: Norton, 1969.

Adomeit, Hannes. "Gorbachev and German Reunification: Revision of Thinking, Realignment of Power," *Problems of Communism,* July-August 1990.

Aslund, Anders. "Gorbachev, *Perestroika,* and Economic Crisis," *Problems of Communism,* January-April 1991.

Aspaturian, Vernon. *The Union Republics in Soviet Diplomacy.* Geneva: E. Droz, 1960.

Battle, John M., and Thomas D. Sherlock. *Gorbachev's Reforms: An Annotated Bibliography of Soviet Writings.* Gulf Breeze, Fla.: Academic International Press, 1988.

Beschloss, Michael R. *The Crisis Years: Kennedy and Khrushchev, 1960–1963.* New York: Edward Burlingame Books, 1991.

Betts, Richard. *Nuclear Blackmail.* Washington, D.C.: Brookings Institution, 1987.

———. *Surprise Attack.* Washington, D.C.: Brookings Institution, 1982.

Bialer, Seweryn. "The Passing of the Soviet Order?" *Survival,* March-April 1990.

———. *The Soviet Paradox: External Expansion, Internal Decline.* New York: Knopf, 1986.

———. "Gorbachev's Program of Change: Sources, Significance, and Prospects," *Political Science Quarterly,* Fall 1988.

Black, J. L., ed. *Origins, Evolution, and Nature of the Cold War. An Annotated Bibliographic Guide.* Santa Barbara: ABC-Clio, 1986.

Bracken, Paul. *The Command and Control of Nuclear Forces.* New Haven: Yale University Press, 1983.

Brown, J. F. *Eastern Europe and Communist Rule.* Durham: Duke University Press, 1988.

Brucan, Silviu. *The Post-Brezhnev Era.* New York: Praeger, 1983.

Brzezinski, Zbigniew. *The Soviet Bloc.* Cambridge: Harvard University Press, 1959.

Bykov, Oleg. *Mery Doveriya.* Moscow: Nauka, 1982.

Dallek, Robert. *The U.S. Style in Foreign Policy.* New York: Knopf, 1983.

Davis, Lynn Etheridge. *The Cold War Begins: U.S.-Soviet Conflict over Eastern Europe.* Princeton: Princeton University Press, 1974.

Dean, Jonathan. *Watershed in Europe: Dismantling the East-West Military Confrontation.* Lexington, Mass.: Lexington Books, 1987.

De Nevers, Renee. *The Soviet Union and Eastern Europe: The End of an Era.* London: International Institute for Strategic Studies, Adelphi Papers no. 249, March 1990.

Edmonds, Robin. *Soviet Foreign Policy: The Brezhnev Years.* Oxford: Oxford University Press, 1983.

d'Encausse, Hélène Carrère. *La Gloire des Nations ou la Fin de l'Empire Sovietique.* Paris: Fayard, 1990.

Fontaine, André. *History of the Cold War.* New York: Vintage, 1970. 2 volumes.

————. *Un Seul Lit Pour Deux Rêves. L'Histoire de la Détente.* Paris: Gallimard, 1982.

Foreign Broadcast Information Service. *Daily Report. Soviet Union.* Washington, D.C.: National Technical Information Service. Translations from Soviet print and broadcast media published five times per week.

"The Foreign Policy and Diplomatic Activity of the USSR (November 1989–December 1990). A Survey Prepared by the USSR Ministry of Foreign Affairs," *International Affairs* (Moscow), March 1991.

Fox, William T.R. *The Superpowers—Their Responsibility for Peace.* New Haven: Yale Institute of International Studies, 1944.

Gaddis, John Lewis. *Russia, the Soviet Union, and the United States.* New York: McGraw-Hill, 1990.

Gaddis, John Lewis, and Thomas Etzold, eds. *Documents on Containment.* New York: Columbia University Press, 1978.

Gardner, Richard N. "The Comeback of Liberal Internationalism," *Washington Quarterly,* Summer 1990.

Garrett, Stephen. *From Potsdam to Poland: U.S. Foreign Policy Toward Eastern Europe.* New York: Praeger, 1986.

Garthoff, Raymond. *From Detente to Confrontation: U.S.-Soviet Relations from Nixon to Reagan.* Washington, D.C.: Brookings Institution, 1985.

Gasteyger, Curt. "The Remaking of Eastern Europe's Security," *Survival,* March-April 1991.

Gati, Charles, ed. *Caging the Bear: Containment and the Cold War.* Indianapolis: Bobbs-Merrill, 1974.

Goodby, James. "Commonwealth and Concert: Organizing Principles of Post-Containment Order in Europe," *Washington Quarterly,* Summer 1991.

Goodman, Melvin A., and Carolyn McGiffert Ekedahl. "Trends in Soviet Policy in the Middle East and the Gulf," *International Journal,* Summer 1990.

Gorbachev, Mikhail. *Perestroika: New Thinking for My Country and the World.* New York: Harper and Row, 1987.

————. *The Ideology of Renewal for Revolutionary Restructuring.* Moscow: Novosti, 1988.

Gordon, Lincoln. *Eroding Empire: Western Relations with Eastern Europe.* Washington, D.C.: Brookings Institution, 1987.

Halle, Louis J. *The Cold War as History.* New York: Harper Colophon, 1967.

Halperin, Morton. *Nuclear Fallacy: Dispelling the Myth of Nuclear Strategy.* Cambridge: Ballinger, 1987.

Institute of World Economy and International Relations (Moscow). *Disarmament and Security*. Published annually since 1987.

Jamgotch, Nish, Jr. *U.S.-Soviet Cooperation: A New Future*. New York: Praeger, 1989.

Jervis, Robert. *The Illogic of American Nuclear Strategy*. Ithaca: Cornell University Press, 1984.

Jones, Joseph M. *The Fifteen Weeks (February 21–June 5, 1947)*. San Diego: Harcourt Brace & World, 1955.

Kahan, Jerome H. *Security in the Nuclear Age*. Washington, D.C.: Brookings Institution, 1975.

Karaganov, Sergei A. "The Year of Europe: A Soviet View," *Survival*, March-April 1990.

Kaufmann, William W. *Glasnost, Perestroika, and U.S. Defense Spending*. Washington, D.C.: Brookings Institution, 1990.

Kennan, George F. *Memoirs*. Boston: Little, Brown, 1967, 1972. 2 volumes.

Kovrig, Bennett. *The Myth of Liberation*. Baltimore: Johns Hopkins University Press, 1973.

Kratochwil, Friedrich. *International Order and Foreign Policy: A Theoretical Sketch of Postwar International Politics*. Boulder: Westview Press, 1978.

Kupchan, Charles A., and Clifford A. Kupchan. "Concerts, Collective Security, and the Future of Europe," *International Security*, Summer 1991.

Kux, Stephan. *Soviet Federalism: A Comparative Perspective*. New York: Institute for East-West Security Studies, 1990.

LaFeber, Walter. *America, Russia, and the Cold War, 1945–1990*. 6th ed. New York: McGraw-Hill, 1991.

Lapidus, Gail. "State and Society: Toward the Emergence of Civil Society in the Soviet Union," in Seweryn Bialer, ed. *Politics, Society, and Nationality Inside Gorbachev's Russia*. Boulder: Westview Press, 1989.

Larrabee, F. Stephen, ed. *The Two German States and European Security*. New York: St. Martins, 1989.

Larrabee, F. Stephen, and Allen Lynch. "Confidence-Building Measures in U.S.-Soviet Relations," in R. B. Byers, F. Stephen Larrabee, and Allen Lynch, eds. *Confidence-Building Measures and International Security*. New York: Institute for East-West Security Studies, 1986.

Legvold, Robert. "Soviet Policy in East Asia," *Washington Quarterly*, Spring 1991.

Lewin, Moshe. *The Gorbachev Phenomenon: A Historical Inquiry*. Berkeley: University of California Press, 1988.

Light, Margot. *The Soviet Theory of International Relations*. U.K.: Wheatsheaf Books, 1987.

Lynch, Allen. *The Soviet Study of International Relations*. Cambridge: Cambridge University Press, 1987, 1989.

———. *Gorbachev's International Outlook: Intellectual Origins and Political Consequences*. New York: Institute for East-West Security Studies, 1988.

Lynn-Jones, Sean M. "A Quiet Success for Arms Control: Preventing Incidents at Sea," *International Security*, Spring 1985.

Malashenko, Igor. "Russia: The Earth's Heartland," *International Affairs* (Moscow), July 1990.

Mandelbaum, Michael, ed. *The Rise of Nations in the Soviet Union: American Foreign Policy and the Disintegration of the USSR.* New York: Council on Foreign Relations, 1991.

———. *The Nuclear Revolution.* Cambridge: Cambridge University Press, 1981.

Maresca, John J. *To Helsinki—the Conference on Security and Cooperation in Europe, 1973–1975.* Durham: Duke University Press, 1985.

Mastny, Vojtech. *Russia's Road to Cold War.* New York: Columbia University Press, 1980.

Meyer, Stephen. "Sources and Prospects of Gorbachev's New Thinking," *International Security,* Fall 1988.

The Military Balance. Published annually by the London-based International Institute for Strategic Studies.

Mlynar, Zdenek. "Neue Ideen in der sowjetischen Aussenpolitik," *Mediatus,* no. 3 (1987).

Motyl, Alexander J. *Sovietology, Rationality, Nationality: Coming to Grips with Nationalism in the USSR.* New York: Columbia University Press, 1990.

———. "The Case for Dissolution," *World Policy Journal,* Summer 1991.

———. "The Foreign Relations of the Ukrainian SSR," *Harvard Ukrainian Studies,* March 1982.

Newhouse, John. *Cold Dawn: The Story of SALT.* Washington, D.C.: Pergamon-Brassey's, 1989.

Nye, Joseph, Jr. "Nuclear Learning and U.S.-Soviet Security Regimes," *International Organization,* Summer 1987.

Nye, Joseph, Jr., et al. *Hawks, Doves, and Owls.* New York: Norton, 1985.

Pipes, Richard. "Gorbachev's Russia: Breakdown or Crackdown?" *Commentary,* March 1990.

Potter, William C., ed. *Verification and Arms Control.* Lexington, Mass.: Lexington Books, 1985.

Report on the USSR. Munich: Radio Free Europe/Radio Liberty Research Institute. Analysis and reportage published weekly.

Schopflin, George. "The End of Communism in Eastern Europe," *International Affairs* (London), April 1990.

———. "Post-Communism: Constructing New Democracies in Eastern Europe," *International Affairs* (London), April 1991.

Shakhnazarov, Georgie Kh. "Renewal of Ideology and the Ideology of Renewal," *Social Sciences* (Moscow), no. 2 (1991).

Shulman, Marshall D. *Beyond the Cold War.* New Haven: Yale University Press, 1965.

Simon, Gerhard. *Die Desintegration der Sowjetunion durch die Nationen und Republiken.* Cologne: Berichte des Bundesinstituts fuer ostwissenschaftliche und internationaler Studien, no. 25, 1991.

SIPRI Yearbook. World Armaments and Disarmament. Published annually by the Stockholm International Peace Research Institute.

Smart, Christopher. "Gorbachev's Lenin: The Myth in Service to *Perestroika*," *Studies in Comparative Communism,* Spring 1990.

Smith, Gaddis. *The United States and the Origins of the Cold War.* New York: Columbia University Press, 1972.

Stefan, Charles G. "The Emergence of the Soviet-Yugoslav Break," *Diplomatic History,* Fall 1982.

Steinmetz, Mark S. "The U.S. Propaganda Effort in Czechoslovakia, 1945–1948," *Diplomatic History,* Fall 1982.

Stillman, Edmund, and William Pfaff. *The New Politics: America and the End of the Postwar World.* New York: Harper Colophon, 1961.

Talbott, Strobe. *Deadly Gambits: The Reagan Administration and the Stalemate in Nuclear Arms Control.* New York: Knopf, 1984.

————. *The Russians and Reagan.* New York: Vintage Books, 1984.

Teague, Elizabeth. "Perestroika: The Polish Influence," *Survey,* October 1988.

Thom, Françoise. *La langue de Bois.* Paris: Julliard, 1987.

Trask, David F. *Victory Without Peace: U.S. Foreign Relations in the Twentieth Century.* New York: Wiley, 1968.

Trofimenko, Genrikh A., and Pavel T. Podlesnyi. *Sovetsko-Amerikanskiye Otnosheniya v Sovremennom Mire.* Moscow: Nauka, 1987.

Ulam, Adam B. *Expansion and Coexistence: A History of Soviet Foreign Policy from 1917–1973.* New York: Praeger, 1973.

————. *The Rivals: America and Russia Since World War II.* New York: Viking Press, 1971.

U.S. Arms Control and Disarmament Agency. *Documents on Disarmament.* Washington, D.C.: U.S. Govt. Printing Office. Published annually.

U.S. Dept. of State. *Documents on American Foreign Policy.* Washington, D.C.: U.S. Govt. Printing Office. Published annually.

————. *Foreign Relations of the United States.* Washington, D.C.: U.S. Govt. Printing Office. See these declassified volumes on U.S. relations with Eastern Europe and the Soviet Union from World War II through the 1950s.

————. *State Department Bulletin.* Washington, D.C.: U.S. Govt. Printing Office. Published monthly.

Ury, William Langer, and Richard Smoke. *Beyond the Hotline: Controlling a Nuclear Crisis.* Cambridge: Harvard Law School, 1984.

Van Evera, Stephen. "Primed For Peace: Europe After the Cold War," *International Security,* Winter 1990/91.

Vestnik Ministerstva Inostrannykh Del. Moscow: Ministry of Foreign Affairs. Official documents on Soviet foreign policy published periodically since 1987.

Weekly Compilation of Presidential Documents. Washington, D.C.: U.S. Govt. Printing Office.

Weihmiller, Gordon A. *U.S.-Soviet Summits: An Account of East-West Diplomacy at the Top, 1955–1985.* Lanham, Md.: University Press of America, 1986.

Wilson, Andrew. *The Disarmer's Handbook of Military Technology and Organization.* New York: Penguin, 1983.

Wolfe, Thomas W. *The SALT Experience.* Cambridge: Ballinger, 1979.

Woodby, Sylvia. *Gorbachev and the Decline of Ideology in Soviet Foreign Policy.* Boulder: Westview Press, 1989.

Woodby, Sylvia, and Alfred B. Evans, Jr., eds. *Restructuring Soviet Ideology: Gorbachev's New Thinking.* Boulder: Westview Press, 1990.

Zhurkin, Vitaly. "The Make-up of the Pan-European Process," *Social Sciences* (Moscow), no. 2 (1991).

Zhurkin, Vitaly V., Sergei A. Karaganov, and Andrei Kortunov. "Vyzovy Bezopasnosti–Starye i Novye," *Kommunist,* no. 1 (January 1988).

About the Book and Author

In this book, Allen Lynch challenges the common wisdom that the revolutionary events in Eastern Europe in 1989 and in the Soviet Union in 1991 marked the end of the cold war. Instead, he argues that the cold war was actually resolved by the early 1970s, as evidenced by the tacit acceptance of a divided Germany and Europe. More recent events thus overthrew not the cold war but the *post*-cold war order in East-West and U.S.-Soviet relations. And—often to their surprise and consternation—leaders of the governments involved must now face formidable new forces created by German unity and nationalism in Eastern Europe and the former Soviet Union, which were contained efficiently—if at times brutally—by the post–cold war order.

In its three sections, the book reviews historical, contemporary, and future-oriented themes, respectively. Lynch begins by exploring the deeper logic of the cold war and how it was resolved by the 1970s. He then presents an overview of recent Soviet domestic and foreign policy processes as they affect East-West relations. The concluding section considers the future, with special emphasis on the implications of a disintegrating USSR for U.S. foreign policy.

Allen Lynch was assistant director of the W. Averell Harriman Institute for Advanced Study of the Soviet Union, Columbia University, until May 1992, at which time he became associate professor of government and foreign affairs at the University of Virginia.

Index